God, Man and Domesticated Animals

God, Man and Domesticated Animals

The Birth of Shepherds and Their Descendants in the Ancient Near East

By

Yutaka TANI

Kyoto University Press

This English edition first published in 2017 jointly by:

Kyoto University Press
69 Yoshida Konoe-cho
Sakyo-ku, Kyoto 606-8315
Japan
Telephone: +81-75-761-6182
Fax: +81-75-761-6190
Email: sales@kyoto-up.or.jp
Web: http://www.kyoto-up.or.jp

Trans Pacific Press
PO Box 164, Balwyn North, Melbourne
Victoria 3104, Australia
Telephone: +61-3-9859-1112
Fax: +61-3-8611-7989
Email: tpp.mail@gmail.com
Web: http://www.transpacificpress.com

Copyright © Kyoto University Press and Trans Pacific Press 2017.
Set by Sarah Tuke, Melbourne.

Distributors

USA and Canada
International Specialized Book Services (ISBS)
920 NE 58th Avenue, Suite 300
Portland, Oregon 97213-3786
USA
Telephone: (800) 944-6190
Fax: (503) 280-8832
Email: orders@isbs.com
Web: http://www.isbs.com

Asia and the Pacific (except Japan)
Kinokuniya Company Ltd.

Head office:
38-1 Sakuragaoka 5-chome
Setagaya-ku, Tokyo 156-8691
Japan
Telephone: +81-3-3439-0161
Fax: +81-3-3439-0839
Email: bkimp@kinokuniya.co.jp
Web: www.kinokuniya.co.jp

Asia-Pacific office:
Kinokuniya Book Stores of Singapore Pte., Ltd.
391B Orchard Road #13-06/07/08
Ngee Ann City Tower B
Singapore 238874
Telephone: +65-6276-5558
Fax: +65-6276-5570
Email: SSO@kinokuniya.co.jp

The editing and publication of this book was supported by a Grant-in-Aid for the Publication of Scientific Research Results (No. 16HP5272), provided by the Japan Society for the Promotion of Science, to which we express our sincere appreciation.

All rights reserved. No reproduction of any part of this book may take place without the written permission of Kyoto University Press or Trans Pacific Press.

ISBN   978-1-925608-92-2

Cover illustrations
Front cover: The 'Peace' panel of the Standard of Ur (circa 2500 B.C., held in the British Museum) from the city of Ur in ancient Mesopotamia.
Back cover: Pashtun nomads in the summer quarter of 1979 at Badakhshan, Afghanistan. Photos by Y. Tani.

Contents

Figures	vi
Tables	vii
Photographs	viii
Preface	ix
Acknowledgements	xxi

Part I: Domestication Process and the Birth of Shepherds

1	Location of Domesticated Sheep and Goats	3
2	Objectives and Methods	9
3	How did Domestication Begin?	17
4	Developments After the Beginning of Domestication	41
5	The Unique Position of Ancient Near Eastern Pastoralists: Overcoming the Physiological Barrier to Milking Cows	77

Part II: Large Household Chiefs, Entrusted Shepherds and Domesticated Animals

6	The Domesticated Animal as Serf: Herd Guide-Wethers and Eunuchs	93
7	Relationship Between Temple Cities and Pastoral Groups in the Ancient Near East	115
8	Mode Analysis of Dietary Narratives in the Pentateuch	165

Notes	193
Bibliography	194
Index	209

Figures

3.1	Origins of the domestication of sheep, goats, cattle and pigs	22
3.2	Archaeological sites in Levant	26
3.3	Kite site at Zeraf area	28
3.4	Hani rock incision	29
3.5	Periodical transition of consumed animals in Levant	31
3.6	Transition towards collective sharing of home range	39
4.1	Archaeological site thought to be an animal enclosure at Beisamoun	42
4.2	Archaeological site thought to be an animal enclosure at Abu Gosh	43
4.3	Inner court thought to have kept sheep/goats at Umm Dabaghiyah	45
4.4	Reconstruction of animal enclosure at Beidha	46
4.5	A Baxtyâri shepherd's campsite	57
4.6	Shepherd's memory of mother-offspring relationships	65
6.1	Group of ewes guided by a herd guide-wether as a leader/follower allegory	94
6.2	Homology of the roles of herd guide-wether and eunuch	96
6.3	Various types of herd guide and the hypothetical process of their elaboration	105
6.4	Geographical distribution of various herd guiding techniques	108
6.5	Data collecting locations of various herd guides	109
7.1	Major Mesopotamian cities around the third millennium B.C.	116
8.1	Edible/inedible fish	179
8.2	Edible/inedible insects	179
8.3	Edible/inedible beasts	181

Tables

3.1 Beginning of agriculture and husbandry	24
7.1 Age distribution of consumed bones in primordial villages	117
7.2 Age and sex composition of entrusted herds for wool production at annual shearing owned by the temple in the old Babylonian city of Ur	128
7.3 Composition of herds owned by Prince Arsham	137
7.4 Compiled tablet of the successive annual accounting of the entrusted herd of a private herd owner, Naab Aha Heshurrim, from 569 B.C. to 559 B.C.	142
7.5 Number of breeding ewes, newborn females and newborn males secured by the owner	145
7.6 Experimental supposition of the owner's share and the entrusted shepherd's share of the newborn female and male lambs according to the variable birth rate (3/5, 2/3 and 4/5 of the breeding ewes) in the early stage (breeding ewes = 100) and the last stage (breeding ewes = 390)	147

Photographs

3.1	Gramineae grass plain in Northern Afghanistan	25
4.1	Large crowd of sheep in a harbouring site (Carpathian summer quarter, Romania)	53
4.2	Suckling assistance for a true offspring, Rajasthan, India	55
4.3	Nursing assistance for newborns at suckling time, Cerqueto, Abruzzo, Italy	56
4.4	Shifting method of adoption stratagems, Rajasthan, India	62
5.1	Depiction of milking in a relief at a Sumerian temple from the Ubaid Period	79
6.1	Eunuch in the period of Sargon the second	97

Preface

It is generally accepted today that preindustrial subsistence economies can be classified into the following four categories: hunting, collecting, husbandry and agriculture. This typology, which is rather common in the European languages, is made according to the following two oppositional criteria that distinguish the objects of the respective economic pursuits: 1) animals or plants and 2) wild or domesticated (cultivated). In order to describe the development of human subsistence economies, this classification is taken for granted and universally recognised and the latter feature—domestication (or cultivation)—is regarded as the product of a more advanced stage in human history. Even the Japanese, the author being one of them, are accustomed to such classificatory principles, having assimilated European culture since the second half of the nineteenth century, and do not look into the fact that in the Japanese tradition there was a different mode of describing subsistence activities.

In fact, from a common modern Japanese dictionary I can identify a pair of oppositional terms concerning subsistence activities: *kari-ba* (*kari* place) and *maki-ba* (*maki* place). The former signifies the 'hunting place' of wild animals and the latter the 'herding place' of domesticated animals. So, taking *kari* to mean hunting acts and *maki* to indicate herding acts, we are likely to assume that the Japanese have formed these categories according to the European classificatory principle. However, if I refer to other idiomatic usages of these words, it becomes clear that such interpretation should be revisited.

Let me check several ways the term *kari* is used, which as employed above seemed to indicate 'hunting act'. First, I can exemplify the following common usages which can clearly be taken to mean the act of hunting wild animals: *kuma-kari* (bear hunting) or *shika-kari* (deer hunting). I can add another to this list: *shiohi-kari* (sea-shell collecting). Even if we do not usually describe sea-shell gathering as an act of hunting, sea-shells too are wild 'animals'. However, after considering the following usages, *kinoko-kari* (mushroom collecting), *ine-kari* (rice harvesting) and *momiji-kari* (maple tapping), we must recognise that *kari* is not a term restricted to the activity of hunting wild animals, but has a wider connotation; that is, it designates certain acts towards living beings without distinguishing between animal or plant. Moreover, any plant, either wild or cultivated, can be regarded as an object of *kari*.

Now, what about *maki*? It is well known that in ancient Japanese texts *maki* indicates the herding place of cattle and horses. In the hillside areas of Northern Japan there are many highland plateaus named with the suffix -*maki* that have been used as herding places for horses and cattle, for example Oomaki and Komaki. From these examples, it is clear that *maki* is a term that has been used to describe acts of herding or the herding places of domesticated animals. However, in the following usage, *ine-maki* (rice sowing) and *tane-maki* (seed sowing), we realise that *maki*, too, does not only refer to domesticated animals, but designates a certain act towards living beings without any distinction between animals or plants.

Now, leaving aside the usages that concern animals, let's try to confront the above-cited two words concerning rice cultivation: *ine-maki* and *ine-kari*. *Ine-maki* indicates the act of sowing rice as it is released from human hands, while *ine-kari* signifies the act of harvesting rice, collected by human hands. *Maki* and *kari* respectively designate oppositional transactions: the former is the act of transferring from human hands to the natural domain and the latter is the act of transferring from the natural domain to human hands. Now, remembering that both terms are used without distinguishing between animals and plants, we may say that in ancient Japanese subsistence economies economic acts are primarily classified in relation to the direction of transfer of the object in question: from the domain of human control to the natural domain or vice versa. No distinction is made in terms of the objects involved, be they animals/plants and wild/domesticated (or cultivated).

According to such perception, collected wild plants and hunted wild animals are living beings that have reproduced and grown in their own natural reproductive domains independently from human control until a certain point in time when they finally fall into human hands. On the other hand, cultivated plants are those that repeat the processes of being released from human hands into their own natural domain to grow and reproduce (to be sown) and then taken into human hands after their growth and reproduction (for human use).

Now, keeping the Japanese traditional perspective regarding subsistence activities in mind, I demonstrate how rural Japanese have used *uma-maki* (horse mustering place) and *ushi-maki* (cattle herding place) since the ancient period when animal husbandry was introduced from civilised China and Korea. In winter they would keep these animals in small barns attached to their houses and in spring would use them to plough the fields. In early summer villagers used to bring their horses and cattle up to *maki* on the hillsides for fattening until autumn when the cold weather approached. When you hear of such old Japanese customs of bringing them to *maki* in summer, you may be reminded of the familiar scene of the summer quarters of shepherds in the Middle East and Mediterranean where sheep or cattle herders follow their flocks or herds from morning to evening. However, against such expectations, you would see quite a different scene at *maki*: horses and cows were left free to wander and graze without any shepherds except when villagers occasionally came up to give them salt. When autumn came, all the villagers would go up to collect (*kari*) these dispersed animals at *maki* places and bring them down to their villages.

In northern China where ancient Chinese civilisation flourished, animal husbandry was common. Cattle, sheep and goats, which are suitable for herding in open grasslands, were kept in the open areas surrounding villages, but pigs that were the most common food animals were kept in the villagers' houses. As seen from the word 牧 *mù*, the cattle and sheep herder had been a well known traditional category since ancient times. However, even if the knowledge of Chinese husbandry as well as milk processing techniques was introduced into Japan from China, sheep as economic animals were not. Herding techniques did not take root and as a result the shepherd, as a professional category, did not exist. Why were these fundamental elements dropped in the course of importing pastoralistic culture from China? To understand the reasons behind this, Japan's climate and flora are particularly relevant.

Japan belongs to the monsoon climate zone where heavy summer rains facilitate the development of dense undergrowth in the forested areas. Sheep are domesticated animals suited to open grassland under a shepherd's guide. If the flock enters a dense forest or shrubby area, they begin to disperse, losing group cohesion. For the purposes of sheep herding, such vegetation that leads to the animals straying must be avoided. However, cattle and horses were imported and began to be seasonally brought up to *maki* in the mountain areas. Given this fact, the cattle herder could have become a profession, but cattle herders, too, were not introduced and these domesticated animals were left to wander free in the sparse forested zone or bamboo grasslands without the attendance of herders.

One reason behind the absence of herders is that the cultivation of rice as a summer crop demands a large amount of labour during summer, and this did not allow villagers any spare time to attend to the animals in the mountains. However, the Japanese traditional attitude toward living beings mentioned above could also be relevant. Even if rice is a cultivated plant, the act of sowing in the artificially prepared fields was described as a *maki* act signifying the release of seeds into their own natural domain for their free growth and reproduction. Despite the fact that the knowledge of animal husbandry was introduced as a higher subsistence technique from the civilised Continent, and the Japanese villagers prepared grazing fields for their domesticated animals, they left the animals free to wander and graze without any human supervision or control and referred to the place with the term *maki* (to be released from human hands into their own natural domain).

Now, to describe such an attitude towards living beings in other terms, one could say that it is the belief that any living being has to be left free in its own growth and reproductive domain independent from human intervention. The following facts can be identified in this regard. First, even if the practice of milking and its processing techniques were once introduced into Japan from China in the ancient period, they soon disappeared in the middle-ages. Also, in the course of the adoption of knowledge, castration techniques seem to have been excluded from the husbandry of these animals; neither draught cattle nor riding horses were castrated until modern times when European husbandry methods were introduced. In these aspects, too, we can identify the basic Japanese attitude of avoiding human intervention into the animal growth and reproduction process as much as possible, even for domesticated animals.

Of course, such an attitude towards plants and animals is not peculiar to the Japanese. Haudricourt (1969) once noted that Oceanian root-crop cultivators try not to enter the fields after having sown their crops so as not to disturb the crop's growth and development processes. Mongolian shepherds, as I will mention later, leave one particularly large or beautiful sheep to die a natural death rather than killing it for meat, regarding it as a representative individual responsible for flock reproduction. They believe that if such an outstanding individual is killed, the innate reproduction mechanism will be destroyed and the flock might die out. In these attitudes the following belief is shared: any living being should maintain its own reproductive domain independent from the arbitrary intervention of humans, otherwise the whole population will die.

Now, after having discussed these East Asian cultural attitudes towards animals that do not distinguish the difference between wild and domesticated (cultivated), let us turn to the European mode of categorising subsistence economies that is considered universally acceptable today. Leaving aside the distinctive feature—plants/animals—the distinction between wild and domesticated (or cultivated) is regarded as a very important feature in describing the historical developmental stages of human subsistence economies. In this regard, it is appropriate to recall the meaning of 'domestication'.

Normally, 'domestication' is defined as acts to keep certain animals' development and reproductive processes under human control. The term is derived from the Latin term *domus*, which signifies 'house' (in a social sense, not material) or 'ruling territorial domain of the household chief' (Benveniste, 1966). So, 'to be domesticated' is originally 'to enter into or to belong to the ruling domain of the household chief as his property'. The original meaning here is not too far from the usual above-mentioned definition; i.e. to keep some animals' development and reproductive processes under human control. Considering how a shepherd in the Middle East and Mediterranean daily and annually intervenes in the life of his flock, we should deem such a definition quite appropriate. Shepherds annually repeat the seasonal separation of breeding rams, joining them later with the ewes' group in order to concentrate lambing within a shorter period. Every day they take their flocks to good grasslands to improve growth. Moreover, the following phrase in Genesis 1:27–29 in the Old Testament is familiar for those belonging to the Judeo-Christian tradition: God created man in the image of himself, in the image of God he created him, male and female he created them. God blessed them, saying to them, 'Be fruitful, multiply, fill the earth and subdue it. Be masters of the fish of the sea, the birds of heaven and all the living creatures that move on earth'. Here God's imperative declaration implies that 'Man is worthy of being the master of all animals because of his similitude to God' and must have had considerable significance in the conceptualisation of human/animal relations. The 'domestication of animals' could be a convincing historical realisation of God's declaration, and the shepherd could be seen as one of the symbolic human figures appointed by God to govern animals. It is not without reason that the Europeans took the typical definition of domestication as being appropriate and drew a decisive line between hunting and husbandry, considering the latter a more developed stage. This occurred because since the beginning of domestication humans have been able to significantly increase the extent of their control over animals: the greater the degree of human control over nature, the greater the advancement of humanity and the better the realisation of God's words. The technological achievements of modern biologists in the fields of bio-tech and clone reproduction can be seen as the final stage of 'domestication' and the complete realisation of God's command in the sense that they have succeeded in bringing the development and reproduction of living beings under total human control.

Now, this is not the right place to argue about the problems of such interventions into the biological processes that entail the latent possibility of destroying the given ecological and biological balance and stability of life on a universal scale. However, after having examined the traditional East Asian attitudes towards plants and animals where an un-violable domain is reserved for their developmental and reproductive processes, we must recognise that such European attitudes that measure human achievements according to the extent of control over nature were not universally accepted, as Ingold points out in *The Perception of the Environment* (2002), but are instead a cultural and historical product of the ancient Near Eastern and Mediterranean world. This book focuses on several notions that can help us understand how such a peculiar attitude towards animals was born.

The book is comprised of two parts with the following subtitles:
    Part One: The Domestication Process and the Birth of Shepherds
    Part Two: Large Household Chiefs, Entrusted Shepherds and Domesticated Animals

In relation to Part One, the questions 'when, where and how' concerning the beginning of domestication have been one of the major topics for scholars of the history of humankind. It was only in the second half of the last century that archaeologists succeeded in giving scientifically acceptable answers to the above questions regarding the domestication of sheep/goats, which has been considered to have preceded the domestication of cattle. If one visits Middle Eastern pastoralists to observe their herding activities, one will realise how closely the shepherds intervene in these animals' life histories and the extent to which they have behaviourally diverged from their wild ancestors. Of course, these shepherds' close technical contact with their animals and the animals' divergence from their progenitors could not have occurred without the beginning of domestication. It must be said, however, that the beginning of this process was not its completion, but instead signifies the initiation of close interactions between humans and animals; it is an accumulative interactional process that occurs via the shepherds' technical interventions and the animals' responses to them that leads the animals to become 'domesticated animals' and to the birth of the typical professional 'shepherds' observable today in the Middle East and the Mediterranean regions.

What I first try to do in Part One is to reconstruct this accumulative interaction process between humans and animals (especially sheep/goats) from its origins, calling it the 'domestication process'. Of course, most technical interventions and animals' behavioural responses do not leave behind material evidence for the archaeologists and archaeozoologists attempting to discover traces of their existence and identify their origins. Despite the fact that, owing to recent archaeozoological innovative investigation methods, we are now informed that several technical interventions including milking were initiated soon after the beginning of domestication, sufficient reliable materials for reconstructing the domestication process are missing. In order to supplement this absence, I refer to observational data on basic and common intervention techniques shared among various contemporary pastoralists in the Middle East and Mediterranean areas that I have collected in my field surveys since 1969 and to detailed ethnographic reports on pastoralist activities in the surrounding areas. In order to determine the relative order of the invention of respective modes of interventions and techniques, I have adopted abductive inference through analyses of the conditions necessary for the respective intervention technique and the animals' supposed behavioural response to that human intervention. After such tentative reconstruction of the domestication process, I will show that a shepherd in the ancient Near Eastern and

Mediterranean areas had to acquire many techniques that intervened in sheep/goats' growth and reproduction. These can be classified as collective bio-control, classificatory bio-control (for example, classified according to gender and age) and personal bio-control (distinguished by an un-substitutable mother-offspring tie or an un-substitutable order-obedience bond between the shepherd and a specific individual animal). From these facts, we will be able to well understand how the original model of the so-called 'pastoral power' in Foucault's sense was conceived (Foucault, 1980 and 1981).

Although in the last chapter of Part One I argue hypothetically that cow-milking was initiated on the premise of an adoption technique for orphaned lambs/kids, which is typical of personal bio-control, my arguments aim to illustrate the birth of shepherds unique to the ancient Near East and Mediterranean areas through the reconstruction of the 'domestication process' of sheep/goats. Taking into consideration recent archaeological and archaeozoological results, I think that a majority of the domestication process was completed rather rapidly and the emergence of professional shepherds equipped with basic intervention techniques was realised a short time after the domestication of sheep and goats commenced.

After showing how the typical shepherd came into being, in Part Two I shift the discussion towards the historical age of the temple city-states in the Near East. With the expansion of city-states' ruling powers over surrounding local areas, the temple cities came to hold sway over the surrounding pastoralist groups, and the cities' ruling class began to own large numbers of sheep/goats and cattle, just as the large household chiefs had, and they employed shepherds, entrusting them with the care of their flocks.

In the first chapter of Part Two, I identify a functional similarity between eunuchs as ruling tools used by the Emperors in the ancient Near East and the herd guide-wether utilised by Middle Eastern pastoralists as an effective technique to make the flock move smoothly according to the shepherd's will. Even if there is a possibility that both techniques—one in the human control domain and the other in the animal control domain—were invented independently, we may suppose that either worked as a model for metaphorical extension that led to the invention of the other. In order to determine which of the two techniques could have been the model for the other, from eunuch to herd guide-wether or vice-versa, I provide evidence that, besides the herd guide-wether, there are simpler flock-guiding techniques employed in the Mediterranean and Middle Eastern areas. This implies that the herd guide-wether could have been invented as a final product in the course of the development of these basic herd-guiding techniques, without any reference to eunuchs as a model. Moreover, I will show that as a facilitating factor for the metaphorical transference, there was a unique perspective among ancient Near Eastern household chiefs who ascribed their household serfs and domesticated animals into the same category as living movable property.

Various cuneiform tablet records concerning animal husbandry in these temple city-states were recently published, from which we can learn that the temples owned and administered large numbers of flocks of sheep not only to satisfy the ritual and food demands but also to obtain wool for their textile industries. Among these tablets are accounting records of the flocks entrusted to shepherds and documentation on the occasion of annual contract renewals. Between the lines one can ascertain the interesting relationship between the large flock owners and the entrusted shepherds. For large flock owners, i.e. large household chiefs living in the city distant from the herding field, it was impossible to know if the shepherds would take good care of their flocks and would provide a correct report on the production of lambs without falsification. For this reason, in the contract, the number of lambs to be delivered to the owner was mathematically calculated at a fixed minimum rate on the basis of breeding ewe numbers. As for loss by accidental death, which is a common feature of sheep/goat husbandry, the owner allowed a certain proportional number of animal deaths imposing on the shepherd the duty of showing skins as evidence. I will demonstrate that, notwithstanding these preventive measures, the shepherd could still find room to cheat the system—by delivering a poorly developed individual taken from his part of the flock, or by bringing the owner the skin of a sheep after eating it and so on. Under such a relationship exposed to deception/suspicion, the only effective measure for the owner to ensure the entrusted shepherds were faithful and honest was to appeal to his moral sentiments using an idealised image of a good shepherd while simultaneously threatening him with dismissal if fraud was exposed. After a close reading of these accounting records, the tense relationship between large household chiefs as flock owners and the entrusted shepherds regarding the appropriation of domesticated animals' lives comes to light.

I mentioned above that in Genesis God assigns man the right to rule over animals because of man's similitude to Him. However, in the subsequent parts of the Old Testament we find repeated assertion of the original belonging of animals to God and His order to carry out redemptive sacrificial rituals when killing animals to eat. Behind these narratives on God's (as Dominus) assertion, can we identify the reflection of the tense relationship between household chiefs as owners and the entrusted shepherds concerning the domesticated animals' lives? Reading the second chapter of Part Two where the relationship between owner and entrusted shepherd is described, we can well understand how God's decree that gave a decisive orientation to the European attitude towards animals was accepted by the Israelites as a message taken for granted.

It is well known that the regulations on edible/inedible animals set out in Leviticus have played a crucial role in the dietary customs of the Judaic and Islamic world. Mary Douglas, an influential symbolic anthropologist, cited these regulations as a typical example to support her taboo theory: i.e. the exclusion of deviators from a classificatory system. Despite the fact that she later withdrew the possibility of the application of her theory to these very dietary regulations (Douglas, 1999), as far as her interpretation once applied to the regulations, all inedible/unclean animals should be morphological or behavioural deviators from any of the well-defined animal classes. It is true that the edible/clean ungulate animals—sheep and cattle—are judged edible because they are equipped with cloven hoof and ruminant characteristics as members of a well-defined class, while the inedible/unclean ungulate animals, such as pigs, camels etc. are deficient of either of these two necessary conditions. However, reading on, we will find that other non-ungulate mammals precisely defined as beasts 'walking with flat of foot' are also judged inedible/unclean. Even if the narratives about the edible/inedible regulations in Leviticus seem logically coherent as Douglas once pointed out, there is not only incoherence in the sense mentioned above, but also unnatural descriptions of certain animal morphology. After applying my analysis of God's utterances to this narrative, one will recognise that the modes of narratives are guided by an underlying implicit motivation: the edible and clean animals, sheep/

goats and cattle, were the same domesticated animals that used to be herded and consumed by the Israelites who were small domesticated animal herders wandering in the wastelands surrounding the dominant civilised power centres. The inedible/unclean ungulates, pigs, camels and so on, were eaten by those of the dominant civilised centres or nomads in the desert. Regarding the preceding narratives on dietary principles, this discussion will elucidate the fact that the narratives in Leviticus on the edibility/inedibility of animals were a message from God to the Israelites, who were going through an identity crisis at the time. At that time they were subordinated as servant shepherds under the Pharaoh, a civilised dominant power. In other words, these narratives were a kind of political discourse which utilised the differences in food habits between the Israelites as small animal herders and the adjacent peoples, and constitute an interesting story that reflects the relationship between large household chiefs (*domini*) in the dominant civilised centres and shepherds living a peripheral life who were liable to fall into subordinated status and become servant shepherds.

I would be happy if, when reading through the three chapters in Part Two, readers came to understand how God's assertions concerning animals in the Old Testament came to take their unique forms reflecting the actual relationships between city-states' ruling chiefs as large herd owners and local pastoralists as entrusted shepherds pivoting around domesticated animal life.

This book was written based on two previous publications (1997, 2010) written in Japanese, but is a completely revised version with reference to recently obtained data and information.

I know that I, as a cultural anthropologist, am going to develop audacious arguments in order to clarify the historical background for the formation of the unique ideas on the human-animal relationship in the Near East and the Mediterranean world. I hope only that my arguments will serve to trigger further clarification on the issue by ancient Oriental studies specialists.

Acknowledgements

I have enjoyed a privileged position dedicating significant time to fieldwork thanks to my professional position for more than twenty years at the Institute for Research in Humanities of Kyoto University as a staff member of the Department of Social Anthropology. I have had the opportunity to conduct fieldwork by visiting various pastoralists in the Middle Eastern and Mediterranean areas taking part in the following projects financed by the Grant-in-Aid for Scientific Research of the Japan Society for the Promotion of Science: Project Nos. x521048(1977), x00160-30413(1978), x0016050413(1980), 57041027(1982), 60041041(1985), 62041051(1987) and 01041055(1989). My visit to the Baxtyâri nomads in Iran and the Bakharwal transhumants in India in 1993 was realized through the Inamori Grant in 1992. As most of the information on pastoralists' management activities used in my reconstruction of the sheep/goat domestication process was obtained during field surveys financed by those grants, I would like to express, first of all, my gratitude to those involved in the Grant-in-Aid process.

During my stay at the shepherds' campsites I was observing, the shepherds all kindly allowed me to stay as long as I wanted and willingly accepted when I asked to follow their daily herding activities and observe their busy nursing assistance. Even though I do not identify all the pastoralists and visiting dates here, I am grateful to all for their warm and kind collaboration.

In Japan there are only a few archaeologists and archaeozoologists specialised in the reconstruction of the domestication process in the Middle East. Among them, I owe much to S. Fujii and K. Hongo with whom I have had the chance to discuss and from whom I acquired significant new information gleaned from recent archaeological excavations and analyses. K. Maegawa, an excellent Sumerologist, was a very close colleague in my workplace. Knowing well what kind of topics I was interested in, he often showed me useful articles and books. Y. Konagaya, a specialist on Mongolian nomadic people and an excellent field observer, always stimulated my interest providing me with observational data on Mongolian shepherd's technical modes of intervention that was very useful in terms of comparison with the practices of Middle Eastern shepherds.

Dr. Juliet Clutton-Brock assisted me by inviting me to read a paper at a session of 'Cultural Attitudes towards Animals' organized by herself and Tim Ingold, held at the World Archaeological Congress in 1986, and at a session entitled 'The Zooarchaeology of Fats, Oils, Milk and Dairying' organized by J. Mulville and A.K. Outram held at the ninth ICAZ Conference in Durham, 2002. R. Ellen and K. Fukui invited me to take part in a MOA Symposium in 1992 with the title 'Redefining Nature: Ecology, Culture and Domestication'. In this symposium I was again able to meet Tim Ingold and had the chance to discuss the European concept of domestication with him. I am grateful for their friendly encouragement to publish my studies in English.

I express my heartful thanks to my wife Anna Salvi who supported me throughout this project. Thanks are also due to Susan Holmes and Miriam Riley who edited the manuscript of this book with great care.

Finally, I would like to express my heartfelt thanks to T. Suzuki and S. Takagaki of Kyoto University Press in turning my manuscript into a book. The publication of this book was supported by a Grant-in-Aid for Publication of Scientific Research Results (Grant Number 16HP5272), provided by the Japan Society for the Promotion of Science, to which I express my sincere appreciation.

I dedicate this book to my dearest wife Anna, son Ken and daughter Yuki.

Part I
Domestication Process and the Birth of Shepherds

1 Location of Domesticated Sheep and Goats

In television documentaries on the Middle East, we often see scenes of domesticated sheep/goats moving across a grazing field. At first glance, their behaviour does not seem so different from that of their wild progenitors. However, after spending time with the shepherds and observing how they take care of their flocks and how the flocks behave in response to these interventions, one begins to realise that these flocks are far removed from the way their wild progenitors lived and that they have acquired unique behavioural characteristics brought about by the various repeated human interventions inherent to domestication.

Firstly, if we consider the locations where shepherds do their herding, we realise that most are far from the original distributional areas where the ancestral wild progenitors lived in the Middle East. Man relocated them from their original habitat to a rather different one and they adapted to a different environment.

Now, looking more closely, in West Asia for example we can see that in most cases two shepherds accompany one flock of sheep: the first goes ahead, in front of the flock, while the other remains at the back to chase individuals left behind, and if the front shepherd calls to the animals the front group responds by following him. In the case of a wild flock, they would not follow a human, even if they were located at the head of the flock. Domesticated flocks are attached to humans, having become intimate with them.

In the evening, the flock returns to their enclosure close to the shepherd's campsite without guidance. It is common in Europe to keep the flocks in a wooden or stone enclosure at night, so we are inclined to believe that unless an enclosure is provided a herd would wander off and by next morning be out of sight, but that is not the case. At the summer quarters of Pashtun nomads in Northeastern Afghanistan (1978) and at the winter quarters of the Marwari nomads of Rajasthan in India (1993) I observed that shepherds never kept their animals in an enclosure: after they returned to the campsite, sheep/goats would wander around the camp for a while and then lie down nearby. The Qashqa'i nomads of Iran also do not keep their flocks inside an enclosure except during winter (Beck, 1991: 296). The domesticated sheep/goats not only follow the shepherds, being 'close to man', but are also 'self-anchored to the human campsite', considering it their home range.

When I visited a village in the Logar province of Afghanistan (July, 1977) I witnessed in the distance two groups of sheep coming in succession from the wild desert accompanied by two different groups of shepherds. They had taken them to drink water at a stream emerging from an underground canal (*foggara*). At first, the sheep of the former group began to drink standing side by side along the stream. Soon after, the second group arrived and began to drink mingling with the first group. Shortly afterwards, the shepherds let them lay down on the ground to rest. There I observed an interesting scene: each flock lay down in a place separate from the other. It is well known that in the case of reindeers kept by Saami herders, some individuals of one herd often transfer to another when two groups of different owners approach. Here in Afghanistan, on the contrary, individuals of the respective groups rested in different places, as if they knew they belonged to a certain group. It is evident that among domesticated sheep/goats, a kind of 'belonging to a particular group' was established.

In order to obtain further knowledge on domesticated sheep/goats under human control, we will examine the proportional composition according to sex and age in a flock of 200–300 head. Except for special cases, we will learn that most in the flock are female. Moreover, most males are young, less than one and a half years old, aside from some breeding males. Such a proportional ratio in sex and age can be attested not only in the Middle East where domestication was initiated, but also in the Mediterranean where pastoralism was introduced at a later stage, indicating that this proportional ratio is one of the common features of domesticated flocks kept by sheep/goat herders.

The respective number of newborn males and females should be approximately equal as is the case with wild progenitors. Why, instead, are male numbers much smaller in domesticated flocks? This is because shepherds intentionally cull most of the males at the age of about one and a half years, when their growth rate decreases. Now, apart from the primary reason for culling these lambs, we know that people in the West eat lamb as a symbolic sacrificial animal in the rituals of Jewish Passover, Christian Easter and Islamic Ramadan. This ritualistic custom can be traced back to the original management practice by Middle Eastern pastoralists of culling male yearlings in spring.

Because the growth rate of sheep/goats diminishes and then stops at maturity, the increase in the rate of meat resource at the age of one and a half begins to ease off. Except for breeding males, after maturity all other males cease to offer an increasing quantity of meat and become unproductive parasitic animals. In fact, the increase in the rate of meat compared to grass consumption goes down to zero, therefore the practice of culling male yearlings among sheep/goat herders is directly economically motivated. The management of domestic sheep/goat flocks follows this general principle: 'females are to be kept alive even after maturity as individuals useful for increasing the flock, while males are to be culled at the age of maturity except for select breeding individuals'.

With such a general view, let us examine the shepherds' herd in autumn. The breeding rams are running after the ewes. The males of their wild progenitors, which usually live separately from the female group, join them in autumn and begin to chase the females. So, we are led to believe that the domesticated breeding males, arriving at the mating season, are also going to freely satisfy their reproductive drive. However, the shepherds tell us that these breeding rams, which have been saved from culling, have been kept under special control prior to autumn. In fact, in summer, they are kept in the village separated from the main flock in which there are only a few castrated rams and yearlings besides the numerous ewes. Whenever the breeding rams cannot be kept in the village and have to be kept in the main flock, a sort of chastity belt is attached around the hips of rams in order to prevent them from mating. It is only in the autumn that the breeding rams are allowed to join the ewes and release their sexual drive. Why do shepherds apply such a practice of seasonal sexual seclusion?

The mating season of the wild ancestor is concentrated in autumn. On the other hand, domesticated sheep/goats are active in terms of mating instinct all year round without a seasonal concentration: this is one of the effects of domestication. If they keep rams constantly in the ewes' group without a seasonal seclusion, mating may occur at any time and the delivery period would extend all year long. As I will describe below, the shepherds are very busy giving nursing assistance to newborns during the successive growth stages. If delivery occurs throughout the year and growth stages among newborns differ, nursing care and milking after weaning cannot be done collectively; the need to economise labour for collective nursing assistance and milking is the reason for applying the fundamental management technique of seasonal seclusion.

By artificially concentrating mating in autumn, delivery occurs only within a short period during winter. Then, many newborns are kept at night in a corner within the shepherd's tent or in a small pen separated from the mother ewes that are kept in a larger enclosure. The following morning, before departing for herding, the shepherd must give the newborns a chance to suckle milk from their mothers. On this occasion, he not only picks up the newborns from the separate pen and brings them near to the mother ewes' group, but he also carries some to their respective mothers and pushes each under the ewe's belly. This form of daily nursing assistance is quite labour intensive.

In the case of wild ancestors, just after delivery, a mother and her newborn by bleating and smelling each other establish imprinting for mutual recognition according to a well-known ethological mechanism. After imprinting is established, they will never fail to recognise each other and the mother ewe will only allow her offspring to suckle. After that each wild newborn always follows its mother in the field and spends the night lying close to her. Whenever a newborn wants to suckle milk from its mother, it has the chance to do so.

On the other hand, in the case of domestic sheep/goats, the shepherd keeps the newborns separate from their mothers as described above and has to give considerable assistance during suckling time the next morning. Of course, during lambing, when a shepherd notices the coming delivery of a ewe he follows her and immediately after delivery he ascertains that the mother ewe and newborn smell each other's odour. If the mother ewe, as sometimes happens, tries to leave her newborn, he keeps her close to it in order to be sure that mutual recognition has been established. It is extremely important that mutual recognition takes place with domesticated sheep/goats. When shepherds keep newborns with their mothers without separation, suckling seems to occur without any assistance, as the ethological mechanism for imprinting is innate and these interventions seem needless. Nevertheless, why does the shepherd keep the newborns in a pen separate from their mothers' enclosure at night and take on the troublesome burden of daily nursing assistance?

In any case, when newborns that grow under the shepherds' nursing care become able to graze by themselves, they are weaned, and from that point on, every day before departing for herding and after returning to the campsite in the evening, the shepherds milk the mother ewes.

There are several milking methods: one is to hold the animal's neck in a loop of rope stretched between two poles outside and to free it after it is milked. The other method is to put all animals into an enclosure with only one narrow exit, then, a boy usually chases them towards the exit. Just outside a shepherd is waiting and as soon as one comes out, he catches and milks her. This continues until all have been milked. Before starting milking the shepherd grasps the udder and pushes it up towards the ewe's belly in a firm manner. This mimics the newborn when it suckles from its mother. In the case of a wild female, if a newborn other than her actual offspring tries to push her udder up, she reacts by fleeing. On the contrary, the domesticated milking ewe obediently accepts the violent human touch before being milked.

The beginning of milking is considered a revolutionary event not only in the history of pastoralism, but also in the food history of human beings. Before this practice began, pastoralists had only used animals for their meat, just as hunters did. It is only after the beginning of milking that humans for the first time acquired the possibility of getting animal proteins from living domesticated animals without killing them.

Modern people living an urban life are likely to think that cows are milk tanks and that one can easily obtain milk by squeezing an udder. In the case of cows, before innovating breeding with modern varieties, the milk cow would not allow milking either by a newborn that was not her own offspring or by any human being. This was because the gland would not open without the stimulus given by her imprinted offspring's call and odour. Nevertheless, the people of the Middle East had begun milking since the prehistoric age, adopting a special method to overcome the impediment of the female's physiological mechanism. It is well known that cattle breeders of Southeast Asia and llama and alpaca herders in South America had not known of milking before the introduction of western milking techniques. How could the shepherds of the ancient Near East have invented a special method to succeed in milking? Knowing the female's physiological mechanism, such a question needs answering, but I will leave it to a later chapter and instead emphasise the fact that domesticated female sheep/goats as objects of exploitation for milk production came to have quite a different life experience from their wild progenitors.

Shepherds usually begin to milk mother ewes after weaning their offspring when they have grown enough to feed by themselves on soft grass. At this stage, the shepherds can let the lambs stay in the adult group for herding. However, they keep them separated from the adults for a period of time. This is a measure necessary to avoid the possibility of offspring freely suckling milk from their mothers. Milking practices also forced the newborns of domesticated sheep/goats to accept a different life to that of their wild ancestors.

2 Objectives and Methods

Objective of discussion

Visiting herding fields each season in the Middle East, one can observe various aspects of the relationship between shepherds and domesticated sheep/goats and realise how far removed these animals are from the lives of their wild ancestors.

Among the shepherds' interventions discussed in the previous chapter, the custom to cull male yearlings can be easily understood as an economic motivation to reduce the number of unproductive individuals. The seasonal separation of breeding rams from ewes is considered a preventive measure in order to lighten the burden of collective nursing care during lambing and milking; this is also motivated by economics in terms of maximising labour efficiency. However, not all forms of intervention discussed in Chapter One can be explained by such simple economic factors.

Every day the shepherds take their sheep to fields to allow them to freely graze. This is not carried out according to the shepherd's unilateral intervention alone. The burden of their shepherding care is also alleviated by the domesticated animals' behavioural characteristics: their willingness to follow the shepherd and self-anchoring to the human campsite. These characteristics must have been acquired through repeated daily human intervention, but what kinds of human interventions were involved and how did they develop?

As discussed in Chapter One, every evening the shepherd separates newborns from their mother ewes and keeps them in an independent pen. Then, the next morning he must collect them one by one to give them a chance to suckle. If he attended to them well at delivery in order to establish imprinting, newborns can be left free to approach their mothers spontaneously to suckle. From the perspective of the economics of labour-power, the shepherd's daily separation of mother ewes from their newborns seems unprofitable. Nevertheless, why do shepherds repeat such seemingly excessive and labour-intensive interventions?

The above practices are generally observable at least among all sheep/goat herders in the Middle East. Moreover, most of them must be considered to have been adopted for the first time after the beginning of domestication. This indicates that the totality of human technical interventions were not established from the outset of domestication. Most of the relationships between humans and domesticates developed after the beginning of domestication. What is observable today can be described as a result of an accumulative process of successive interactions between humans and animals, even if the foundations of this process were initiated by humans.

According to this perspective on the domestication process, I first reconstruct the initiation of sheep/goat domestication in the Middle East and later delve into the processes developed by various human interventions after the advent of domestication. After such tentative reconstructions, I demonstrate the unique characteristics of professional shepherds in the Middle East and the Mediterranean areas. The first half of this book is dedicated to such endeavour. Incidentally, my discussion is limited to sheep/goats, which are considered to be the first animals domesticated in these regions.

Methodological issues: Limits of archaeozoological approaches

In order to reconstruct the beginning of the domestication of sheep/goats in the Middle East and the subsequent processes that developed between humans and animals, I propose a methodological premise as follows: these processes must be described as successive interrelationships between human interventions and the animals' responses to them, as an accumulative process of successive interactions between humans and animals. However, after having put forward such a perspective for the reconstruction of domestication, we immediately bump into a methodological hurdle.

According to archaeozoologists, the domestication of sheep/goats occurred far earlier than the advent of written documentation, i.e. in the later half of the ninth millennium, in the middle of Pre-Pottery Neolithic Culture B (Zeder, 2006; Hongo, 2009). The practice of milking sheep/goats has recently been estimated to have begun in the middle of the seventh millennium B.C. at the latest (Evershed et al., 2008). How and with what kinds of materials can we reconstruct these events? Even if I outlined a methodological approach, we would have to contend with the scarcity of available materials. Most human interventions that were adopted to achieve domestication, or were initiated after domestication, must have been carried out without the use of tools. Evidence of these various kinds of interventions immediately evaporated on completion of the process.

Incidentally, hypothetical arguments have been outlined on the beginning of domestication to determine the developmental stages of the main subsistence economies: hunting, gathering, cultivating and herding. We can find an example in a monograph by Morgan (1877) published in the latter half of the nineteenth century, who tried to reconstruct the developmental stages of humankind. He compared agricultural peasants in the ancient Orient with 'contemporary nomads' who in those days were regarded as having maintained the original form of pastoralism. Paying attention to the fact that the nomads had few material tools compared to agriculturalists, he concluded that the ever-migrating pastoralists with poor material culture belonged to a more primitive developmental stage (Morgan, 1877). Friedrich Engels, in *L'Origine de la Famille, de la Proprieté Privée et de l'E'tat* (1884), adopted Morgan's thesis and defined pastoralism as the stage prior to agriculture in the subsistence economy hierarchy. Behind such judgment was not only a historical prejudice that considers nomads who wander in peripheral regions far from civilised urban centres as more primitive, but also a historical progressivism that emerged after the industrial revolution according to which the progress of civilisation can be measured by the abundance of material culture: i.e. tools and mechanical instruments.

However, we may pose the following question: do technical acts rely on tools and instruments? Leroi-Gourhan, a celebrated archaeologist, once asked what tools were in relation to techniques, and found that a technique is a program of a series of action chains conceived in the relationship between a subject and their natural environment: the instrument constitutes only an indispensable element of the technical program (1964–1965, 1: 164; 2: 35). An instrument is at most a partial link in the action chains memorised in the human brain that acts intellectually.

Let me discuss one of the above-mentioned management techniques in relation to domesticated flocks—the culling of male yearlings. This technique that involves culling all young males aside from breeding rams is a practice established on 'the knowledge that animals stop growing at the age of maturity and their quantity of meat does not increase further' and on the following resultant management strategy: 'such unproductive males are better culled when they reach maturity'. This technique is organised via several action chains according to this knowledge and strategy. A culling knife as a necessary tool is only the last step in this chain. There is no need to employ any tool other than a stone knife, which had been adopted since the hunting stage.

Let's discuss another example. In summer, shepherds keep breeding rams separated from ewes and only in autumn do they join the ewe group. This is another strategy employed in order to easily facilitate subsequent collective interventions in winter. Just after delivery, every evening shepherds separate newborns from their mothers by keeping them in a corner of their tent. No material tool is necessary to effect separation. We can easily point out other important technical interventions that do not rely on material tools such as nursing assistance and leading and chasing the flock during daily herding. These are achieved using only human intervention through physical, visual and acoustic stimuli.

Let me compare the above technical interventions with agriculturalists' interventions regarding cultivated plants. In agriculture, human hands are not sufficient to turn the ground or drive water for irrigation, therefore digging tools are indispensable.

The scarcity of material tools in pastoralism does not prove its technical primitiveness compared to agriculture, thus there is no necessary reason for pastoralism to be allocated to a stage preceding agriculture in the developmental stages of the human subsistence economy.

In the latter half of the twentieth century the basis of scientific evidence provided by archaeologists and archaeozoologists identified the place and time of the beginning of plant cultivation and sheep/goat domestication in the Middle East. According to these results, the cultivation of grains began in the Levant Corridor from 9000 B.C. to 8500 B.C., and the domestication of sheep/goats emerged between 8300 B.C. and 7500 B.C., even though the respective locations of sheep/goat domestication differ. This indicates that pastoralism, which in the past had been regarded as a subsistence economy more primitive and prior to grain cultivation, unexpectedly happened to appear on the scene of human history about a thousand years after the advent of grain cultivation. Independently from the fact that pastoralists had fewer tools compared to agriculturalists, the transition from hunting to pastoralism could only be achieved when certain supportive conditions came to fruition and when it became clear that herding provided more efficient productivity and a more stable subsistence economy than hunting.

In spite of the scarcity of materials available, how did archaeozoologists and archaeologists obtain scientific clues to approximate 'when' humans initiated the domestication of sheep/goats? Later I will show the results of the extensive excavations at numerous archaeological sites in the Middle East and their method of analysing the remains of consumed bones excavated there. Important clues were found that suggested a gradual transition from a hunter's pattern to a pastoralist's pattern in the so-called killing profile deciphered from the bone assemblages.

However, even if archaeozoologists could succeed in identifying 'where' and 'when' domestication was initiated utilising the data on the 'killing profile', this evidence is drawn from material signs that remain in the consumed bones that depended on the new killing strategy adopted by those who initiated domestication. Even though archaeozoologists could determine the 'where' and 'when' of the advent of domestication, the question 'how' is left unanswered—even if there are several 'how' hypotheses, we have not yet arrived at a unanimous agreement on 'how' and 'under what conditions' humans succeeded in domestication. In order to answer the question 'how', it is necessary to obtain information on intervention processes used prior to domestication. These people may have chased or approached a wild flock in a particular way and finally succeeded in keeping a certain individual group on hand. Most of the modes of intervention involved left no material evidence because they could be carried out without tools.

Moreover, I have suggested that domestication achieved through human interventions was not completed at the time of the success of domestication. In fact, there are several modes of intervention used by shepherds that were adopted for the first time after domestication was first achieved. For example, the seasonal separation of breeding rams from the female group for mating control, the daily separation of newborns from the mother ewes' group soon after delivery and the temporary herding of weaned juveniles separated from the group of mother ewes did not leave any archaeological evidence. Moreover, there are no traces of shepherds' involvement in morning feeding, when he carries the newborns kept in his tent to the respective mothers and helps them to begin suckling by grabbing the teat. These interventions into the social relationships of sheep/goats do not leave material traces.

Archaeozoologists' investigations based on the killing profile analysis do not provide effective means to reconstruct 'how' humans succeeded in domestication or 'how' various deliberate technical interventions came to be successively adopted after the beginning of domestication. In order to reconstruct these processes we must look for other methods.

A proposal of methods

Firstly, for the reconstruction of the process that led to domestication, it is important to be informed about the following two facts: 1) chronological knowledge of the beginning of sheep/goat domestication and 2) information about the livelihoods and natural environmental conditions of those who carried out the domestication of sheep and goats. Archaeologists have demonstrated that domestication proceeded on the hillside area of the Fertile Crescent after the expansion of grain agriculturalists into that area. This fact may be useful to identify the surrounding environmental conditions and how and why the people, already hunting-agriculturalists, came to domesticate wild sheep/goats. In this context, we can also refer to zoological knowledge of the behavioural characteristics of these animals. Furthermore, for a useful comparison we may refer to what we know about the relationships of the Saami people with the so-called semi-domesticated reindeer. Reindeer differ from sheep/goats in behavioural characteristics, however that knowledge can be utilised as lateral evidence.

On the other hand, 'man-domesticated animal' relationships are not solely achieved through unilateral coercive physical modes of intervention derived from human economic motivations, even if the starting point of the process must have been initiated by humans. After humans began to keep animals in an enclosure under their control, the animals must have begun to regard this space as their home range. Being touched and fed by humans, they also must have begun to follow them, departing from the behaviour of their wild ancestors. Such behavioural changes on the part of animals made it possible for humans to begin several other modes of intervention: for example daily herding. Through repeated daily herding, humans must have invented a range of herd-guiding techniques.

In other words, some techniques might have been invented on the basis of a pre-existent man-animal relationship established by previous technical interventions, while the newly invented processes could in turn add something to the human-animal relationships to open up the possibility of future technical steps. The relationship we can observe today in the herding field is not a product of the first human interventions in the early period of domestication, but is the final result of a chain of successive events produced by the interactions between humans and animals continually promoted even after the beginning of domestication. If we can presume a previous and later relationship between various modes of technical intervention, we may have a clue to reconstruct the domestication process by taking into consideration the necessary conditions for each technical intervention and relating it to others.

In addition, we know that domesticated animals return to a wild state if people leave them free and abandon all the daily repeated actions. As for reindeer, Paine points out that domesticated reindeer regain their wild characteristics after relinquishing human intervention, just as a rubber band goes back to its original state after the external force is released (Paine, 1994: 30). Even if it is not always true that feral sheep/goats regain all the original characteristics of their wild ancestors, knowledge of the social and behavioural characteristics of feral sheep/goats can provide important referential clues to the effects of man's influence, because the characteristics peculiar to the domesticated flocks can be considered to be results brought about by humans through daily and annual routines.

Returning to the so-called semi-domesticated flocks of reindeer of the Saami, we know that they are kept under a kind of control that differs from that of the domesticated sheep/goats and that they have different behavioural characteristics. Taking the differences into account, we can infer the kinds of interventions shepherds used that brought about the peculiar social and behavioural characteristics of domesticated sheep/goats.

When one tries to reconstruct the domestication process, which must have progressed successively in the prehistoric age, the archaeozoological and archaeological investigations that depend on the excavation of consumed bones have a methodological limitation. In order to overcome that limitation, one can resort to comparison with the behavioural characteristics of feral sheep/goats and semi-domesticated reindeer. By examining the respective indispensable conditions for each intervention, we may be able to abductively decipher the prior-posterior order of the introduction of the techniques that we can generally find among pastoralists today.

I have engaged in collecting observational data on the technical interventions of various sheep/goat pastoralists over more than twenty years, extensively visiting groups from the Mediterranean area in the west to the west of India in the east. Of course, there were regional and ethnic differences between the pastoralists I visited, however among them I found that they had fundamental technical practices in common. Further, from ethnographic monographs I could add information concerning the intervention techniques of other pastoralists I was unable to visit. From all this data, I have learnt that beyond the Middle Eastern pastoralists these fundamental techniques are commonly adopted extensively from Mongolia to Africa. This indicates that these commonly shared technical practices came to be universally adopted as necessary and fundamental, to the extent that pastoralists want to efficiently obtain animal food resources from their flocks.

I now try to reconstruct the beginning of the domestication of sheep/goats in the Middle East (Chapter Three) and look at how the fundamental intervention techniques commonly adopted among the various pastoralists today have successively been developed since the beginning of domestication (Chapter Four).

3 How did Domestication Begin?

How did humans succeed in domesticating sheep and goats? I noted earlier in this book that to answer this question it is useful to refer to the knowledge of 'when' and 'where' domestication took place, i.e. chronological conditions. I now discuss the methods archaeozoologists have used to identify them.

When and where? Achaeozoological methods and their results

In the second half of the twentieth century archaeologists Child and Braidwood began studies based on reliable material evidence to chronologically determine the beginning of grain cultivation and domestication in the Middle East. The earlier archaeological materials they used, however, were not appropriate for looking into Pre-Pottery Neolithic Culture B, which was later identified as the beginning of domestication. It was only after the 1970s in the twentieth century that it became possible to start reliable discussions based on data from climatic change, dwelling sites, excavated stone utensils, geographical distributions of ancestral wild sheep/goats and the analysis of carbonised grain and animal bone remains excavated at various archaeological sites.

As for the beginning of grain cultivation, the most important discovery was the oldest carbonised grain at Jericho on the northwestern coast of the Dead Sea. After further extensive excavation in neighbouring areas, botanical archaeologists confirmed that grain cultivation began in the period of the middle and late Pre-Pottery Neolithic Culture A in the lower wetlands of the Levant Corridor (Bar Yosef and Belfer-Cohen, 1989: 447–498; Fujii, 2001: 92–93).

On the other hand, no evidence of the initiation of sheep/goat domestication was found at this archaeological stage, even though after the beginning of grain cultivation the subsistence economy began to shift from hunting-gathering to hunting-cultivating. It was only in the middle and late periods of Pre-Pottery Neolithic Culture B that evidence of the domestication of sheep/goats can be attested, about 1,000 years after the beginning of grain cultivation.

What kinds of materials did the archeaeozoologists rely on in order to identify the beginning of sheep/goat domestication? The information came mostly from the analysis of consumed bone remains excavated at various archaeological sites belonging to various chronological stages. The next question is what aspects of the excavated bones did they pay attention to and what criteria did they adopt in order to reach such conclusions? The main methods were as follows (Meadow, 1989: 80–90).

Changes in the 'killing profile'

It is possible to ascertain the sex and age of bone samples from the growth rate and morphological characteristics of bone fragments. The age of the male or female individuals identifies the age at which they were killed and consumed by humans. From statistical data of the age at death of each individual according to gender, we can reconstruct the killing profile respectively of each sex group at a given chronological stratum of a certain archaeological site and check the diachronic change in successive killing patterns.

Now, let us imagine the respective killing strategy of hunters and herders.

The hunting stage

Especially in the stage of hunting with arrows, the sex and age of the hunted individuals must have been mainly incidental, therefore randomness in age and sex distribution is inevitable. Of course, we know that hunters in general adopt a selective hunting strategy to ensure the reproduction of the game group; as far as possible they must have avoided hunting females as they played a reproductive role, and instead must have favoured hunting males. However, hunting newborns must have been avoided to allow for their growth, even if they were easy prey. It must have been a common habit for hunters to try to hunt larger individuals in order to obtain more meat with less energy expended.

In the archaeological assemblies of bones at the hunting stage, we may be able to find more bone samples of fully-grown individuals and aged males compared to those at the post-domestication stage.

The post-domestication stage

It is likely that humans adopted a different killing strategy after domestication. As I mentioned in the previous chapter, the meat available from an individual animal does not increase after maturity, which in the case of sheep/goats is around one and a half years. For this reason it is most likely that humans in the post-domestication stage began to adopt the following killing strategy: 1) all newborns were allowed to grow until they were one and a half years old; 2) females were left alive to reproduce and ensure the future of the flock; and 3) most of the rams, aside from the breeding males, were culled and consumed at a young age. As a result, in an archaeological assembly of bone remains in the post-domestication stages ewes after the age of maturity should represent a large proportion, while rams after the age of maturity should be proportionally smaller as most of the male yearlings were culled.

To sum up, we may describe the contrasting aspects of the interventions carried out by hunters and herders in the following two ways: 1) different possibilities to intervene in the animal group—shooting wild animals with arrows (element of luck beyond human intentions)/slaughtering domesticated animals under human control (high possibility of carrying out human intentions); and 2) different economic criteria in the killing and consumption strategy—maximisation of the obtained meats against labour energy consumed/maximisation of the meat obtained against grass consumption. As a result of these two different ways of obtaining meat, the killing profile reconstructed from the respective sex and age of the bones consumed produces different curves in the hunting and herding stages.

Of course, this is only a theoretical assumption, based on the premise of ideal models of killing methods by both hunters and herders. Actually, even after finding evidence of a certain transition towards a new killing strategy among herders during a certain period, it has been possible to attest the killing pattern unique to hunters, too, at a particular point in time. There was a certain transitional period between the early stage of domestication and its completion, and we can suppose that during this period, hunting may have accompanied domestication until the community was able to sufficiently satisfy its demand for meat through pastoral activities. However, even though such a transitional stage could be verified, at a certain final stage, as dependence on domesticated animals increased, the killing profile should begin to demonstrate the herder's pattern without leaving any trace of the hunter's strategy. By meticulous observations of the shifts in killing patterns at many archaeological sites, archaeozoologists have been able to determine the approximate time and place of the development of domestication.

Reduction in body size

This generally occurs when a limited number of animals of a species find themselves isolated in a small, restricted area, either by artificial transfer onto an island or by the separation of the island from the mainland. In such a situation, reproduction is repeated within a restricted gene pool cut off from the flow of genes from outer areas. Under such conditions the body size of individuals reduces. The same gene isolation must have also occurred in domesticated flocks under human control and as a consequence the body size of domesticated individuals must have reduced in comparison with their wild progenitors. Of course, the reduction may not have become evident in the immediate period following the beginning of domestication, but would have emerged only after a certain expanse of time. In any case, the reduction of body size can be taken as evidence of gene isolation and can be used to determine the beginning of domestication.

According to such inference, this second marker was first proposed by Hans-Peter Uerpmann in the late 1970s (Uerpmann, 1978). In analysing assemblages of archaeological caprovine bones in the Fertile Crescent area, he found a remarkable downward shift in body size after about 9500 BP uncalibrated. On confirming the subsequent absence of further body size reduction in the later prehistoric assemblages, he suggested that it was caused by domestication. By using the same body size marker, many archaeozoologists provided similar evidence in order to chronologically determine the beginning of domestication.

Recently, the reliability of body size reduction by gene isolation as a marker of domestication has been questioned; in fact reduction in body size can occur for various reasons, for example the deterioration of life conditions after domestication and early weaning of animals under human control. Moreover, Zeder (2006) has recently questioned the data processing of previous analysts; they had analysed bone samples regardless of different growth rates between sexes. Sheep and goats are animals that display sexual dimorphism and the age/size co-relational curve may change in relation to sex. Zeder, paying attention to the different growth rate, remeasured many bone samples at Ali Kosh and Ganzi Dareh taking note of sex and reconstructed the specific killing profile of each sex. She found that the central value of size in male samples moves towards a smaller size compared to the central value in the previous (probable hunting) stages, and that many males were killed around the age of one to two years. On the other hand, in the female samples, she was unable to find remarkable size reduction between the hunting stage and later periods, which can be assigned at the stage of domestication. Moreover, from the killing profile of females, she showed that no significant number of females were culled at a young age (Zeder, 2006: 184–185).

If the reduction in body size had been caused by gene isolation, it should have been attested equally in males and females regardless of sex. Instead, if not observed in the female samples, the cause of the size reduction of males in the killing profile should be attributed to some other reasons. Taking note of these facts, Zeder suggested that the de facto transition of the central value of size in the male samples towards a smaller size is the result of the culling of not yet fully-grown males that was begun after domestication. So the general body size reduction in the bone samples, which has been confirmed and was regarded as the result of gene isolation by preceding archaeozoologists, was caused by the pastoralists' strategy of culling male yearlings after the beginning of domestication. Her argument is persuasive.

Of course, that does not mean that the marker of body size reduction has lost its relevance in the quest to identify the beginning of domestication. By adopting the culling strategy regarding male yearlings after domestication, the shift of the central value of size towards a smaller size in the male samples is inevitable. Even though there may be many factors involved in the reduction of body size, this one-sided size reduction in the male samples could suggest the transition from the hunters' killing strategy to that of the pastoralists and remains the basic marker testifying the beginning of domestication.

Changes in horns

One of the most distinctive morphological differences observed between wild and domestic caprovines is found in the horns: changes in the shape of the cross section, the degree of helical twisting and horn length. However, these kinds of variations are also attested among wild individuals. Therefore, these morphological markers are not regarded as effective evidence of domestication.

Location of bone samples

If a sheep/goat bone sample is excavated in an area far from the original habitat of its wild progenitors and it shows some domesticated characteristics, it is very probable that it comes from the bone remains of consumed domesticated animals that had been transported to the place after domestication. This suggests that the sheep/goats had already been domesticated in a previous period at a different location. This knowledge too is useful in order to determine the latest date for the beginning of domestication.

Among the above four markers, the first one, i.e. the change in the killing profile, is considered at present as the most effective and reliable criterion. Of course, the actual shift from the hunters' to herders' profile is not immediate. In the earliest stage of domestication, it must have been impossible for shepherds to get sufficient meat just from the domesticated flock. The shift from hunting to pastoralism as a subsistence economy must have been achieved gradually. However, after archaeozoologists' extensive excavations of archaeological sites in the Middle East and their meticulous and painstaking analyses of bone samples, they have been able to identify the approximate location and period of the earliest domestication of sheep and goats. The following are the current results of their investigations (see Figure 3.1)

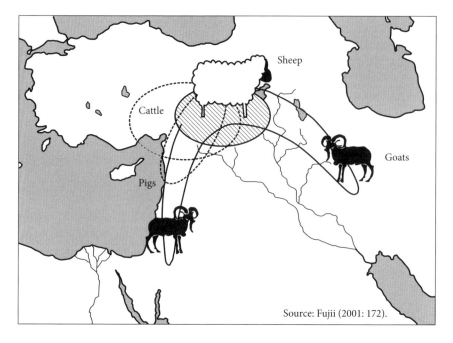

Figure 3.1 Origins of the domestication of sheep, goats, cattle and pigs

Firstly, regarding goat domestication, it is said that the shift towards this process initially took place in the middle and late periods of Pre-Pottery Neolithic Culture B in the Fertile Crescent: the southern and northern Levant, the southern foothills of Taurus in Turkey and Zagros in eastern Iraq. Due to the extensive size of the geographical area of sites where the earliest traces were found, researchers have refrained from determining the original centre of domestication. Some suppose that domestication was initiated and progressed in parallel in each area highlighted in Figure 3.1. On the other hand, in terms of sheep domestication, the earliest evidence of the shift from hunting to herding is found in the archaeological stratum of the Middle period of Pre-Pottery Neolithic Culture B in the area extending from the southern foothills of the Taurus to the western foothills of the Zagros. According to current archaeozoological studies, this indicates that the domestication of sheep and goats had been started around the middle and late periods of Pre-Pottery Neolithic Culture B, from 8300 to 7500 B.C., even though the place of domestication is different for sheep and goats (Zeder, 2005: 141–42; 2006: 202). At this point, it is worthwhile taking note that the earliest evidence of domestication has been found on hillsides where the earliest hunting-agriculturalists living on the lower wetlands progressively expanded their domain towards the hillsides and started rainfall cultivation (Fujii, 2001: 138–140).

Environmental/technical conditions favourable to domestication

Now, after the archaeozoologists provided answers to the 'when' and 'where' in terms of the beginning of the domestication of sheep/goats, we must tackle the question of 'how' it was carried out. Before starting this inquiry, it is necessary to know the specific environmental and historical conditions that shape any event.

For a long time before the beginning of domestication, the hunters of those regions must have encountered and hunted wild sheep and goats, but they did not or could not domesticate them prior to the beginning of wheat cultivation during Pre-Pottery Neolithic Culture A. Moreover, the domestication of sheep/goats was not initiated on the low wetlands where wheat cultivation was first achieved, but on the hillsides where the wheat cultivators had later expanded their living sites and had begun rainfall cultivation. This signifies that some kind of catalyst more important than simple encounters with sheep/goats had matured during that period and that certain environmental conditions must have been present. Let me outline the periodical and environmental conditions in the location where sheep/goats were first domesticated.

Before the beginning of wheat cultivation, people lived by hunting and gathering. In the Pre-Pottery Neolithic Culture A period, around 9000–8500 B.C., the first wheat cultivation was attempted in the lowlands and wetlands in the form of small-scale garden cultivation. Then, during Pre-Pottery Neolithic Culture B, it expanded towards the hillsides in the form of rainfall cultivation. Evidence of sheep/goat domestication came to be present on those same hillsides at the archaeological layer of the middle and later period of Pre-Pottery Neolithic Culture B, about 1,000 years after the beginning of wheat agriculture.

Now, let me summarise these facts in a different way. For a certain period after the age of Pre-Pottery Neolithic Culture A, people in the lowlands and wetlands in the Levant corridor had practiced so-called garden cultivation near springs and marshlands maintaining at the same time the former hunter-gatherer way of life. On the other hand, people in other places, including the hillsides where the lowland hunting-agricultural people later came to expand their domain, still remained at the hunting-gathering stage. Before the middle period of Pre-pottery Neolithic Culture B, domesticated sheep/goats were nowhere to be found in the Middle East (see Table 3.1). Then, after Pre-Pottery Neolithic Culture B and on the hillside areas, sheep/

Table 3.1 Beginning of agriculture and husbandry

	Natufian Culture	Pre-Pottery Neolithic Culture A	Pre-Pottery Neolithic Culture B (Middle and Late Period)
Lowland			
Plants	Collecting	Gathering and horticulture agriculture	Gathering and horticulture agriculture
Animals	Hunting	Hunting	Hunting
Hillside			
Plants	Collecting	Collecting	→ Gathering and rainfall agriculture
Animals	Hunting	Hunting	→ Hunting and beginning of domestication

goats began to be domesticated. This suggests that the people on hillsides—hunter-gatherers until then who had begun rainfall cultivation in this period—were the initiators of the first steps toward the domestication of sheep/goats.

If we take into consideration the vegetational conditions on the hillsides where rainfall cultivation began, we know that it was undulate immense Gramineae grasslands including the ancestral species of our cultivated wheat. Even today if one visits the hillsides in the Middle East where rainfall cultivation took place, one can find extensive Gramineae grasslands (Photo 3.1). In spring, annual grasses begin to ripen. The hunter-gatherers seasonally visited to collect the grains of wild Gramineae long before the middle and late periods of Pre-Pottery Neolithic Culture B and before the beginning of rainfall cultivation (Fujii, 2001: 96). It was this Gramineae grassland that ungulates, too, had frequently visited to feed on grasses and grains. The hunter-gatherers who used to come to collect the wild grains must have frequently encountered flocks of ungulates. However, after the agriculturalists' expansion towards the hillsides, sedentary populations began to live there. In middle and late Pre-Pottery Neolithic Culture B, larger sedentary villages appeared and the cultivated lands began to expand more extensively on the hillside grasslands. The inhabitants must have not only more frequently encountered wild sheep/goats, but they must also have become competitive with noxious animals for agricultural products. Uerpmann states that the wild sheep/goats, which until then were considered targets for hunting, might have come to be seen as potential enemies that would invade the cultivated lands and damage the harvests (Uerpmann, 1978).

Photo 3.1 Gramineae grass plain in Northern Afghanistan

I am also inclined to think that these historical and environmental conditions were important promoting factors towards the beginning of sheep/goat domestication, but they are insufficient to explain why and how domestication was effected in this area and in this period. There must have been a certain change in the man-animal relationship, especially in terms of human intervention techniques. In fact, we are informed by archaeologists that before the Pre-Pottery Neolithic Culture A period, in the middle and late Natufian Culture, new hunting techniques different from arrow hunting, called 'drive in hunting', came to be adopted in the ancient Near East, even though the game targets were not sheep/goats but plain gazelles. This 'drive-in hunting' seems to have been an important and effective technique to foster the domestication of sheep/goats. I now discuss several archaeological facts on 'drive-in hunting' techniques.

Drive-in hunting techniques

At archaeological sites of the middle and late periods of Natufian Culture (prior to Pre-Pottery Neolithic Culture A), for example at Hayonim, Ain, Mallaha and Hatula in the Levant Corridor, significant numbers of consumed gazelle bones were found. Compared to other animal bones, its numerical dominance was

Figure 3.2 Archaeological sites in Levant

remarkable, indicating that in this period people would hunt and consume mainly these animals (Davis, 1982). The dominance of gazelle bones is not characteristic only of this period as it is also found in preceding periods.

However, archaeozoologists who had conducted a comparative analysis of the bones of each period of Natufian Culture discovered the following interesting change in their composition: in the earlier period, the proportion of male and female bones was almost equal, suggesting that they had been hunted equally without preference as they were encountered by humans. On the other hand, in the middle period of the Natufian, the proportion of hunted males conspicuously increased and came to occupy about eighty percent of the total hunted animals (Cope, 1991: 341–358). This would have been impossible to achieve using arrows as the only means of hunting, and the question arose as to how such exclusively selective killing could have been realised: hunters must have begun to adopt a kind of elaborate selective hunting method. Cope suggests the adoption of 'drive-in hunting', i.e. a method to collectively chase a whole group of gazelles and drive them into a net or stone circle prepared beforehand (1991: 351). By such drive-in hunting, they could capture all individuals alive and then deliberately free females responsible for reproduction, while killing and consuming the males in high proportion.

At other sites of the late Natufian Culture, archaeologists actually discovered evidence suggesting the adoption of drive-in hunting. One is an assemblage of consumed bones, mostly gazelles, excavated at Salibiya in the lower area of the Jordan valley. Crabtree and others (1991), analysing their age distribution, showed the respective percentage of animals younger than eight months old and less than one year and eight months old corresponding to the age distribution found in wild flocks. As long as humans had adopted arrow hunting, they did not (could not) hunt them according to such age distribution. Moreover, arrow hunters tend to selectively hunt older and larger individuals so as to conserve energy. Crabtree and others maintain that the Salibiyan hunters must have obtained the whole of the wild flock of gazelles by driving them in a circle or chasing them against a cliff and then consuming them all (Crabtree et al., 1991: 165).

The Natufian Culture Period is the last period of the Paleolithic age just before Pre-Pottery Neolithic Culture A when wheat agriculture was begun and people were still engaged in hunting and gathering. However, as archaeozoological evidence on the middle and late periods of Natufian Culture suggests, the hunters of the Levant Corridor must have adopted drive-in hunting and succeeded in collectively obtaining entire flocks of plain gazelles by driving them into a restricted space.

In terms of the adoption of drive-in hunting, we have other interesting forms of evidence. In the deserts of Syria, Transjordan and Saudi Arabia, many stone constructions called 'desert kites' were discovered in the first half of the twentieth century. They have the form of a kite with two long tails. From a stone circle several long lines of stone-heaps extend, giving the shape of an open mouth (see Figures 3.3 and 3.4). When they were discovered, it was unclear as to the use they had been built for. In later archaeological surveys, archaeologists concluded that they were permanent constructions for drive-in hunting, designed to capture whole flocks of ungulates (mainly gazelles). Chasing them between the extended stone mound lanes, humans drove them into the stone circle at the end (Helms and Betts, 1987).

Moreover, at the kite sites many stone spears were found which might have been attached to arrowheads. This suggests that they shot or captured gazelles driven into the stone circle or who had fallen into holes dug along the wall of the stone circle. After identifying the chronology of each morphologically different type of 'kite' from the stone tools found there, archaeologists have suggested that

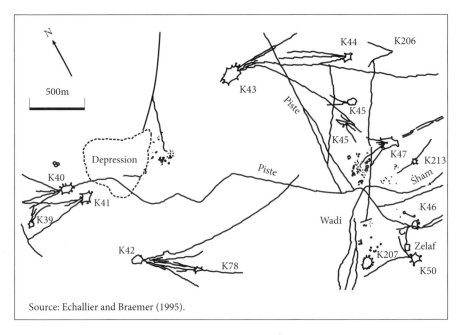

Figure 3.3 Kite site at Zeraf area

the oldest construction type belongs to the late period of the Natufian Culture (Helms and Betts, 1987: 50).

Of course, the geographical distribution of these 'kites' is restricted within a desert area of the southern Levant except for a few other examples (Damascus and Palmira). In archaeological sites out of the Levant desert area (Umm-Dabaghiyah in the north of Iran and Nahal Hemar on the highland area of Israel), net ropes were also found which must have been used for drive-in hunting (Fujii, 2001: 178). As I mentioned earlier, from the bone analysis at the archaeological sites of the middle and late period of Natufian Culture in the Levant Corridor, Cope and others suggested that the hunter-gatherers might have begun drive-in hunting in the semi-desert area of the Levant Corridor where no stone 'kite' constructions were discovered. We may also suppose that on the plains area in the Levant Corridor far from the distribution area of 'kites', hunters may have begun a kind of reduced size drive-in hunting using two rows of people and an innermost net circle in order to capture an entire flock of gazelles.

How did Domestication Begin?

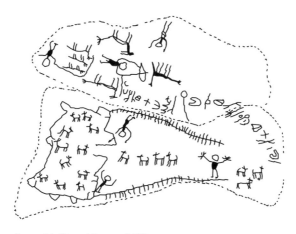

Source: Echallier and Braemer (1995).

Figure 3.4 Hani rock incision

Without sophisticated knowledge of the animals' behaviour, acquired through frequent encounters and patient observation, any inappropriate approach to a wild flock may have startled them and resulted in their fleeing as a group. Even if the hunters carefully approached a flock, they might not always have succeeded in chasing them towards the kite circle, depending on land conditions and the position of the chasers. With regard to this knowledge, after careful observation of how Afghan shepherds chase their flock, Matsui (1989) illustrated an interesting technique for inducing the flock to move in the expected direction by vocal interference and special positioning. He suggested that such knowledge must have already been acquired at the stage of semi-domestication before the beginning of sheep/goat domestication (1989: 159–89). On the other hand, Paine shows how the Saami reindeer herders adopt special inducing techniques when they drive their herds into a fenced enclosure for ear-marking or for catching particular individuals for consumption (Paine, 1994: 72–4). We may suppose that the Levantine hunters, who had begun drive-in hunting since the middle and late periods of Natufian Culture, must have also developed inducing techniques. The advent of drive-in hunting accompanied by these inducing techniques may be called 'preadaptation towards domestication'.

Of course, even if we imagine the beginning of drive-in hunting of gazelles in the middle and late periods of Natufian Culture as preadaptation, neither gazelle nor sheep/goat domestication was carried out in that period. Why could/did they not achieve this? Why must we wait for the beginning of sheep/goat domestication until the middle and late periods of Pre-Pottery Neolithic Culture B? To answer the first question, we can point to the difficulty in establishing intimacy between gazelles and humans that can be facilitated with sheep/goats, and their inadaptability to the densely crowded living conditions of an enclosure, which domesticated sheep/goats can bear. We can suppose that such behavioural differences between gazelles and sheep/goats are the reason why gazelles remained in a wild state, even if they were collectively captured alive. The drive-in hunters of gazelles who succeeded in capturing whole flocks alive must have killed and consumed them immediately.

With respect to this, moreover, archaeozoologists have found interesting evidence: in Levant a rapid shift from gazelles to sheep/goats as the targets of hunters took place in Pre-Pottery Neolithic Culture B (Davis, 1982: 10; see Figure 3.5).

As one probable reason for the shift, we may presume a population reduction of gazelles caused by collective capturing by drive-in hunting. However, we can also take into consideration the following fact: hill-living wild sheep/goats migrate vertically from the hills to the plains within a short range, while plain gazelles migrate horizontally and with a very wide range. The hunter-rainfall agriculturalists on hillsides must have come into contact more frequently and chased more easily these wild sheep/goats as they wandered within a short migrating range. The period of the rapid shift in game from gazelles to wild sheep/goats approximately coincides with the period of the expansion of wheat cultivation towards the hillsides where wide fields were covered by Gramineae grass. As I have already cited above, Peters et al. (2005: 119) suggest that when rainfall agriculturalists on the hillsides began to expand their cultivated land, they may have more frequently come across larger numbers of wild sheep/goats than gazelles as natural enemies damaging their crops. The rapid shift of hunted game from gazelles to sheep/goats can therefore be explained by taking into consideration 1) the chronology of the period of agriculturalist expansion on hillsides, 2) hillside vegetation and 3) a difference in the migration pattern between gazelles and wild sheep/goats.

Summing up, drive-in hunting had the potential to bring about the beginning of domestication because it was a hunting method that made it possible to collectively capture animals alive, which had not been possible with the previous arrow hunting. It had already been adopted in the Natufian Culture in the ancient

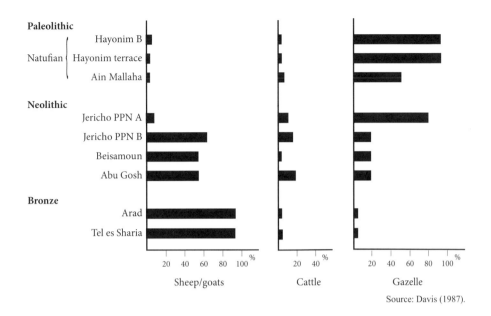

Figure 3.5 Periodical transition of consumed animals in Levant

Near East, however, as long as they hunted plain gazelles, domestication could not occur. It was necessary to wait until the transition from hunting gazelles to wild sheep/goats, which were easy to establish intimate relationships with. This shift was rapidly achieved in the period of Pre-Pottery Neolithic Culture B, and as a reason for this transition we can presume a population reduction of gazelles by the diffusion of drive-in hunting. Moreover, the period of Pre-Pottery Neolithic Culture B coincided with that of the hillside expansion of wheat agriculturalists that favoured encounters with wild sheep/goats more frequently than before. Under these promoting circumstances preceded by the historical expansion of the hunting-agricultural people in Pre-Pottery Neolithic Culture B, the technique of drive-in hunting adopted already in the middle or later period of Natufian Culture pushed towards the next step in the beginning of sheep/goat domestication.

Origins of domestication (1): 'drive-in hunting'

Presupposing the above-mentioned promoting factors towards domestication, how was the domestication of sheep/goats actually carried out in the middle and later periods of Pre-Pottery Neolithic Culture B? Even if the hillside people could obtain whole flocks of wild sheep/goats alive by drive-in hunting, this does not immediately sanction the beginning of domestication, as they probably killed and consumed them soon after capture. It is important to underline, however, the fact that individuals captured by drive-in hunting were alive, while with arrow hunting, the animals were already dead before the hunters laid hands on them. According to a clever definition by Fujii, arrow hunting can be classified as 'kill and collect' hunting, while drive-in hunting can be seen as 'collect and kill' hunting (Fujii, 2001: 176). In the second case, humans were able to wait before killing and consuming. Domestication consists of actions carried out by humans in order to collectively keep individual animals alive under their control. In this sense, we can say that the hunters who had begun to hunt sheep/goats by drive-in hunting were only on the path towards domestication.

Initially drive-in hunters might not even have had any intention of domesticating the animals they captured. They had succeeded in driving many animals into the corner of a stone circle and they must have shot and killed them, as attested by the gazelle hunters at Salibiya. Sometimes it may have been the case that the number of wild dead animals was too large to transport to the residential sites. They presumably must have left some of them alive in the net or stone circle to retrieve at a later stage. Among the captured prey, there must have been various males and females at different stages of growth: adults, juveniles and newborns. In front of such group, the first thing that comes to mind might be to kill the adults and wait before killing the juveniles and newborns. Such a selective slaughtering practice had already occurred and is attested in the high proportional killing (eighty percent) of male gazelles at the Levant sites of the middle and late periods of Natufian Culture. On the other hand, especially when drive-in hunting was carried out in spring, they may have found not only numerous mother-offspring pairs, but also many pregnant females wandering in the enclosure. It is reasonable to suppose that the hunters waited for the lambs/kids to be born and grow to a certain size before killing them. I will call such strategy 'survival strategy of the mother-offspring pair'.

Of course, in order to continue such a strategy, they must be able to feed them daily by collecting and bringing grass to the hunting site. The drive-in hunting site must have been distant from their residential site, not only for the early drive-in hunters of gazelles in the Natufian Culture but also for the hunting-agriculture people before their expansion to the hillsides. It must have been rather difficult for them to collect and transport the necessary amount of grass to feed the captured animals on a daily basis. Even if they succeeded in keeping them alive, the amount of grass they could provide must have been very limited. On the other hand, in the middle and late periods of Pre-Pottery Neolithic Culture B when people started rainfall agriculture on the hillsides, the situation was quite different. At this stage the drive-in hunting site would have been close to their residences as wide Gramineae grasslands spread around the villages. Under such new environmental conditions, it would have become easy for them not only to collect abundant grass and feed many mother and newborn pairs, but also to continue to keep lambs even after weaning. For the first time after adopting 'the survival strategy of the mother-offspring pair' under such favourable conditions, a new kind of individual born and fed in the artificial enclosure must have appeared. Its meaning is important, because these animals would become collectively self-anchored to a man-made enclosure, and this location would begin to become the place where they were born and grown and signify their own home range.

Of course, the mothers artificially fed after being captured must have remained wild, as they had lived in the wild until then and their home ranges remained on the original wild grasslands. Had they been set free from the enclosure they would have tried to return to their original wild home range. On the contrary, the newborns raised in the man-made enclosure would not have escaped. These newborns of 'the survival strategy of the mother-offspring pair' are the first generation to obtain the distinct behavioural characteristic seen in domesticated sheep/goats today. Following Fujii's definition, we can call them 'the (domestic) game that do not escape' (Fujii, 2001: 168), i.e. the first generation of domesticated sheep/goats.

In the early periods such individuals must have been small in number, and hillside people could easily feed them because of the proximity of drive-in hunting places to their residences. By regularly feeding the first generation, females born there delivered their offspring of a second generation that would emerge as a nucleus of individuals collectively sharing a common home range in the same artificial enclosure.

Of course, the human intervention process, which I have supposed and explained above, cannot be proven by any archaeological data. It simply represents a hypothetical reconstruction of the process leading to the advent of sheep/goat domestication, taking into consideration the environmental conditions of the place where evidence of the earliest domestication was attested and supposing that the people there would use the drive-in hunting technique for which the records of stone circles and 'kites' are an important clue. In this hypothesis, the crucial points are the presumptions of capturing numerous live individuals in an enclosure by drive-in hunting and of sparing and feeding the newborns at the artificial enclosure applying 'the survival strategy of the mother-offspring pair'. The favourable circumstances behind such behaviour are the proximity between human residential sites and the homeland of the wild sheep/goats on the hillsides and the abundance of Gramineae grasses. This presumption seems apt to well explain the process as the decisive move towards the domestication of sheep/goats.

Such a hypothesis on the beginning of sheep/goat domestication has already been suggested by Cope, Matsui and Fujii (Cope, 1991; Matsui, 1989; and Fujii, 2001: 175–8). Especially Fujii, as discussed above, defined the adoption of drive-in hunting as a transition from 'kill and collect' hunting using arrows to 'collect and kill' hunting, and proposed the 'survival strategy of the mother-offspring pair' as decisive intervention leading to the first domesticated individuals. He defined the final result of this strategy as the advent of '(domestic) game that does not escape'. My reconstruction outlined above was guided by the work of these scholars. However, there is a difference in my argument as follows.

I have described the first evidence of the nucleus of the domesticated group not only as the advent of '(domestic) game that does not escape' as Fujii defines it, but also as the emergence of a sheep/goat group collectively sharing their respective home range through self-anchoring to the same artificial enclosure. I would like to emphasise the event of sharing an enclosure as a common home range as an important shift introduced by the beginning of domestication: this renders many aspects of human intervention after the beginning of domestication more understandable.

However, before discussing the implications of this fundamental shift in the beginning of domestication, I would like to test another hypothesis on sheep/goat domestication besides drive-in hunting.

Origins of domestication (2): 'intimacy establishment'

This hypothesis proposed by Imanishi (1948) and Umesao (1965) imagines the process of domestication through the establishment of intimacy with the whole flock of sheep/goats achieved through the hunter's constant proximity. As useful comparative data to check the validity of this hypothesis, we can first refer to the relationships of the Saami of the Arboreal zone with reindeer, a related species to sheep/goats.

The Saami are often described as reindeer nomads, which may give the impression that their reindeers are fully domesticated. However, as shown in Paine's (1994) detailed descriptions, these animals must be characterised as being half domesticated because except for a few individuals that are tamed as riding or transport animals, the Saami allow them to repeat their own seasonal migration over a very wide range of 200–300 kilometres according to their original behavioural pattern. The herders follow them all year round and when they want to catch a number of individuals for slaughtering, they drive them into a fenced enclosure prepared beforehand. As far as such 'drive-in' intervention is concerned, what they do does not differ from the presupposed drive-in hunting of Natufian Culture in the ancient Near East. The Saami's intervention is not restricted to such drive-in inducement, however, as herders often dare to enter into the midst of a wandering herd to catch some by lasso or by hand. They have established a close level of approachability with them. If we describe the relationship from the reindeer's side, we may say that the herd allow such a close approach by humans (Paine, 1994: 129). Through constant following and by attending wild herds, the Saami have succeeded in establishing intimacy with the reindeers and in taming some selected individuals. We may describe this as 'intimacy establishment with the herd as a whole'.

Of course, aside from the tamed individuals, most of the reindeer are left free to migrate according to their own behavioural characteristics. During daily attendance to the migrating herd, the most important matter for the herders is to avoid the mingling of their animals with those owned by other herders. They generally do not carry out daily herding in the way of the sheep/goat shepherds in the Middle East, who every day guide their flocks to a different pasture and herd them back to the campsite in the evening. They do not intervene in the animals' activities through nursing assistance during delivery and at suckling time, which are commonly carried out among sheep/goat shepherds. As one reason why the Saami leave the reindeer herd free to follow their own innate migration, we may take into account the scarcity of grasses in the boreal area. In those vegetation conditions, it may be wiser to allow reindeers to follow their instinctive ability to find the growing moss that varies yearly and seasonally.

Even though they are not fully domesticated, the important fact in this context is that the Saami succeed in establishing sufficiently intimate relationships with reindeers to allow humans to enter into the herd. The relationship between the Saami and the herd provides us with lateral evidence for the validity of the hypothesis of 'establishing intimacy with the flock as a whole' as a prerequisite for the process of domestication.

It is not important whether we call the intimate relationship between Saami and reindeers 'semi-domestication' (Matsui, 1989) or 'proto-domestication' (Cope,

1991: 357). As far as the herd is left free to migrate following their own behavioural instinct, we cannot define this stage as domestication. However, it is important that thanks to the established intimacy with the herd as a whole, the Saami succeed in capturing some individuals and in taming them.

Taking such facts into consideration, we may presume a similar initial condition in the process of sheep/goat domestication. Given the characteristics of sheep and goats, it is easier for humans to establish intimacy with them than with reindeer. We have already learnt that in Pre-Pottery Neolithic Culture B, people who began rainfall cultivation on hillsides covered by wild Gramineae must have had more frequent and close encounters with wild flocks of sheep/goats. It was during that same period that the shift from gazelles to sheep/goats as game targets took place. Given these chronological and environmental conditions, we may suppose the possibility that the hunting-rainfall agricultural people deepened their intimacy with wild flocks of sheep/goats through constantly following them and succeeded in catching some of them. Then, by feeding the captured mother-offspring pairs at their campsite, they could obtain the first core of domesticated individuals self-anchored to a human residential site. So, during the initial phase of domestication, to the drive-in hunting hypothesis we may add the process of 'establishing intimacy with the flock as a whole' as another possibility.

Until now, these two hypotheses have been regarded as incompatible with each other. Researchers have long discussed which hypothesis ought to be acceptable, because drive-in hunting—chasing into an enclosure and capturing wild animals—seemed an aggressive method incompatible with the establishment of intimacy. However, are these two approaches really incompatible? We have seen how the Saami adopt these two methods of approach in parallel: 1) by following the migrating reindeer, they succeed in establishing intimacy with the whole flock so that the animals allow humans to closely approach in order to catch them and 2) by driving the whole flock into an enclosure they succeed in capturing several individuals to tame them or to ear-mark newborns. From the above description it is clear that the 'drive in' and 'establish intimacy' methods are not incompatible and can in fact coexist.

It is very likely that by constantly chasing and following wild flocks of sheep/goats in order to keep them away from cultivated fields, humans were able in turn to establish intimacy with them. It is easily imaginable that taking advantage of such a favourable intimate relationship they drove them into previously prepared fenced areas to catch whole groups of them. I will leave checking the validity of the two hypotheses and the final judgement on the process to future scholars, because more important matters concerning our context here are the actual results and implications in relation to these animals that come from the human attempts at domestication presumed in these hypotheses.

Until this point, presenting two possible hypotheses on the initial process of domestication, I have implicitly supposed 'effective and constant procurement of meat' as a latent driving motive towards domestication. However, Vigne and Helmer (2007) recently suggested the possibility that the domestication in the ancient Near East could have been at least partly motivated by milk procurement.

Until about two decades ago, milking was regarded as one of the secondary products in the domestication process and was thought to have been initiated at the earliest at the beginning of the fifth millennium B.C. (Davis, 1984; 1993: 3–5). Owing to the advanced technique of analysing fatty acids from milk attached to shards of Neolithic pottery vessels, however, we are now informed by Evershed et al. that milking had been practiced at least by the seventh millennium B.C. (Evershed, et al., 2008). On the other hand, Vigne and Helmer (2007), who elaborated a more precise method to determine the culling age of consumed bones and tried to infer the beginning of milking from the culling profile, supposed that milking was probably practiced in the early period of the eighth millennium B.C. However, as suggested above, the milk glands of the cow do not open without the stimulus of its true offspring, indicating that there was a physiological impediment to be overcome by milk-ejection inducing devices, which I will discuss later. Conversely, though a milking ewe tends to avoid a suckling approach except by her true offspring, sheep/goats do not have such a physiological impediment. Therefore humans could have exploited milk without inventing any device whenever they had access to a mother ewe and took to milking in order to drink. Even though it is not yet scientifically possible to distinguish the milk residue of either sheep/goats or cows, the first animals pastoralists began to milk would likely have been sheep/goats.

Besides this material evidence for the beginning of milking, Fujii, an archaeologist, recently demonstrated that nomadic expansion from mother villages towards deserts was already initiated soon after the beginning of domestication at the Jafr Basin sites in southern Jordan (Fujii, 2013). Referring to the above knowledge on the very early stages of milking, he proposed a hypothetical assumption that milking was initiated via the motivation of these first nomadic pastoralists to quench their thirst in the extremely dry environment (Fujii, 2015). If the first milkers were the early nomadic pastoralists who advanced across the desert, the first animals to be milked would likely have been sheep/goats.

Even though Vigne and Helmer's arguments on identifying the chronological date of the beginning of milking are based on several unreliable presuppositions, it is, as they suggest, most likely that the milking practice was initiated by 'hunter-cultivators' who began to keep a number of sheep and goats. However, such hunter-cultivators, too, could have caught those animals after having succeeded in establishing a kind of intimacy with wild flocks, as is assumed in the second hypothesis.

What did the beginning of domestication mean?

When I, following the drive-in hunting hypothesis, supposed the 'survival strategy of the mother-offspring pair' and daily feeding of the captured animals by collecting grass as preconditions for beginning the process of domestication, I emphasised that consequently some individuals would have been born and raised in the artificial enclosure. In fact, it may not be the only end result brought about in the course of the 'drive-in' hypothesis, but also in the course of the 'intimacy establishment' hypothesis. Independently from the difference between these two processes, as far as keeping and feeding captured animals in an enclosure goes, the final result is the same: the advent of a group of animals self-anchored to an artificial enclosure and sharing the same restricted site as their common home range.

Until now, archaeologists and archaeozoologists have analysed the killing profile of bone assemblies in the Middle East and paid attention to the primordial construction of enclosures where people must have kept animals, but their prime interest was to identify 'where' and 'when' the domestication of sheep/goats was carried out. They did not question what it had meant to those animals to be brought into an artificial enclosure and to be reared there in terms of their behaviour and living conditions.

Fujii first discussed it as the advent of '(domestic) game that does not escape'. Being fed by humans in the enclosure, newborns developed high levels of intimacy with them and became self-anchored to a human residential site. Supposing a group of sheep/goats attached to an artificial enclosure, we can understand why pastoralists could begin daily herding. The definition by Fujii is right and important as far as the behavioural shift is concerned, but the implications of collective self-anchoring to the same artificial enclosure are not completely accounted for by his definition alone.

How did Domestication Begin?

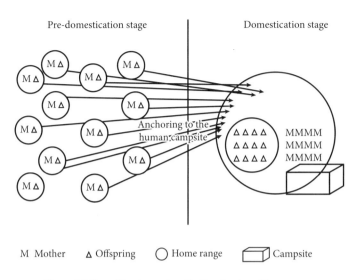

Figure 3.6 Transition towards collective sharing of home range

I have described the self-anchoring of newborns to an enclosure as collectively sharing the same restricted site as their common home range. With regard to this, it is fitting to cite the following information obtained by Jewell, Milner and Boyd from their field observation of feral sheep at St. Kilda in the U.K. (Jewell, Milner and Boyd, 1974). Except for migration, each individual occupies its own home range separate from others, even if their respective home ranges sometimes partially overlap. Conversely, sheep/goats after the beginning of domestication began to collectively share the same artificial enclosure as their common home range. From an ethological point of view, the domesticated sheep/goats found themselves in quite a new situation that differed from that of their progenitors, as seen in Figure 3.6, and we cannot ignore this shift in their living conditions. In the wild stage, pregnant ewes could deliver their offspring in their respective home range separated from others. Instead, after domestication, delivery occurred in a closed crowded space in the harbouring site or during herding migration. In the wild stage, newborns after birth could freely follow their mothers for suckling, while in the domesticated situation they must approach their mothers in the midst of a crowd of animals in a limited space. The emergence of this new situation forced pastoralists to engage in various new ways of intervention. In compensation for the new possibility of obtaining meat resources at any time, people who had succeeded in keeping many sheep/goats were obliged to carry out new burdensome duties to care for them.

At the beginning of this book, I pointed out many aspects of human intervention towards domesticated sheep/goats commonly found today among pastoralists of various areas, and I stated that one of my aims was to reconstruct the process of how the relationship between man and domesticated flocks successively progressed. The next chapter features a reconstruction of the stages concerning the time after the beginning of sheep/goat domestication, i.e. the implications of the new conditions in which these animals, now domesticated, began to find themselves and the approaches and solutions invented and carried out by shepherds.

4 Developments After the Beginning of Domestication

Given the new life conditions brought about by artificial enclosures, what forms of human intervention were now possible or necessary? Regarding a group of animals confined in an enclosure, the first necessity is to provide grass. How was this achieved? Being raised together in an enclosure was quite a new situation that differed markedly from their wild progenitors, each of whom could independently reserve their own home range. Were the effects on animals positive or negative? And if negative, what kinds of countermeasures were adopted by early pastoralists? In earlier chapters I noted that the fundamental technical interventions commonly adopted by various pastoralist communities should be described as a process of successive steps of interaction between man and animals. Taking into consideration the conditions that emerged after the advent of domestication, I now try to reconstruct how shepherds coped with the new challenging situation and the tools and techniques they used and investigate how the animals responded to their actions.

Male culling strategy

Among the excavated residential sites of the later period of Pre-Pottery Neolithic Culture B, archaeologists found a few examples of piles of stones that from their shape can be deemed enclosures for domesticated animals. One is located at Beisamoun in the Jordan Valley (Israel)—a little removed from the human residential district is a rectangular form surrounded by stone walls, each measuring about fifteen metres in length (Figure 4.1). Archaeologists were unable to find any trace of pillar-like suspensions designed to support a roof and it is unimaginable that such a large space could be covered by a roof without any such structure, indicating that it was an open-air enclosure. Moreover, the wall was too thin to support stone piles of more than one meter in height. From these observations, archaeologists judged that it was not a construction for human residence, but a stone enclosure for domesticated sheep/goats (Lechevallier, 1978; Fujii, 2001: 179).

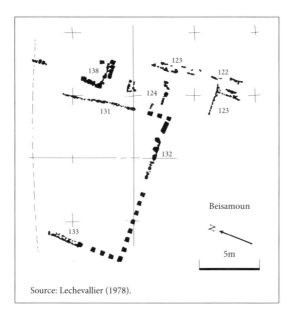

Figure 4.1 Archaeological site thought to be an animal enclosure at Beisamoun

On the other hand, had it been a typical enclosure for domesticated sheep/goats, there should have been an open gate to let them out for daily herding. Instead, there was no gate. Considering that this site has been assigned to the earlier period when sheep/goat domestication was in its initial phase, they supposed that it was utilised to keep and feed sheep/goats captured according to a survival strategy. The same type of stone wall is also found at the archaeological site of Abu Gosh (Lechevallier, 1978; see Figure 4.2).

However, considering that pastoralists kept the captured sheep/goats in a closed enclosure collecting grass to feed them, the number of animals would have increased through the generations unless a culling strategy was adopted. Let's suppose that among the flock ten newborn females had been initially captured along with several breeding rams. After two years, those newborn females would begin to give birth. Even estimating a newborn mortality rate of forty percent under unhygienic conditions and supposing that the shepherds culled and consumed four year old individuals, in five years time the total average number would be thirty. In ten years it would be eighty, and 160 in twenty years. In twenty years, the flock size would

Developments After the Beginning of Domestication

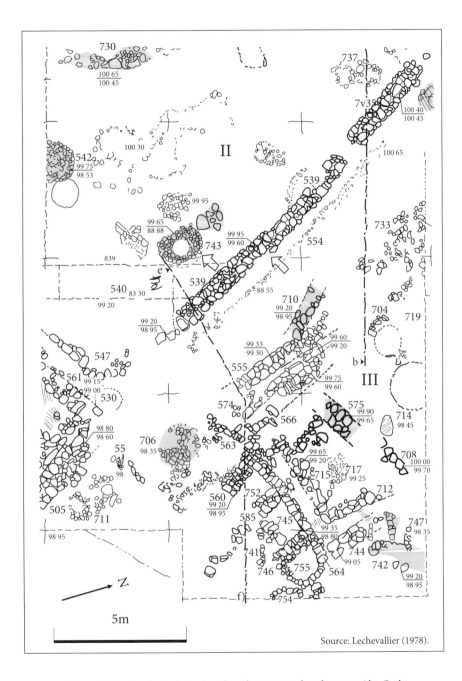

Figure 4.2 Archaeological site thought to be an animal enclosure at Abu Gosh

grow to sixteen times the initial number. Pastoralists must have quickly encountered the problem of securing sufficient grass to feed such a large number of animals. Of course, the earliest animal owners were rainfall agriculturists on the hillside areas who fed their flocks with collected wild Gramineae grasses that grew close to their place of residence or with the straw harvested from cultivated wheat. If we calculate the quantity of grass they had to secure for only one individual per year, we can conclude that as the flock size increased, owners must have gone to more distant places to obtain sufficient grass.

What measures might they have taken in the face of constant grass shortages? As mentioned in the previous chapter, during the stage of the mother-offspring survival strategy adopted after drive-in hunting, males were selectively slaughtered and consumed. This was because after maturity males become unproductive as meat suppliers, and to economise grass-collecting labour it was better to consume them when they were one and a half or two years old. Archaeozoologists have attested that the number of males beyond this age decreased markedly in the bone remains they examined among the consumed animals from this period compared to that of the previous period. They took this fact as evidence of the beginning of domestication.

From these facts, we can suppose that early pastoralists began to adopt the following management strategies within the period immediately after the beginning of sheep/goat domestication: keeping the ewes responsible for flock reproduction alive and culling the rams as unproductive, except for breeding rams. Since then, this culling strategy has become one of the customary management practices used by pastoralists in the Middle East. The sacrificial male lambs slaughtered and consumed at the Passover rites of Hebraism, at the Christian Easter Festival and during the Islamic celebrations after Ramadan are male yearlings culled according to the traditional management strategy.

Now, if we try to define this culling strategy from the standpoint of 'bio-control' (in association with Foucault's 'bio-politics') we can describe it as 'classificatory bio-control' over the domesticated sheep/goats according to sex and age distinctions.

The beginning of daily herding and its conditions

People in the early stage of domestication must have provided their animals with grass collected in the neighbourhood of their living sites on a daily basis. Even if they had culled the males in order to economise grass-collecting labour, females were to be kept alive to continue to produce offspring and the flock size must have grown as a result. It must have been only a matter of time before the labour

Developments After the Beginning of Domestication

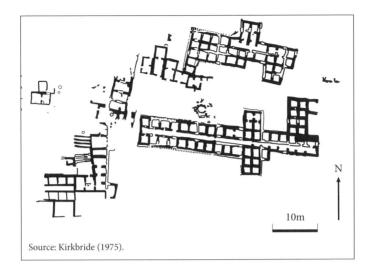

Figure 4.3 Inner court thought to have kept sheep/goats at Umm Dabaghiyah

capacity for grass collection reached its limit: the measure to resolve the problem was to take the flock to the fields and let them graze freely. In fact, we have early evidence of herding.

At some residential sites from the late period of Pre-Pottery Neolithic Culture B to Pre-Pottery Neolithic Culture C, archaeologists found inner courts surrounded by dwelling rooms, one corner of which was open, like an exit. If it were used as a storeroom, it would have been better to have been completely enclosed by walls in order to protect the goods against robbery. Archaeozoologists judged that these courts were used to keep domesticated sheep/goats and that people must have taken their flocks out for herding every day (see Umm Dabaghiyah (Kirkbride, 1975) plate I and the former half of the Beidha II (Kirkbride, 1966: 12); see Figures 4.3 and 4.4). Of course, in the earlier periods the herding place must have been close to the residential sites. What favourable conditions facilitated the beginning of herding?

Self-anchored animals and their intimacy with humans

At least in the Mediterranean area, we often see shepherds who keep their flocks in stone enclosures or wooden pens. If someone sees for the first time sheep/goats kept in an enclosure at night, they would likely think that this is used to confine animals that would otherwise escape.

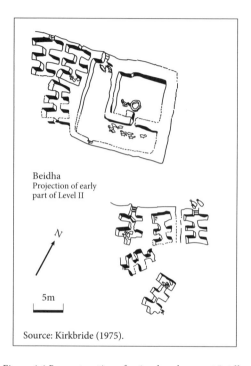

Figure 4.4 Reconstruction of animal enclosure at Beidha

However, I stated above that I witnessed in the summer quarter of the Pashtun nomads of Afghanistan the flock of sheep/goats returning by themselves to the human campsite, even without the shepherds' guidance. After having wandered for some time around the campsite, they lay down to rest in the adjacent open space. Even without an enclosure, they regarded the human campsite as their home. In the past after the initial moves towards domestication, when pairs of mothers and offspring were kept at artificial dwelling places, newborns would be fed and raised in the enclosure. From that life experience, they began to regard the site as their own home range and became attached to the man-made enclosure.

This phenomenon does not, however, automatically develop into herding. The following must therefore have occurred: discovery—in the early days of domestication, owners may have found that some of their animals were grazing at a neighbouring field after escaping from their enclosure. They would not have gone far, and they would have returned near to the enclosure at sunset. The shepherds had already established an intimate relationship with their animals through daily feeding and learned that these animals would follow them when enticed with handfuls of grain or grass. This must have given them confidence in guiding their flocks to distant grasslands, as they would follow them back to the campsite. In so doing they could preserve their cultivated fields and resolve the issue created by the limits of their capacity to collect grass. The larger the flock, the farther the shepherds would take them.

Tendency to follow a leading individual

Daily herding is generally achieved by two shepherds. The shepherd in front leads the flock while the other walks behind and has the task of checking slow or straying animals and chasing them back into the main group. The back shepherd intervenes in the flock by force and coercion. On the contrary, the leading shepherd walks ahead in front of the herd sometimes calling them. Coercive physical intervention is not necessary and the shepherd will be followed meekly by some individuals, which are in turn followed by the rest. This stems from their behavioural characteristic of followership, i.e. to follow the individuals that walk in front. As a result, the whole flock moves smoothly after the leading shepherd. Followership is a very important behavioural characteristic that makes herding easy, but why do some individuals follow the shepherd notwithstanding the fact that in a sheep/goat flock there is no natural leader?

The shepherds carry out nursing care for newborns for several weeks after their birth, as I will specify later. This is a very important time for the establishment of a close human-animal relationship. A shepherd knows well which individuals are more obedient and intimate and, as I often observed among various pastoralists, they favour that attitude and strengthen the link by rewarding them with grain fed by hand.

In the morning when the shepherd opens the exit of the enclosure to begin daily herding, one would think the flock would immediately move out of the enclosure and begin walking away to graze. In fact, except for goats that are more active, the timid sheep do not dare to move, instead they observe the situation around them and even when they have moved out, pushed by the shepherd's chasing from behind, they tend to lie down at a place near the exit. (Very often I personally observed such scenes at the campsites of the Carpathian shepherds in Romania or the Marwari nomads in western India). On such occasions, the shepherd takes a handful of grain out of his bag and shows it to some individuals, those more intimate with him, who run to him to get the grain and this movement induces others to follow creating a chain reaction until all follow in turn. This taming via ordinary food provisioning lets the shepherd guide the flock at his will.

On the other hand, the shepherd at the back of the flock chases them also on the basis of the knowledge of the special behavioural characteristics of sheep/goats. As mentioned above, the chasing techniques based on this kind of knowledge must have been already learned in the semi-domestication stage of drive-in hunting (see page 29). Strong intimacy, however, the most important feature in the shepherd-sheep/goats relationship, is established through the nursing care that every shepherd has been obliged to carry out since domestication.

Formation of flock boundary

Beyond intimacy, I want to point out another favourable behaviour characteristic of domesticated sheep/goats that can be defined as the formation of a flock boundary.

During herding time, it sometimes happens that two flocks of different herding groups encounter each other; it is a shepherds' greatest fear to see two flocks mingling. In the case of reindeer, the core preoccupation of herders is the transmigration of individuals from one flock into another (Kuzuno, 1990: 18; Tei, 1992: 70, 148). With domesticated sheep and goats, the risk can be diminished by the formation of a flock boundary.

At the beginning of this book, I mentioned an interesting fact observed in Afghanistan: two different flocks guided by different shepherds to a stream to drink intermingled, but when they returned to rest on the banks of the stream, the members of each flock sat down at a place separate from the other, as if each knew which group they belonged to.

This behaviour, which I observed with the sheep flocks of the Pashtuns of Afghanistan, was also observed by Ohta with the goat flocks of the Turkana in East Africa. When two flocks guided by different owners intermingled, Ohta says that by the shepherd's slight body movements, the respective members of each flock separated from each other and returned to their own group (Ohta, 1982a and 1982b). Shikano, who observed goat flocks of the Samburu people in East Africa, reports a similar finding (Shikano, 1984).

In the case of the reindeer herds of the Saami, when two different flocks approach each other, the herders nervously control the movements of their herds in order to prevent mixing. If, however, some individuals transmigrate into the other herd, the owner asks the owner of the other herd to drive them into a fenced area nearby and confirm the ownership of each individual by checking their ear marks (Kuzuno, 1990; Paine, 1994: 23–24).

Contrary to domesticated sheep/goats, why do such reindeer transmigrations easily occur? First of all, the Saami do not bring their herd back to their residential site daily, unlike shepherds of sheep/goats in the Middle East. They leave their herds free to wander and migrate as they like. New offspring are born and grow with their mothers in the fields living in conditions quite different from the newborns of domesticated sheep/goats, which are born in and raised at the same man-made residential site. These reindeer are neither self-anchored to the same artificial harbouring site, nor collectively share the place as their common home range. On the contrary, domesticated sheep/goats in the Middle East born and raised at the same harbouring site experience intensified belonging to their group and form a sort of flock boundary.

Of course, there are different methods of organising the herding units. In some cases, several owners join their animals into one large herding unit and take turns at herding. At night, the groups of different owners return to the respective harbouring site and spend the night there. However, every morning they meet again and join the other groups. By such treatment, group cohesion can be decreased and some individuals may move into the other herding group when two groups approach each other. In Central Italy, during such joint herding activities I observed this phenomenon several times (at Cerqueto in the province of Abruzzo), and the shepherds had to spend lots of time catching the migrated individuals. From this example, we can learn how the formation of a flock boundary is important in order to carry out smoother herding control. Because of the daily experiences that differ from those of wild sheep/goat progenitors and semi-domesticated reindeer, a flock boundary is created in domesticated sheep/goat flocks. This flock boundary formation must also have been one of the favourable conditions for early herders that made flock guiding smoother.

To sum up, I have identified three favourable conditions that facilitated daily herding: 1) the advent of a group of individuals self-anchored to a man-made residential site, 2) the establishment of a lead-follow relationship between man and animal by means of intimacy created by providing for them from birth and 3) the formation of a flock boundary fostered by sharing the same place as a common home range, which, in the case of the Saami reindeer herders, is missing.

We can call all these favourable conditions the 'positive effects of domestication'.

Of course, in the earliest period of daily herding, the distance between the camp and the grazing field must have been short and the flock size rather small, just enough to satisfy all the meat demands of the villagers. Hunting must have been maintained in parallel in order to account for meat shortages. In fact, in the consumed animal bone remains of the middle and late periods of Pre-Pottery Neolithic Culture B, wild animal bones are also found. It is after the last period of Pre-Pottery Neolithic Culture B or the beginning of Pre-Pottery Neolithic Culture C that people were able to successfully satisfy all their meat demands via domesticated sheep/goats. We may suppose that in this period, by shifting daily herding from short to long distances, pastoralism as a subsistence economy was eventually fully established. Daily herding allows herders to keep and feed larger flocks with a small labour force. Just two shepherds are needed to guide a large flock of 300–400 head by using the lead-follow relationship. If we want to describe such a herding technique, we can use the definition of 'total collective bio-control'.

With regard to daily herding, I have noted the favourable conditions found in the domesticated flock's behaviour as the positive effects of domestication, but we should not ignore the negative aspects of domestication for both herders and animals, which must also have been a consequence of the collective use of the same home range. In order to cope with these negative effects, pastoralists even now have to adopt various taxing interventions regarding sheep/goats that were unimaginable prior to domestication. These interventions mainly deal with mother-offspring relationships during lambing and the nursing care that follows and can be witnessed not only among the pastoralists in the Middle East, but also wherever pastoralism of sheep/goats has spread to. In the next chapter I show what kinds of negative effects emerged and how interventions were adopted to cope with them. Archaeozoologists dealing with the domestication processes have seldom discussed these issues, even though they had extremely important implications for the subsequent development of human-animal relationships. Also, ethnographers who have observed pastoralists' activities have not paid much attention to either the negative effects of domestication or to these technical modes of intervention.

Negative effects of domestication and nursing care of newborns

Negative effects during lambing compared to the pre-domestication stage

Of course, we have no possibility of observing the situation of the wild progenitors of sheep/goats during lambing, however we have reports of a goat flock left abandoned centuries ago by the Americans on an island of the Ogasawara Archipelago in Japan who have been living since then without human intervention. They can be considered wild because to some extent they returned to their original wild behaviour. By comparing characteristics between these feral goats and domesticated ones, we can imagine the new conditions in which the domesticated goats found themselves after domestication and daily herding.

Incomplete imprinting in the herding field and newborn intervention

As ethologists say, imprinting between a mother and her newborn at delivery is crucial and indispensable in order to establish mutual recognition. Sheep and goats are no exception. Immediately after delivery, a mother ewe licks her newborn for a period and they exchange bleating sounds. Through the exchange of smell and voice, mutual recognition is established, but it is necessary to have such interaction for at least ten minutes, otherwise a good mother-offspring relationship cannot be established and the mother tends to avoid her offspring's suckling approach (Lent, 1974; Craig, 1981). In order to establish a perfect mother-offspring relationship, shepherds try to keep them close to each other for a certain period of time.

Given the importance of imprinting, what were the conditions in which feral goats found themselves at kidding time?

On the behavioural characteristics of feral goats, we can refer to the observational reports of the zoologists mentioned above (see page 39: Riney and Caughley, 1959; Jewell, Milner and Boyd, 1974; Shikano, 1984). According to them, during migration feral goats aggregate, but in other situations each individual stays separate from the others and occupies its own independent home range, even if it happens to partially overlap some other individual's. In such a dispersed flock formation, a pregnant female can deliver at its own home range and there is no evident obstacle in terms of achieving successful imprinting. After having established imprinting, a newborn kid can easily follow its mother and suckle; in the wild, there are few negative factors to disturb delivery, imprinting and suckling. One can guess that mother ewes and offspring of wild sheep/goats in the pre-domestication stage, too, must have enjoyed such favourable conditions for imprinting.

Conversely, the situation in which the newborns of domesticated sheep/goats find themselves is quite different. The delivery may occur at any time, either during herding migration in the daytime or in the enclosure where all the animals collectively spend the night.

Delivery during herding migration

It is general knowledge that a lambing ewe that is going to deliver in the herding field moves away from the main flock to avoid any disturbance from the other animals. Soon after delivery, she licks her newborn for a while and exchanges sounds exactly as her wild progenitor would have done, however, at this critical time for imprinting, it often happens that the ewe delivering for the first time refuses to attend to her newborn. This occurs because she seems to be afraid of being left alone behind her migrating fellows, so she often tries to catch up with the main flock, leaving her newborn alone at the delivery place (Beck, 1991: 106).

Due to this, when the lambing ewe detaches from the flock to deliver, the shepherd follows her and attends to her delivery. If, in order to catch up with the main group, the ewe leaves her newborn without any exchange of sounds and licking, the shepherd catches her and holds her close to her newborn (I myself observed this intervention by the Marwari nomads in Rajasthan in India in 1993).

Of course a newborn lamb/kid cannot follow a migrating flock of adults. The shepherd, after confirming that the imprinting has been well established, picks up the newborn and brings it back to his campsite by carrying it on his shoulders or in a bag. Sometimes he takes another measure in order to secure a more stable mutual recognition. He picks up the newborn and shows it closely to its mother, then he begins to slowly walk backward thus inviting the mother to follow him and finally brings the pair back to the campsite. By utilising the mother-offspring tie, the shepherd can maintain the relationship between them and reinforce their mutual recognition by keeping them in a small enclosure at the campsite. This technique was initially reported by Konagaya among the Mongolian shepherds (Konagaya, 1989: 10-11). Later, I observed the same method adopted by the Sarakatsani of Greece and the Baxtyâri of Iran (in winter, 1993).

Dangers of campsite delivery and newborn seclusion

Apart from happening during daily herding, delivery may occur in the campsite enclosure at night. On such an occasion, the lambing ewe tries to give birth in a separate free space in the enclosure and to lie down close to her newborn. However, the newborn lamb, as long as it is left in the enclosure, is exposed to another type of danger stemming from all the ewes' sharing the same harbouring site in a dense crowd. While the lambing ewe of wild progenitors could deliver in her own independent home range, the domesticated pregnant ewe must give birth in the enclosure amongst a dense crowd of adult ewes. In the case of a flock size of some

Developments After the Beginning of Domestication

Photo 4.1 Large crowd of sheep in a harbouring site (Carpathian summer quarter, Romania)

scores, the density is not very high, but let us imagine a situation when, after the initial phases of daily herding, the flock size grew to 200–300 head after thirty to forty years.

In the evening, after the ewes return to the campsite, a large flock is generally driven into a closed enclosure or an inner court of residence, or even a cave dug into a cliff. The enclosure size is not very large and the sheep begin to lie down very close to each other, the density being akin to that of a crowded train at rush hour (see Photo 4.1). In such compact circumstances, whenever an adult wakes up, stands and moves, the others around it begin to animate and move as well. If a weak newborn just after delivery is left among these adults, it can be easily trampled under the feet of the adult animals, or suffocated by pressure against its nose by an adult's heavy body (for an example see Beck, 1991: 148).

The safe way to avoid such accidents is as follows:
1. Remove the lambing ewe from the main adult group and let her deliver in a safe place.
2. After confirming that imprinting has been established, seclude the newborn lambs in an independent pen at night, in order to avoid any danger of injury or death caused by the adults, and keep the mother ewes in the enclosure with the main adult group.

3. The next morning, at suckling time, pick out these newborns from the pen and carry them to their respective mothers to give them the chance to suck milk.
4. Return them to the pen and keep them there during daytime, until the ewes return after daily herding.
5. In the evening at milking time, repeat nursing care and then take the lambs back to the independent pen for newborns in order to have them spend the night peacefully.

The same daily routine is repeated for some time until the newborns are well grown. Aside from such daily seclusion from the adult group, there is no other way for newborns to be kept safe. At night, seclusion is a general measure applied to all lambs. During delivery season, several lambs can be born within a short period. In a large herd of 200–300 head, most of which are ewes, the number of newborns to fetch and take to the pen at every suckling time becomes quite large and the work is strenuous.

I have observed several methods of daily seclusion: one was a small stone enclosure constructed inside the main stone enclosure for adults (observed amongst the Shagni people of Badakhshan in Afghanistan and Baxtyâri of Iran), another was a separate wooden fence beside the main enclosure (Bakharwal of India) and yet another was a small space inside the shepherd's tent (Baxtyâri of Iran). The point is that the seclusion of newborns from the adults' harbouring place was universally adopted without exception by all the pastoralists I visited in the Middle East.

We can regard the danger of death for newborns in the adult ewes' harbouring enclosure as something new and a negative effect brought about by domestication. If we try to describe the daily seclusion of newborns from the standpoint of bio-control, we can define it as another kind of 'classificatory bio-control' different from the culling of yearling males.

Mother-offspring encounter failure at suckling time

The seclusion of newborns was an indispensable nursing measure, however, if the newborns are secluded from their mothers after delivery, the shepherds must give them the chance to encounter their mothers to suckle milk from them the next morning. As described above, they pick up the newborns one by one from the separate pen and take them to the adults' enclosure. On such occasion, we may think that the lambs, which have established imprinting with their mothers, can

Developments After the Beginning of Domestication

Photo 4.2 Suckling assistance for a true offspring, Rajasthan, India

easily approach the respective ewe invited by her calling sounds, but it does not necessarily occur this way.

It would be a happy situation if a newborn could arrive at its mother by passing through a narrow open path between densely aggregated individuals. However, if the ewe is in the midst of the crowd, a weak newborn finds itself facing a wall of aggregated adults. As the lamb calls to its mother and the mother answers back and this goes on for some time, the shepherd following the calls picks up the lamb and brings it close to its mother and pushes it under the udder to suck. If a shepherd by mistake takes it to a different ewe, she tries to avoid the lamb's attempts to suckle.

Shepherds spend a significant amount of time on this job and finishing all the nursing assistance. I have observed such burdensome nursing among many pastoral peoples, but aside from a few examples, this assistance has received scant attention from ethnographers (see for example Matsubara, 1983; Konagaya, 1989; Beck, 1991). I now describe an example of this type of intervention that I observed amongst the Baxtyâri nomads of Iran (1993).

Photo 4.3 Nursing assistance for newborns at suckling time, Cerqueto, Abruzzo, Italy

The shepherds used a cave dug into a clay cliff as the enclosure for their flock and set their tent just beside the cave's entrance. As their daily routine, in the morning they chased the flock out of the main cave where they had spent the night and during the day they herded them in a distant field. Newborns, however, were kept in a dark, small, hole dug into the clay wall inside the tent. In a small side room prepared on the side of the main cave, two to three week old newborns were kept at night, but during the day they were taken to the field independently from the adult group. I will call the separation of the newborns 'primary seclusion' and that of the grown lambs, 'secondary seclusion' (see Figure 4.5).

In the evening, the adult group returned to the campsite. The shepherds scattered grain in the open space in front of the campsite in order to attract the adults and chase them into the main cave. As soon as the animals entered the cave and began to lie down, the shepherds began to pick the newly born lambs out of the first seclusion hole, one by one, taking them to their mothers to suckle. After this procedure, the shepherds picked the grown lambs out of the second seclusion room and carried them to the adult group for suckling. The shepherd, having exactly fixed the pairs in his memory, took them to their real mothers, pushing them one by one under the

Developments After the Beginning of Domestication

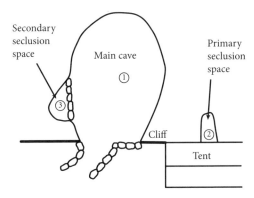

Figure 4.5 A Baxtyâri shepherd's campsite

ewe's breast and keeping the ewe's neck firmly between his legs to let the newborn suck milk quietly.

I observed the same nursing assistance practiced by Marwari nomads in Rajasthan, India who let the adult group pass the night in an open space close to the campsite free from enclosure. In the evening, when they returned after daily herding, the adult group wandered for a while near the campsite and began to lie down in a certain area. The shepherds then freed the one to two week old newborns to give them the chance to meet their mothers. In this case, too, many newborns were unable to approach their mothers. The shepherds immediately located the unhappy ones, then, one shepherd picked up one small lamb and tried to approach the mother ewe, while another attempted to catch her as she was reluctant and kept fleeing. After some effort, the first shepherd pushed the newborn under the ewe's udder, while the second man kept her neck between his legs. In order to catch the escaping ewe, they expended lots of labour and time and it was almost one hour later that they were able to finish the nursing assistance of matching the animals for successful suckling. This burdensome task was repeated twice per day, in the morning before departure for daily herding and in the evening after returning to the campsite.

Beck, who achieved a very detailed observation of the pastoral activities of the Qashqa'i nomads of Iran, also reports that they had spent more or less one hour matching sixteen pairs of mother ewes and newborns.

The shepherds' assistance to newborns during suckling time is extended not only towards the newborns unable to get to their mothers in the midst of a crowd of ewes. As I said above, the imprinting between a mother and her offspring is likely to be insufficient in the case of delivery during herding time. Especially a ewe delivering for the first time tends to refuse to attend to her newborn at mutual imprinting establishment interactions just after delivery. Therefore there are always several newborns that cannot easily suckle from their mother because of insufficient imprinting. Shepherds not only apply a measure for reinforcing the mother-offspring tie, but must also carry the newborn to the mother's udder to allow it to suckle (Matubara, 1983; Konagaya, 1989).

Let's call such work 'artificial nursing for a happy suckling relationship between a ewe and her newborn'.

In short, I pointed out the following three modes of intervention that the shepherds had to adopt in response to the negative effects created by domestication: 1) nursing assistance to avoid imprinting failure during delivery time, 2) seclusion of newborns from the adult group at night in order to avoid newborn injury or death in the midst of highly dense crowds of adults and 3) nursing assistance for newborns to achieve happy suckling relationships. These burdensome modes of intervention were unexpected but absolutely necessary work for the people who had taken to the domestication of sheep/goats. However, they can be observed among sheep/goat herders not only in the Middle East but also in all areas of the Eurasian Continent from the Mediterranean in the west (from my fieldwork at Abruzzo in Central Italy (1971) and Sarakatsani in Greece (1993)) to Mongolia in the East (Konagaya, 1989). Of course, this suggests that the negative effects of domestication were caused universally and these were necessary and fundamental interventions for managing domesticated sheep/goats.

It is appropriate to examine what stage of the domestication process these interventions were initiated in.

Now, let us suppose the following initial conditions. At the initiation of the domestication of sheep/goats, one captured ten ewes with breeding rams and began to feed them. The mortality rate of newborns was rather high, at forty percent. Male yearlings were culled and ewes were kept alive until they were four years old for the production of offspring. Supposing such conditions, let's calculate how many sheep the shepherd would have in forty years—about 270 head. The number would be sufficient to bring about large crowded groups of ewes difficult for the newborn to pass through in order to arrive at its mother ewe. We must recognise that the negative effects caused by the collective sharing of their home range in the same enclosure would have emerged not particularly long after the beginning of domestication, forcing the shepherd to extend emergency nursing assistance.

Previously I mentioned the presence of an enclosure for domesticated sheep in the middle period of Pre-Pottery Neolithic Culture B at the archaeological site of Abu Gosh (see Figure 4.2). Interestingly, we can find there the remains of a small stone circle inside the large enclosure. In the archaeological site of Beida II in the same period, too, we can find a small circle within the larger enclosure for adult animals (see Figure 4.4). As it is in the residential site of the Umm Dabaghiyah IV, which can be attributed to the later period of Pre-Pottery Neolithic Culture B, there we find a small enclosure in the inner court where sheep must have been kept at night (see Figure 4.5). These sites do not tell us what use they were constructed for. They might have been used to segregate pregnant ewes for safe delivery, or they might have been used to establish stable, steady mother-offspring imprinting (Fujii, 2001: 181). We can, moreover, suppose that these structures were utilised for the seclusion of newborns, which could otherwise be trampled and injured if left at night with the adult group. Had they been used for the overnight seclusion of newborns, every morning someone must have collected the newborns for nursing assistance to form the suckling relationship. Taking this archaeological evidence into account, we may suppose that the seclusion of newborns and nursing assistance began not particularly long after the beginning of sheep/goat domestication.

Incidentally, regarding the negative effects of domestication, archaeozoologists have flagged these in the past. In this sense, the theme itself is not new, but their concern was quite different from the topic discussed here. For example, they paid attention to the specimens of poorly grown individuals among the excavated bones of sheep/goats of the earlier period of the post-domestication stage. They supposed that the rapid increase in animal numbers after domestication had accelerated the deterioration of grassland around the residential site and led to the malnutrition of mother ewes, who would therefore produce underdeveloped newborns. The other possible cause they identified was a deterioration of hygiene under the crowded cohabitation of animals in the relatively narrow space of enclosures (Meadow, 1989: 86). Instead, the negative effects of domestication I discuss here are of a different nature in that they derive from the same conditions repeatedly reproduced over the centuries since the beginning of domestication. In fact, these negative consequences are really fundamental and fatal to newborns under domestication in general unless artificial modes of intervention are implemented.

I now describe forms of nursing assistance used in order to achieve a happy suckling relationship between a mother ewe and her newborn from the perspective of 'bio-control'.

The kind of delivery assistance during daily herding and the daily seclusion of newborns from the adult group can be described as 'classificatory bio-control', because shepherds extend their assistance as far as newborns are exposed to the general risk of imprinting failure and eventual injury or death. Conversely, nursing assistance to achieve a happy suckling-sucking relationship is quite different from the other two kinds of assistance. The shepherd's awareness is, at the same time, directed towards the suckling newborn who wants milk and the ewe who is ready to be suckled. The particular fact the shepherds pay attention to is neither a general attribute as 'suckling newborn' nor a general attribute as 'milking ewe', but an unhappy situation that can occur between a particular suckling newborn which cannot approach its mother and a mother ewe which can be identified as the mother of this unhappy suckling newborn. The combination here is determined by the unique mother-offspring pair relational tie that is perfectly fixed in the shepherd's memory. In this sense, we can describe that kind of nursing assistance as 'personal bio-control by the respective distinction of mother-offspring tie'.

In fact, this intervention is a peculiar job, quite different from other collective or classificatory forms of bio-control. Apart from that, it is very important because the shepherd's knowledge obtained through his assistance provides at least the following two secondary intervention techniques, also fundamental to flock management: 1) the adoption strategies for orphans and 2) the identification of strayed sheep.

Secondary nursing assistance intervention techniques

Adoption strategies for orphans

Sometimes it happens that a ewe dies from a difficult delivery. We usually call the offspring of a dead mother an 'orphan'; however, besides real orphans there is another type of orphan. I have already mentioned that, especially in deliveries during daily herding, imprinting failure may occur because of a mother's avoidance of attending to her newborn at the crucial time of imprinting. On such occasions, the shepherd tries to keep the mother close to her newborn by force and by bringing them back to the campsite where the pair are kept in a small pen in order to reinforce their mutual recognition. In spite of these attempts, it sometimes happens that a mother ewe refuses to let her offspring suckle milk because of insufficient imprinting.

In order to distinguish such an orphan from a 'real orphan', we may call these offspring 'de facto orphans'.

Independently from the difference between a 'real orphan' and a 'de facto orphan', both are destined to die from starvation unless shepherds take some emergency measures to ensure they receive milk from some other milking ewe. If an alien mother is approached by an orphan without any intervention from the shepherd, the only result is the alien mother's avoidance. To overcome such ethological difficulty, it is necessary to take special measures called 'adoption strategies for orphans'.

Casimir (1982) identified three types of adoption strategies. I will provide outlines of these and add the locations where each was observed according to his classification.

The first type is by using force. A nursing ewe and an orphaned lamb are kept in a small enclosure until the ewe allows the unfamiliar lamb to suckle. This strategy is observed among the following ethnic groups: in the Mediterranean area, the people of Abruzzo, Central Italy (Trinchieri, 1953); in the Middle East, the Pashtuns of Afghanistan (Casimir, 1982) and the Yöluk of Turkey (Matsubara, 1983); and in Northeast Asia, the Mongols (Konagaya, 1991).

The second type is where the olfactory system is blocked. There are several methods of doing this, for example in Mongolia, the muzzle of the mother ewe or the nanny goat is tightly held against the shepherd's body, whereas the Pashtuns wet the muzzle with a strong smelling decoction of juniper so that she cannot discern the smell of the alien lamb or kid. On feeling the touch against her udder, she allows the orphan to suckle. This strategy is observed among the following ethnic groups: in South Asia, the Kashmiri of India (Casimir, 1982: 25); in the Middle East, the Pashtuns of Northeast Afghanistan (field observation, Tani, 1978); and in Northeast Asia, the Mongols (Konagaya, 1991).

The third type of strategy involves the use of a dummy and can be defined as the deception of a mother by using the scent of her genuine offspring. The following variations may be found. Firstly, rubbing with skin: if for some reason a lamb or kid dies, its mother becomes available as a potential surrogate mother, and the shepherd rubs the skin of her dead offspring on the body of an orphaned lamb/kid and presents it to the surrogate ewe. Secondly, rubbing with urine: if a mother who has lost her offspring cannot be found, the shepherd chooses a ewe with her suckling lamb and rubs the urine of her genuine offspring on the body of an orphaned lamb.

These two types of strategies are observed among the following ethnic groups: in the Mediterranean area in Abruzzo, Central Italy (Trinchieri, 1939); in North Africa amongst the Tuareg, Niger (Bernus, 1981); in the Middle East, in Yöluk, Turkey (Matsubara, 1983), Baxtyâri, Iran (Digard, 1981), Qashqa'i, Iran (Beck, 1991)

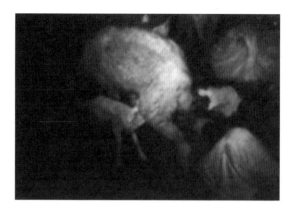

Photo 4.4 Shifting method of adoption stratagems, Rajasthan, India

and Pashtun, Northeast Afghanistan (Casimir, 1982); and in Northeast Asia, the Mongols (Konagaya, 1991).

To these two deception strategies, a third method can be added, which I observed in India among the Marwari shepherds of Rajasthan in 1992.

At suckling time, three shepherds gathered around a mother ewe. One held her by the neck, the second one removed the true offspring from her side, while at the same time the third slipped an orphaned lamb from the other side under her udder, giving it a chance to suckle (Photo 4.4). In this way, the shepherds made use of the true offspring, rather than its skin or urine, as a trigger for releasing milk for an orphan. This device can be classified as a third type and I will call it the 'shifting method'.

This last type can be observed among the following ethnic groups: in India and the Middle East, Marwari, Rajasthan of India (field observation, Tani, 1992) and Qashqa'i, Iran (Beck, 1991); and in Northeast Asia, the Mongols (Konagaya, 1991 and 1996).

The former two adoption strategies are achieved by force, but in the third type the shepherd makes use of the real offspring as a decoy in order to overcome the ethological difficulty. On this occasion, they rely on the memory of the unsubstitutable mother-offspring bond and utilise it as a trigger. When did shepherds learn the importance of such memory and invent such a cunning strategy? When they had to assist with nursing daily to achieve a successful encounter between mothers and offspring, they had to memorise the particular pairs, otherwise a matching failure would bring about the mother ewe's refusal to suckle with extreme consequences. There is therefore no doubt that they learned it through such nursing assistance. The marked aspects of the first two adoption strategies are general classificatory facts: the adopting mother is a milking ewe and the lamb to be adopted is an orphan. On the other hand, in the third type of adoption strategy, what is utilised as a trigger is an un-substitutable personal relationship between a mother and her offspring. From the standpoint of 'bio-control', we can define the third type of adoption strategy as a secondary intervention technique based on 'personal bio-control' with the respective distinction of the mother-offspring tie.

Identification of strayed sheep

During daily herding, when the flock grazes through bushy areas, the sheep tend to disperse. When faced with a small gap the sheep have to cross, those timid in nature tend to avoid it and move around, following the same contour line. On such occasions, some sheep deviate from the course intended by the shepherd, so that if he inattentively leaves them without any intervention, they stray out of sight. This is the so-called 'strayed sheep' emergency. One of the abilities of a shepherd is to realise that this has occurred as early as possible and immediately take action to locate the missing animals. It is obvious that shepherds in general have such ability (Beck, 1991: 118), but it is less evident that shepherds know which individuals are missing. How is it possible to identify them? Of course, we are not able to observe directly their mental process of identification, so I cannot help but infer it.

I will imagine a similar case frequently occurring at elementary schools. A mother comes to collect her child and the teacher who sees the mother immediately calls her child by name, instantly matching the mother and child in their mind. Of course, the teacher is not identifying the child by meticulous memory so that 'this mother has the physiognomy A and the child of the mother with physiognomy A has the physiognomy a and the name N-a'.

Here is another example: on a school excursion, the teacher allows the children to take some free time for a while and tells them to meet at a certain time and place. The children, observing the order, return at the promised time. The greatest concern for the teacher is that all the children are present, so the best way to check is to call them one by one from the list of names. A teacher who knows all the pupils well may do so without consulting the list. They would observe the children gathering and immediately notice who is absent. On such an occasion, too, the teacher is not consciously checking the missing children by matching each child's physiognomy in his memory with the corresponding children in front. What is actually happening in the teacher's brain is a process comparable to computer scanning on a subconscious level. All the information on the physiognomies and names of each pupil must be stored in the teacher's brain.

It is through the same scanning process at a subconscious level that a shepherd can see at a glance that some sheep are missing and can at once realise which individuals are not present. If this is the way it works, how could a shepherd have registered in his memory the different physiognomy of each individual sheep in a flock of 300 head?

The most important memorised information is the visual image. Fortunately, each sheep/goat has a different colour pattern, which becomes a distinctive clue for the shepherd: i.e. one has a black nose, a black band on its shoulder or a black stripe around its neck etc. It is common for shepherds of the same herding group to give and share a certain number of names to distinguish each individual according to different colour patterns: for example 'black nose', 'black shoulder band' or 'black stripe on neck'. However, such naming is not sufficient for individual identification because in a flock of hundreds of head there may be several individuals with a similar colour pattern. Memorising the sex and age of each animal is indispensible in terms of distinguishing them. So a combination of colour pattern, sex and age raise the level of univocal identification. In fact, when the shepherds talk with each other, for example, about which individual should be slaughtered or about which individual is sick, they indicate it using a combination of these individual features. For somebody who does not belong to their pastoral world, it seems quite impossible to keep in mind such a large number of peculiarities of hundreds of head. Once I tested two shepherds, one belonging to the Bakharwal in Kashmir and another from the Carpathian shepherds of Romania. It was in summer when newborns had already grown and joined the adult group. In front of a Carpathian shepherd, I indicated a certain ewe in a herding flock and asked him to indicate her offspring. Passing his eyes as if he were sweeping over the whole flock, he began to indicate the lambs one after another saying 'this' and 'that' and so on. Moreover, he added 'this one' is the first offspring and 'that one' is the second one, etc. (see Figure 4.6). This means that he had not only memorised the respective combination of the peculiar features of colour pattern, sex and age, but he also remembered the respective birth order (a_1, a_2, a_3....) among offspring of the same mother ewe A. As for the Turkish Yöluk nomads, Matsubara reports that they also distinguish all the members of a matrilineal line and refer to each with a special term.

Developments After the Beginning of Domestication

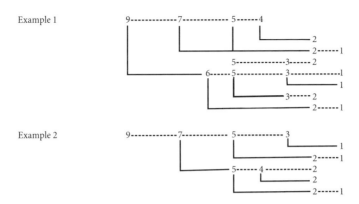

Source: Collected by the author in the village of Ardan in the Province of Nasaud, Romania (Oct. 1978).
Notes: Arabic number = age; dotted line = sibling; line = mother-offspring relationship (except for males).

Figure 4.6 Shepherd's memory of mother-offspring relationships

To summarise, the above indicates that an individual animal in a flock that to a stranger seems anonymous is easily and immediately recognisable by the shepherd according to its peculiar features: 1) a combination of physiognomy, sex and age as individual attributes, 2) a specific mother ewe-offspring relational tie ('this' yearling is the offspring of 'that' mother ewe) and 3) the position in the birth order of a ewe's offspring.

How can a shepherd memorise such precise and numerous pieces of information? In this regard, I noted above that already at a lamb's birth the shepherd is present and has to extend nursing assistance to the mother-offspring pair to establish imprinting. After birth, on the occasion of daily suckling, morning and evening, a shepherd must assist with matching and maintain those pieces of information of the distinctive attributes of each mother and of her offspring acquired as long-term memory through the repetition of daily nursing assistance.

Now, let us suppose the situation of a flock of 300 head as an average. Mother-offspring pairs come to be present one after another during the delivery period. Given that most males are culled except for breeding rams, most individuals in the flock are female. Supposing now that breeding males occupy at a maximum ten percent of the whole, the rest constitutes ninety percent = 270 head of ewes, which can potentially give birth, even if all of them do not necessarily do so. If the birth rate is eighty percent, there will be about 210 newborns. The lambing period is in general concentrated over about one month in winter. This means that on average about seven (210 divided by thirty) newborns would be born daily. Now, let us suppose that these newborns should receive the shepherd's nursing assistance at suckling time for four to five days until they become strong enough to approach their real mothers by themselves, bringing the shepherd's nursing assistance at suckling time to an average of thirty head. This number approximately corresponds to the number of newborns kept in the primary seclusion space (reserved space in the shepherds' tent) or in the secondary seclusion space (reserved space within the adults' enclosure), which I observed at the camp of the Baxtyâri nomads of Iran.

In such case, every day shepherds must memorise seven newborn lambs as offspring of their respective mother ewes and extend nursing assistance for each pair twice a day at suckling time for four to five days, therefore repeating the mother-offspring pair matching about ten times. Each newborn has its special physiognomy, but the growth of newborns is very rapid, so the distinction between 'yesterday's newborns' and 'today's newborns' is not difficult. After ten occasions of providing nursing assistance to the same pair, the memory of each lamb's physiognomy and mother-lamb pair combination will become stored indelibly in the shepherds' long-term memory. It is because of such memorisation that when I asked a Carpathian shepherd to indicate the offspring of a mother ewe I randomly selected, he was able to easily point them out.

Incidentally, Saami reindeer herders who take care of a mixed flock involving plural ownership are anxious to know which owner a newborn belongs to. They cannot identify which mother an offspring belongs to, because they do not assist at deliveries. In order to confirm this, they chase the whole flock into an enclosure and observe which newborn follows which female. After that they make a cut on its ear in the same ownership mark as the mother's (Kuzuno, 1990: 157–179). This is the only way the herders are able to recognise them, as the flock is left free to migrate and is not brought back daily to a harbouring site. Newborns freely approach their mothers in the field to suckle and herders have no need to extend nursing assistance for matching. This is why the Saami do not have the opportunity to precisely memorise the individual physiognomy of each reindeer.

Once, when I stayed at the summer quarters of a group of Carpathian shepherds in Romania, I attached a red ribbon to some yearlings and their mothers in order to observe their behaviour in the herding field. One day, during a herding march, I did not notice that the ribbon of a yearling had fallen off. The leading shepherd, who looked back at times to check if all the animals were following, presently advised me that the yearling's ribbon was missing. So, we retraced our path and found the ribbon entangled in a bush about one hundred meters behind. The shepherd had not seen it fall, but he realised it had just a few minutes later. Even if it was unusual for him to attach a ribbon around the neck of a sheep, he kept it in mind, indicating that he was always alert to anything concerning his flock. There is no doubt that a shepherd in the herding field frequently scans his flock in order to notice eventual straying as early as possible.

Technical interventions concerning milking

Until now, I have dealt with the shepherds' interventions in relation to the positive and negative effects brought about after the beginning of the domestication of sheep/goats. However, we have learned from archaeozoologists' recent analyses of fatty acids adhered to shards of pottery vessels that milking, contrary to the usual assumption until now, was initiated soon after the beginning of domestication. Sheep/goats do not have the physiological impediment of the cow, by which its milk gland does not open without her true offspring's stimulation. During the early phase after the beginning of milking, the flock size must have been small. However, as time passed, the size of flock grew. During this stage it is almost certain that shepherds invented some forms of technical measures to obtain more milk and to make milking labour more time efficient when dealing with hundreds of milking ewes.

Milking facilitation device
Aside from the earliest milking practices, shepherds must have begun milking for their use after weaning. Even without the physiological hurdle, milking ewes do not easily allow creatures other than their true offspring to squeeze their udders and try to free themselves from squeezing human hands. Before milking, shepherds in the Middle East and the Mediterranean areas chase animals into enclosures, waiting for the milking ewes to emerge from a small open exit as they are chased by an assistant and catching them to milk one after another. Alternatively, the Middle Eastern nomadic pastoralists do not always keep their flocks in enclosures, instead leaving them free to sit down in close proximity to their tents. In such case, at milking time they hold and fix each animal's neck in the loop of a rope stretched between two poles and proceed to milk.

While visiting pastoralists in the Middle East and Mediterranean areas I observed the same scene; shepherds thrust the udder of the milking ewes upwards before beginning to squeeze the teat. It is said that this simulates the act of a newborn pushing up its mother's udder just before suckling. In Abruzzo in Central Italy, I observed that when shepherds milked they voiced the same special lip sound as that uttered when they take the true offspring to its mother's breast for suckling (Tani, 1996a[1976b]). There is no doubt that they were intentionally producing the same sound the milking ewes were used to hearing when their true offspring were suckling. Konagaya reports the same simulative vocalisation by Mongolian shepherds (Konagaya, 1983, 1989 and 1991). Leaving aside the actual effect of such simulative acts, it is certain that the shepherds, recreating the mother ewe's experiences during suckling time with her true offspring, are taking steps to induce her to accept the alien human approach to grab her teats. We may call these acts 'milking facilitation devices'. I do not have any clues as to when and where such devices were invented, but they seem to be straightforward ideas for shepherds of the earlier period to have thought of.

Seasonal separation of breeding rams

Milking is a kind of repetitive process similar to the operation of an assembly line. In the first part of this book where I mentioned how domesticates have quite a different life history from their wild ancestors, I pointed out that breeding rams are seasonally separated from the female group during the mating season in order to prevent them from mating freely.

In the case of wild sheep and goats, males and females live naturally separated except for the mating season of autumn when they join together. The mating period is naturally concentrated in autumn, but after domestication it expanded and if the breeding rams were introduced into the main ewes' group, mating could occur outside the mating season and this would result in the extension of the delivery period. In such a situation, it happens that some ewes are ready to be milked after weaning, while others have not yet delivered. As milking is the mechanical and collective work of squeezing a mother ewe's udders in turn, it is impossible for a shepherd to carry out this work regularly. It is better to concentrate delivery within a shorter period to be able to milk collectively and efficiently from a large flock of 200–300 ewes. Restricting the mating period within a shorter season became a strategically desirable measure for shepherds who began to have a large number of sheep/goats. Of course, concentrating delivery time must have previously been considered useful for collective nursing assistance at suckling time, however, milking a large group of ewes must have made restricting mating and delivery within a shorter timeframe a more urgent issue.

By visiting pastoralists who practice milking in the Middle East and the Mediterranean areas, I was able to observe this seasonal mating control in the following two ways. First, in the summertime the breeding rams are kept in the pastoralists' winter village separated from the main flock at the summer quarter in which there are only a few castrated rams and yearlings besides numerous ewes, and in the autumn they are joined into the main flock. Second, the breeding rams are kept with the main flock even in the summertime, but a cloth band is attached around the hip of rams in order to prevent them from mating and in the autumn the band is removed. I believe that the separation of breeding rams and their introduction into the ewes group only in autumn must have been generally adopted by milking pastoralists by not much later than the beginning of milking, whenever the flock size increased to 200–300 head.

To sum up, the seasonal separation of breeding males from the ewes' group is motivated by the realisation of collective and efficient milking labour by concentrating the delivery period into a shorter timeframe. In order to make milking labour more effective, shepherds intervene into the animals' reproductive processes that could have been smoothly realised without human intervention. From the standpoint of 'bio-control', we can define this technical intervention as 'classificatory bio-control' as well as taking note of the categorical attribute of rams, but it is an important control measure in the sense that shepherds keep the animals' reproductive process under control for their collective management.

Change in the female culling strategy

As far as domesticated sheep/goats were considered as only grass consumers and meat suppliers, even the females as lamb producers might be considered for culling at a certain age. But later, when ewes began to be used as milk providers, shepherds must have changed the culling strategy for ewes and begun to keep them alive as long as they were able to deliver and provide milk until the age of five or six. In fact, archaeozoologists attested to the delay of the ewes' slaughtering age by using the killing profile at a certain period and used it as criteria to identify the advent of the practice of milking. The same killing profile is present among the pastoralists at the beginning of the historical age in the Middle East where milking was generally practiced. Here the contrast in the killing age between rams and ewes became distinctively sharper.

Temporal separation of mother ewes and offspring during herding

The practice of milking signifies the human exploitation of milk that was originally reserved for newborns. This does not mean that humans monopolised all the milk, as newborns must be fed with their mother's milk for some time until weaning. Theoretically, after weaning when newborns are well grown and able to graze, shepherds could let them join the adult herding group, but shepherds herd newborns as an independent group for a certain period. This is because, if they herd newborns along with their mothers soon after weaning, the memory of their mothers would be maintained and they would continue to follow them and suckle milk. Shepherds want to obtain milk, so they keep them separate for the period necessary to erase this memory[1]. Among the pastoralists I visited, I was usually able to observe the temporary separate herding (except with the Bakharwal people in Kashmir where milking was not practiced, as they herd newborns together with their mother ewes and therefore separation is unnecessary). Weaning does not, however, always coincide with the beginning of milking. For example, Pashtun nomads in Afghanistan gave the sufficiently grown newborn group, which was already herded separately from the mother group, the chance to encounter their mother ewes' group daily in order to let them suckle the milk remaining after milking. By this repeated encounter the offspring-mother memory was maintained. After bringing the suckling newborn group close to the adult group, the offspring dashed to their respective mothers, invited by their calls (as I observed in 1977).

However, the temporal separation of mother ewes and their offspring in the herding situation is a kind of 'classificatory bio-control', which could not have been observed in the wild prior to domestication.

I have pointed out several technical interventions that came to be adopted because of the beginning of the practice of milking. I suspect that all of them could have begun to be adopted within a short timeframe after pastoralists began to rely to a greater extent on it as a food resource.

Conditions for the emergence of 'professional shepherds'

Thus far I have attempted to reconstruct the process of how the relationship between humans and sheep/goats successively progressed after the beginning of domestication. This involved human–animal interactions and at the same time led to the development of certain techniques. As most of the modes of intervention mentioned here were indispensable for sheep/goat management, they were adopted and have been maintained even today by professional shepherds not only in the Middle East but also in the neighbouring areas of Europe where the management techniques of Middle Eastern origin diffused. Now, in order to well understand the conditions of 'professional shepherds', I will return to the development process I have talked about.

1. At an early stage of domestication, sheep/goats were fed with collected grass. Under such conditions, the most economic management strategy was to keep females alive as elements necessary for reproduction and to cull males that reached maturity. Male culling became a general consumption strategy among pastoralists in general.
2. Individuals that were born and raised in artificial enclosures acquired the behavioural characteristic of returning by themselves to their harbouring site, even when they were left free from the enclosure.
3. Being human-fed, they established an intimate relationship with humans, and this fostered the lead-follow relationship between people and animals.
4. Individuals that shared the same site as their common home range developed a flock boundary: they became individuals that do not mix with another group, even if they approach it. These three behavioural characteristics obtained after domestication are factors favourable for daily herding.
5. After discovering that individuals did not escape even if they were left out of the enclosure, shepherds began daily field-herding and as time passed the herding distance grew. With the beginning of long distance herding, people could keep larger flocks to meet their meat demands without depending on hunting. It was at this very time that pastoral husbandry became an independent subsistence economy.

In this sense, the animals' behavioural characteristics (2), (3) and (4) obtained via domestication were positive effects for the development of pastoralism, while collective sharing of the same man-made residential site as a common home range and daily herding by a human guide were the two main factors producing negative effects on newborns at delivery and suckling time.

6. Delivery during herding time is often accompanied by a destabilising factor for the successful mother offspring imprinting that is indispensable for their mutual recognition. Shepherds are required to attend them at delivery time to try to establish perfect imprinting. It is on this occasion that shepherds memorise exactly the respective mother ewe-offspring pair according to their peculiar physiognomic features.
7. Even though the shepherds attend the delivery to facilitate mutual recognition between a mother and her newborn, imprinting is not always well established. In that case, shepherds try to keep the pair in a small pen.

8. Lambs born in the harbouring site as well as those born during daily herding pass the night in an artificial enclosure. It is inevitable for shepherds to seclude newborns in a separate pen if they want to save them from being injured or killed by being trampled in the dense crowd of adults.
9. In secluding them from adults, shepherds became obliged to give the chance to newborns to encounter their respective mothers at every suckling time. It would not be sufficient to bring newborns into the enclosure where the adult group was kept, because they would face the wall of the crowd. In a lucky situation, sometimes a newborn would find itself close to its real mother, but usually there were several newborns far from their mothers and unable to reach them. Shepherds had to pick up each newborn and bring them to their real mothers to give them the chance to feed, which was a labour intensive job for the shepherds and occurred twice in a day.
10. Among newborns, apart from orphans resulting from dead mothers, there have always been de facto orphans, i.e. those who were prevented from suckling by their real mothers because of imprinting failure. For both of these types of orphan, shepherds must implement adoption strategies in order to avoid their starvation and death. Among the various modes of intervention was the method to induce an alien mother ewe to allow an orphan to suckle by having her sniff the odour of her real offspring. There is no doubt that this method, making use of the real offspring as a trigger, was based on the shepherds' knowledge of imprinting and of a mother's reaction in allowing only her real offspring to suckle. This knowledge ought to have been obtained through the shepherds' attendance to the delivery and daily nursing of newborns. In this sense, the adoption technique can be considered as a secondary one discovered through the primary intervention techniques (6), (7), (8) and (9) implemented to deal with the negative effects of domestication. Achieving nursing successfully was possible only if shepherds memorised the respective mother-offspring pairs perfectly.
11. During daily herding it may have happened that some sheep strayed from the main flock, usually in the face of dense bushes or some other obstacles causing the flock to disperse and eventually divide into two groups. On such occasions, it is necessary for a shepherd to realise as soon as possible if some animal is missing by doing a prompt scan on the basis of his recall. To my surprise, shepherds could often identify which individuals were missing immediately.

The adoption strategies (10) and the ability to promptly identify strayed sheep (11), which can be described as 'personal bio-control', are by-products of the shepherds' primary daily repeated 'personal bio-controls' to cope with the negative effects of domestication: these are (6) attendance at delivery time, (8) seclusion of newborns from the adult group at harbouring time and (9) providing nursing assistance to newborns that cannot encounter their mothers at milking time.

Having pointed out the technical interventions initiated to counterbalance the consequences of domestication, you may wonder why I have not mentioned the technique of 'castration' generally adopted by pastoralists. By castration, not only do males become obedient and their meat is more tender, but also the heated competition between breeding males can be cooled down. Even if the competition can be restricted by the strategy of culling male yearlings, it is advantageous for shepherds to castrate and consume males after fattening, as long as they can find abundant grass in the fields. Moreover, the soft wool of castrated males was considered a precious textile material. As there was no need for specialised technological tools for castration except for a simple knife, this practice must have been widely adopted as early as the very beginning of domestication. In fact, we know that castration is commonly adopted among most pastoralists. Archaeozoologists tried to identify the beginning of castration by paying attention to slender male bones, which are the consequence of castration. However, given the fact that castration itself does not leave any clear evidence behind, they have not yet succeeded in identifying its chronology. The reason why I have not introduced it in my discussion on the reconstruction of the developmental process of domestication is because castration could have been adopted at any stage after domestication.

Apart from the problem of the beginning of castration, I underlined the fact that shepherds began not only 'collective bio-control' in daily herding and 'classificatory bio-control' in culling male yearlings, but also operated 'personal bio-control' for the wellbeing of newborns by paying immediate attention to the peculiar attributes of individuals and their respective mother-offspring bonds. I now discuss the reason why a professional category of 'shepherds' emerged in the ancient Near East and Mediterranean areas where sheep/goat herding widely developed.

The birth of professional shepherds

To urbanites who see shepherds herding their sheep/goat flocks in a field, the management of domesticated sheep/goats may appear to be realised only by collective intervention into a mass of anonymous individuals. Haudricourt once compared root crop cultivators in Oceania with wheat cultivators and sheep/goat herders in the Mediterranean and Near Eastern areas (1969). He wrote that the former take care of the plants by individualistically paying attention to each root crop, while the latter take care not only of grain plants, but also of domesticated flocks collectively. In fact he defined the intervention of the Near Eastern and Mediterranean people with domesticated plants and animals as 'collective'. As far as attention is focused only on the shepherds' activities to guide his flock during herding, Haudricourt is correct, and also the interventions in wheat and grain such as sowing, irrigating and harvesting are achieved without any attention to the plant's individuality, but given the shepherd's 'personal bio-control' in the nursing assistance provided to sheep/goats at delivery and suckling time as noted above, one must admit that in the case of pastoralists such a generalisation is not appropriate.

It is true that during daily herding domesticated sheep and goats are regarded as objects to be treated collectively; i.e. objects of 'collective bio-control'. On the occasion of male culling and the seclusion of newborns from the adult group, they are categorised by sex and age: i.e. objects of 'classificatory bio-control'. However, things differ in terms of nursing care at milking time and with adoption of the orphaned, where the animals are regarded as individuals bearing specific physiognomic features, sex and age and having personal ties, such as 'this' offspring of 'that' mother ewe where the attributes are not interchangeable. During infancy, each lamb receives the shepherd's individual attention to its peculiar characteristics and even after weaning when it is brought out to the herding field, it continues to be recognised by its individuality when going astray or missing. The animals' wellbeing is of great importance to the shepherd who makes a living from them. They are individuals who receive 'personal bio-control'. Now, I demonstrate such personal bio-control applied to sheep/goats from the flock-managing shepherds' point of view.

Judging externally, one may think that a shepherd who technically intervenes in a flock can be substituted for somebody else to the extent that both have learnt requisite technical knowledge. We know that such a substitution is allowed among machine operators. Conversely, what is asked of shepherds is not knowledge written in machine operation manuals, but a personal knowledge of each individual animal, as each has a unique life trajectory and a particular physiognomy. These personal pieces of knowledge can be memorised only by someone who has actually been living with them attending to each delivery and who has carried out nursing assistance daily to the same newborn. Therefore, shepherds of a different group or a farmer of a neighbouring village could never act in substitute. There are sufficient reasons why in the Bible, Cain and Abel were described as independent professional farmers and herders, even if they were brothers. The reason why the profession called 'shepherd' emerged as quite a different and independent one in the ancient Near Eastern and Mediterranean areas can be found in the above-mentioned un-substitutability.

After explaining how the figure of 'shepherd' took form as a unique professional category in the Near Eastern and Mediterranean areas, I would like to discuss another unique aspect of the pastoral culture in these areas: the practice of milking.

5 The Unique Position of Ancient Near Eastern Pastoralists: Overcoming the Physiological Barrier to Milking Cows

Ancient Near Eastern pastoralists as unique initiators of milking

Today archaeologists and archaeozoologists do not question that the practice of milking sheep/goats and cattle was uniquely initiated in the Near East where the domestication of these animals was first realised. Even though the milking of these animals is widely practiced among pastoralists in the surrounding areas of Eurasia and Africa, they were not initiators of the practice of milking, but instead received this culture from the Near East. Despite the fact that llama and alpaca herders in South America and buffalo breeders in the Asia-Pacific have a long history of husbandry, they never initiated milking of their animals (Bernot, 1988; Simoons, 1970). The position of Near Eastern pastoralists as the unique initiators of milking practices is solid. Because of this, archaeologists and archaeozoologists have dedicated significant time to clarify 'when' and precisely 'where' the practice of milking began. Recently, as mentioned in earlier chapters, based on the chemical analyses of dairy residue adhered to pottery shards and the more precise analyses of culling profiles, Vigne and Helmer supposed the beginning of milking had already occurred by the early period of the eighth millennium B.C. (2007).

Milking is the human act of squeezing the teats of sheep/goats or cows, which are used to being suckled only by their true offspring. Being accustomed to watching farmers who easily get milk from cows by squeezing their teats, we are prone to thinking that milk will flow just by extending hands towards a cow and squeezing her teats, provided that human-animal intimacy has been established. In fact, it was only after breeding improvement by gene selection that such a scene became common in Europe. Until then, even there, a cow's milk glands would not open except for the stimulus of her true offspring—the ancestor cows, before the modern improved varieties, had a physiological impediment to being milked. Conversely, sheep/goats never had such an impediment.

In other words, in order to begin milking from sheep/goats there was no hurdle to clear through the invention of a technical device. Whenever people needed or wanted to drink milk from the animals in their possession, it was easy to obtain milk from sheep/goats. As Fujii recently suggested, it is possible that the earliest nomadic pastoralists advanced into the desert soon after beginning of the domestication of sheep/goats and began milking motivated by the need to quench their thirst in the extremely dry environment. Or, as Vigne and Helmer suggest, it is probable that the hunter-cultivators who began to keep a small number of wild sheep or goats at their residential sites as the first initiators of domestication were already partially motivated by obtaining milk, which cannot be provided by hunting, to quench their thirst in the Near Eastern dry climate. The Near Eastern pastoralists' unique position as the earliest initiators of milking was achieved due to favourable faunal conditions where sheep/goats were on hand to be domesticated and through the climatic environment in which the need to quench thirst was constantly present.

Overcoming the physiological milking hurdle

On the other hand, it must have been difficult to succeed in getting milk from cows in the face of the physiological impediment. Evershed et al., from chemical analyses of dairy residue, cautiously draw the conclusion that at least by the second half of the seventh millennium B.C., the northwestern Anatolian cow-breeders had milked and processed the milk (Evershed et al., 2008). Vigne and Helmer, who applied the hypothesis of the so-called 'post-lactation slaughtering peak' in the culling profile for determining the beginning of cow milking, suggest that it began in the early stage of the Neolithic, in the eighth millennium in the Near East. But this hypothesis, I think, is not reliable in terms of judging the presence of cow milking[1]. I would like to continue my argument on the premise that the milking of cows began at a slightly later time than that of sheep/goats, after the invention of devices to clear the physiological hurdle.

Now, after confirming the recent archaeozoological knowledge on the beginning of milking, I would like to point out the following fact: ungulate animals with a physiological impediment to milking include not only Bovidae, but also Camelidae (llama and alpaca), long kept by South American herders. In spite of facing the same physiological hurdle, the Near East and Mediterranean pastoralists cleared it by some method and began milking cows, while the South Americans did not or could not begin milking llamas and alpacas. Where did the reason for such diversion

The Unique Position of Ancient Near Eastern Pastoralists

Photo 5.1 Depiction of milking in a relief at a Sumerian temple from the Ubaid Period

originate? Of course, there might be physiological and ethological differences between these two animal groups. However, the Near Eastern pastoralists' position as uniquely overcoming the physiological barrier to milking is firm, in addition to their position as initiators of milking practices in general.

Were there favourable conditions that allowed the Near Eastern pastoralists to overcome the physiological hurdle? The meaning of the beginning of milking in cultural history is important, and I would like to dedicate this chapter primarily to answering this question and discuss the meaning of the beginning of milking not only for the history of nutrition, but also in terms of sociocultural history.

Milk-ejection reflex-inducing device

To the question of how ancient Near Eastern pastoralists were able to overcome the physiological impediment to milking cows, Amoroso and Jewell (1963) propose one possible answer by pointing out the so called 'milk-ejection reflex-inducing devices' adopted in general among pastoralists in various areas since ancient times.

The oldest historical evidence of these devices in the Near East can be found in a relief of the Ubaid period of the third millennium B.C., excavated at a Sumerian temple in which a milking scene is depicted (see Photo 5.1). In the relief, several milking cows are depicted with a man sitting behind each animal extending his hands to their teats. There is no doubt that it represents the scene of milking. Interestingly enough, beside each milker without exception we find a calf depicted.

If someone does not know about the milk-ejection reflex-inducing device, they would not be able to understand why a calf is depicted thus. After reading ethnographic descriptions of milking practices among cow herders in Africa and India for example, we learn that the calf is the true offspring of the cow and the relief truthfully represents a scene of milking depicting one of the milk-ejection reflex-inducing devices already in use.

I now present an ethnographic description of milking practices among the East African cow herders of Datoga (a tribal group in Tanzania), as reported by Umesao (1966).

Datoga cow herders use a common name to label each mother-offspring pair. Adults and newborns are separately brought to a herding field during the day, however, after returning to the campsite, a cow herder standing between the two groups loudly calls out the respective name. Then, the mother and her offspring that have always been called by that common name, draw near to him. He brings the newborn close to its mother and makes it take a teat, but he allows it to suckle milk for only a very short period, as presently he pulls it away and quite strongly pushes up the teat of the mother cow by hand and begins to milk. This is a kind of cunning method of overcoming the physiological impediment.

As mentioned above, not only does a mother cow allow suckling only to her offspring with whom she has established mutual recognition, but also her milk gland will only open when she smells the odour of her true offspring. By making the true calf approach her, the milk gland will start releasing milk: this is a milk-ejection reflex-inducing device. With this measure herders can easily milk successfully.

Of course, the Datoga custom of giving a common name to each cow-offspring pair has no direct relevance to the application of the device. In fact, it would be sufficient to bring the offspring close to its mother according to the herder's memory of the pair and have the mother cow smell her offspring's odour in order to make the milk gland open.

What Amoroso and Jewell showed in their pioneering article was that as an old technique to overcome the cow's physiological impediment to milking, the milk-ejection reflex-inducing device had already been practiced in the Near East since the third millennium B.C. and widely diffused throughout Europe, Africa and India together with other pastoral techniques of Near Eastern origin (Amoroso and Jewell, 1963). From the apparent antiquity of the device in the Near East and the wide extension of its technical diffusion, we may suppose that it had been practiced in the Near East since far earlier than the historical ages. Even so, was such a cunning device invented without any prior technical condition? In the article by Amoroso and Jewell there is no reference to such a question.

Technical conditions behind 'milk-ejection reflex-inducing devices'

Now, let us recall that in terms of milk-ejection reflex-inducing devices, Amoroso and Jewell identify the following three strategies.
1. Prior to milking, the milker shows the lactating female her true offspring or makes the lamb hold the mother's teat in its mouth.
2. The milker makes use of the offspring's urine or skin (in the case of the offspring's death) as a releaser.
3. The milker provides physical stimulus to the utero-vaginal tract by breathing into it or by manual manipulation.

All three are methods to make a mother cow's milk glands open in order to succeed in obtaining milk, generally impeded by her physiological hurdle. The former two methods make use of knowledge that her milk glands will open by the stimulus of her true offspring. The third is based on the knowledge that strong physical stimulus on her sexual organ makes her milk glands open.

Now, leaving aside the last method, are we not reminded of some similar intervention techniques mentioned above? In the previous chapter (pages 61–62) regarding sheep/goats I presented three types of adoption strategies that allow an orphan to get milk from an alien mother ewe, as follows.
1. The first type was by using force: a nursing ewe and an orphaned lamb are kept in a small enclosure until the ewe allows the unfamiliar lamb to suckle.
2. The second type is where the olfactory system is blocked. There are several methods of doing this, for example to tightly hold the muzzle of the mother ewe or the nanny goat against the shepherd's body or to wet the muzzle with a strong smelling decoction of juniper so that she cannot discern the smell of the alien lamb or kid. On feeling its touch against her udder, she allows the orphan to suckle. Both the above methods use force, unlike the following.
3. The third type of strategy involves the use of a dummy and can be defined as the deception of the mother by making her smell the scent of her genuine offspring using the following three methods.

a. Rubbing with skin. If for some reason a lamb or kid dies, its mother becomes available as a potential surrogate mother. The shepherd rubs the skin of her dead offspring on the body of an orphaned lamb/kid and presents it to the surrogate ewe.
b. Rubbing with urine. If a mother who has lost her offspring cannot be found, the shepherd chooses a ewe with a lamb and rubs the urine of her genuine offspring on the body of an orphaned lamb/kid.
c. Shifting method. While a shepherd holds a mother ewe by the neck, a second shepherd brings her true offspring close to her and makes it momentarily hold the mother's teat. The lamb is then removed out from one side, while a third shepherd slips an orphaned lamb/kid under her flank from the other side. The mother thus cheated gives the orphan a chance to suckle. Here the true offspring is used as a trigger rather than its skin or urine.

The final three strategies (3a, 3b and 3c) share the same ethological knowledge.

Now let me compare the milk-ejection reflex-inducing devices (1) and (2) noted by Amoroso and Jewell with the third adoption strategy regarding sheep/goat orphans. Both of these devices are based on the same knowledge used in the adoption strategies for an orphan and especially the first one corresponds exactly to the adoption strategy (3c)—the shifting method. By substituting 'orphan' with 'milker's hand', it becomes the first strategy adopted in milking practice. The same strategic procedure can be found in parallel with the adoption strategies for orphaned lambs/kids as well as in the milk-ejection reflex-inducing devices (1) and (2) applied to milking cows.

Let's now confirm that the milking of cows began a little later than that of sheep/goats. As for the delay, we can attribute its reason not only to the delayed beginning of the domestication of cows in comparison to that of sheep/goats, but also to the differences between the two animals: unlike for sheep/goats, shepherds had to find some technical device to overcome the cow's physiological impediment. Moreover, at the beginning of this chapter, I raised another question with regard to the unique position of Near Eastern pastoralists pointing out the following fact. Faced with the same kind of physiological hurdle, the Near Eastern pastoralists cleared it by using a certain method and began milking cows, while South Americans did not begin milking llamas and alpacas. Why and how were the former able to clear the hurdle?

Of course, as the reason for such diversion between two peoples, there would have been ethological differences between cattle and llamas/alpacas as well as different attitudes towards respective animals. However, it is an undeniable fact that the Near Eastern pastoralists overcame the cows' physiological impediment by adopting the milk-ejection reflex-inducing devices that share the same strategic process with the adoption strategies for orphaned lambs/kids. As the reason why the Near Eastern pastoralists uniquely overcame this problem, I would like to emphasise the existence of the adoption strategies as a precursor.

Regarding the existence of this prior model, I would like to point out that the South American llama/alpaca herders had no knowledge of the adoption strategies, even though they extended nursing assistance to newborns experiencing difficulty suckling from their mothers, though not so frequently as the Near Eastern pastoralists (verbal report of Toritsuka and Tukuda 2015)[2]. This indicates that they did not possess promoting factors and direct clues that would have motivated and facilitated the invention of milk-ejection reflex-inducing devices.

On the contrary, the Near Eastern pastoralists had direct clues for their invention of the adoption strategies for orphaned lambs/kids. Moreover, as mentioned in the previous chapter, these adoption strategies can be regarded as a secondary product that emerged from the knowledge obtained through the repetitive nursing assistance provided during suckling time. Orphans have always existed. Even if shepherds tried to force an alien mother ewe to allow an orphan to suckle, she must have tended to avoid its approach. Facing such a situation, shepherds must have invented the adoption strategies in order to avoid the orphans' death by starvation on the basis of knowledge acquired through the daily repeated nursing assistance. It is this nursing assistance that was considered to be the shepherds' inevitable response to the negative effects of sheep/goat domestication.

Domestication was not only the beginning of keeping the animals' growth and reproduction processes under human control, but also the beginning of the collective sharing of a home range in an artificial harbouring site that did not exist at the wild stage. This lead to the emergence of a highly crowded group of ewes held in the same narrow space. If newborns were left in such a site at night, they would likely be trampled or suffocated to death. So, every night it was necessary to seclude newborns from the adult ewes' group and give them a chance to encounter their mothers for suckling the following morning. However, it was inevitable that some newborns would be unable to approach their mother, being blocked by other ewes. It was in this sense that nursing assistance began as the shepherds' necessary response to the negative effects caused by the beginning of domestication. In contrast to llamas and alpacas, which do not adapt to high population density environments, sheep/goats do adapt. Compared to the former's flock size at a maximum of seventy to eighty head, sheep/goat flock sizes can easily reach 200–300 head. To the shepherds after the domestication of sheep/goats, nursing assistance to newborn lambs was an indispensable emergency measure they had to adopt. When we consider the development of these matters peculiar to the sheep/goat domestication process, and the shared nature of the technical strategy behind the adoption strategies for orphaned lambs and the milk-ejection reflex-inducing devices for milking cows, we may come to understand how important the domestication of sheep/goats was for Near Eastern pastoralists to be able to obtain unique positions not only as the earliest initiators of milking in general, but also in terms of developing the techniques to clear the physiological hurdle to allow them to milk cows.

To sum up, through a unique development process of matters supposed above, the milking of cows with their calves present must have been practiced by Near Eastern pastoralists far before the same scene was depicted in the relief of a Sumerian temple, already in play since the later period of Pre-Pottery Neolithic Culture B. Moreover, because of its importance as a food procuring technique, along with milking practices for sheep/goats, the milk-ejection reflex-inducing devices for milking cows widely diffused in the surrounding areas of the Old Continent and Africa, as Amoroso and Jewell described.

The beginning of milking and sociocultural history

The meaning of the beginning of milking is not restricted to the context of the management techniques that I discussed in the previous chapter (pages 67–70). As I have already stated, without the practice of milking, domesticated sheep/goats were just objects to be killed and eaten by pastoralists and hunters. With the beginning of the practice of milking, pastoralists were not only provided with a walking cistern, but also the means to obtain animal proteins without killing their animals as capital resources. Moreover, by processing milk into dried cheese, they were provided with animal proteins throughout the year. From the standpoint of food procurement, too, this development signified an epoch-making event. However, leaving aside these topics, usually discussed in the context of the beginning of milking, I would like to dedicate several paragraphs to its social and cultural meanings that have seldom been discussed.

As for the social and cultural meanings of milk use, what first comes to mind is feeding human infants with cow's milk. Especially in the last century when powdered milk came to be easily procured owing to the development of milk processing techniques, women were freed from the burden of breastfeeding and could enter into the labour market as part of the workforce next to men. This prepared favourable conditions for women to participate in the workplace on par with men.

Moreover, I think that the beginning of milking for human consumption was a very important event with regard to dietary ethics. In contrast to the previous stage where animals were only a meat resource and their killing was inevitable, the practice of milking opened up the possibility for humans to gain animal proteins without killing. This means that with the beginning of the practice of milking, a contrasting perspective between two food-taking modes emerged: killing versus not killing animals. In other words, it became possible to settle the following contrasting ethical criteria in the way of life preservation: animal killing = unclean and criminal, non-animal killing = clean and innocent.

We know that there is an ethical principle called *ahinsa* in the Hindu world in which a negative value is attached to life sustained by meat eating and animal killing, and the ritualistic observation of a meat taboo is considered a superior way of life. In the Old Testament, in the ideal Garden of Eden, God gave only grain and fruit to Adam and Eve. It was only to their descendant Noah after the flood that God allowed the killing and consumption of animals with a yielding tone in these words: 'I will no more curse the earth by reason of man, because the design of the human heart is originally wicked from their adolescence' (Genesis 8:21). In the world of the Old Testament, too, a negative value is attributed to life maintained through meat eating. Both of the above are examples of dietary ethics born in the Western and South Asian agro-pastoral worlds.

Of course, hunting peoples did feel a sense of shame in killing animals. Lot-Falk reports that Siberian hunters murmur words of excuse before shooting game: 'I am not shooting with the intention of killing you. By chance you have come up in front of the shot arrow' (Lot-Falk, 1953). They regarded hunted animals as nature's gift (Ingold, 1994). However, not only for hunting peoples, but also for pastoral peoples, who before the beginning of milking obtained animal proteins only by killing them, it was not possible to establish an ethical principle that ascribes a negative value to consuming meat. I suspect that with milk at their disposal for the first time, the possibility of establishing a dietary ideology that attributes a negative value to consuming meat came about.

Haudricourt proposed 'vegetarianism' as the term to indicate the dietary attitude where a negative value is given to meat eating by killing animals and a higher value is instead bestowed upon vegetarian food consumption habits, while he defined 'phytophase' as a consumption pattern evident in Oceania where vegetable consumption predominates without any contrasting value judgement (Haudricourt, 1978). His distinctive definitions, which avoid the confusion between two different food habits, are important. The term 'vegetarianism' should be better expressed as a 'no meat eating (no-animal killing) ideology'. In fact, in Hindu vegetarianism (*ahinsa*), eating meat is not allowed, but eggs and milk are permitted.

In the sociocultural history of humanity, the meaning of the practice of milking for human use is not restricted to the advent of new food ethics. As mentioned previously, the beginning of milking opened up the idea of keeping the mother ewes' group alive longer to enable them to deliver more lambs and by keeping more ewes, more milk for consumption could be assured. Ewes are the original capital, producing meat and milk as a profit. Actually, they are the original capital in the sense that every year they deliver offspring among which males can be consumed as a meat resource and females add to the productive capital. Every year this productive capital provided profit through larger and larger amounts of meat and milk products, growing in geometrical terms. In tablets of the Neo-Babylonian period, we can find the numbers of ewes and newborns in the same entrusted flock, which were annually recorded. Thanks to those registers we can learn that the annual rate of increase of lambing ewes was an average of fifteen percent and the flock multiplied by four times within ten years. From such a record, too, we can realise how high the profit rate in pastoral management was.

In agriculture, wheat and other grains multiply several tens of times the amount sown, and with the annual repetition of sowing, the size of the harvest increases geometrically. However, since the arable land as productive capital is limited with the increasing of the farming population, the extension of available land for each farmer sooner or later reaches its limit. On the other hand, in West Asia immense grassland that extended beyond the irrigated cultivated land was available for herding. The shepherds who became able to provide milk could utilise far wider expanses of grassland, like the nomads or seasonal transhumants, and could further increase the size of their productive capital, i.e. the ewes. Through the shepherds' management strategy of keeping procreating ewes alive, they could not only obtain meat from the ever increasing yearling males, but also milk as goods to be exploited for consumption and circulation. We can find here a primordial form of capitalistic management that continuously aims at more profit as a surplus value with an ever-increasing productive capital.

At the beginning of Part One of this book, I stated that to somebody who, for the first time, observes a scene of sheep/goat herding in the Middle East, Central Asia or Europe, the animals do not look very different from their wild progenitors, wandering in the fields. However, I added that after having closely observed the interactive relationship between the animals and the shepherds, one will recognise that the domesticated sheep and goats came to pass their lives quite differently from their wild progenitors through the shepherds' various technical interventions successively invented in the past. Defining this process of divergence from the wild progenitor temporarily as the 'domestication process', I posed the question of how and under what conditions such technical interventions were developed and how these domesticated sheep/goats came to reach a far distant status from that of their progenitors. Part One was dedicated to mainly reconstructing the domestication process of sheep/goats.

For this reconstruction, I consulted archaeozoological data on the domestication process. However, as the archaeological approach cannot analyse many modes of intervention that do not leave any material evidence, it is impossible to reconstruct the process completely. The development process of management intervention must have been a successive interactive process between human intervention initiated since the beginning of domestication and the respective responses of the animals. That is, the process must be described as an additional and accumulative process of mutual involvement between man and animal. I thus proposed an approach by abductive inference.

We have sufficient information on the modes of behaviour of feral sheep/goats left without any human intervention and on the behavioural characteristics of semi-domesticated reindeer and the modes of human intervention in relation to them. If we can point out certain behavioural characteristics in domesticated sheep/goats that cannot be attested in feral sheep/goats and reindeer, we can take them for traits obtained through repeated technical interventions by shepherds. From them we will be able to retrieve more exact knowledge on the meaning of human intervention into animal behaviour.

Until now, with such methodological approach, I have tried to reconstruct how human-animal relationships attested today among sheep/goat herders have been developed, dividing the discussion into three chapters: 1) the beginning of domestication, 2) technical developments soon after domestication and 3) the unique position of Near Eastern pastoralists concerning milking.

Regarding my tentative reconstruction, one could raise the question as to why I failed to devote a chapter to the beginning of nomadism, which is an important issue in the history of pastoralism, aside from a short page dedicated to discussing the motive to obtain milk from sheep/goats. The meaning of nomadism cannot be ignored both in the development of pastoralism and in the history of civilisation. However, even if the nomads repeatedly migrate seasonally from one campsite to another with animals, what they actually *do* is daily herding from their campsite. Ancient nomads therefore did not add any technical intervention apart from those I have dealt with above.

At the end of Part One above I have included a chronological list outlining most of the technical modes of intervention respectively positioned somewhere during the domestication process developed after the beginning of the domestication of sheep/goats. As mentioned above, I think that these interventions, including cow-milking techniques, came to be successively invented in the ancient Near East within a rather short period after the beginning of domestication and began to spread into surrounding areas as a total set of husbandry techniques. They are observable today not only among the pastoralists in the Middle East, but also among those in the Mediterranean regions and Europe, Central Asia, India and Africa. The ethnographical fact that these techniques have been commonly adopted among all pastoralists across such a wide area suggests that these techniques were important as fundamental intervention techniques.

Alternatively, even if all of these techniques are shared by various pastoralists across these wide areas, this does not mean that the repertoire is the same for different pastoralists of different areas. For example, Mongolian shepherds take one special sheep, usually a large one, as an individual responsible for reproduction in the herding flock. They keep it until it dies of natural causes without slaughtering it. This practice must have derived from the traditional custom and belief of Siberian hunters in Northeast Asia: a beautiful or large marten or bear in the forest is considered the master and key individual of the species on whom the reproduction of the group exclusively depends and as a result will never be hunted (Lot-Falk, 1953; Konagaya, 1991). Even though Mongolian shepherds adopt the same fundamental technical modes of intervention with their sheep/goats as the Middle Eastern pastoralists do, they believe that the life of domesticated animals fundamentally belongs to the natural process and they reserve a domain independent from human intervention. So, even though they mostly apply the same fundamental techniques as other sheep/goat herders, they add other idiosyncratic forms of intervention according to their own cultural beliefs and attitudes. As for pastoralists in the Middle East, also, I wondered if there were certain peculiar modes of intervention unique to the Middle Eastern peoples. One is the technique that I call 'herd-guiding technique by means of a castrated and instructed male'.

In Part Two of this book, entitled 'Large Household Chiefs, Shepherds and Domesticated Animals', I discuss several topics concerning the unique destination of domesticated sheep/goats and the political-economic position of shepherds after the emergence of the civilised city-states in the ancient Near East because of their importance in understanding the historical background of Judeo-Christian discourses on animals that determined the orientation of European attitudes towards animals. It is not without reason that I deal with the instructed herd-guiding wether in the first chapter of this part, not only because it is a technique peculiar to the Middle Eastern and Mediterranean pastoralists, but because it provides a clue to understanding the special perspective of ancient Near Eastern large household chiefs towards domesticated animals and subordinate people.

Part II
Large Household Chiefs, Entrusted Shepherds and Domesticated Animals

6 The Domesticated Animal as Serf: Herd Guide-Wethers and Eunuchs

An incident

At the beginning of July, 1987, I was with the Gujar Bakharwal[1] shepherds who were migrating to their summer quarters in Indian Kashmir. We were set to arrive at the summer quarters in the upper part of the Dachinpole valley after long days of marching. It was a difficult time: it was raining, a heavy mist covered everything and the torrent in the valley had swollen due to melted snow. By four o'clock in the afternoon it was already dark. To reach our final destination, the shepherds had to get their flock across a torrent about six to seven meters wide. On the incline there was a gap between the bank and the water, and the sheep did not dare jump down and cross the torrent. The shepherds knew that if they could succeed in pushing any individual animal into the torrent, all the others would begin to jump into the water following the first one: it was, however, very difficult to achieve this. Despite strenuous attempts on the part of one shepherd to push the first sheep that came to hand, it went gliding away nimbly. He tried with another animal, and failed again. After repeated attempts, the terrified sheep got out of the shepherd's control. He was quite desperate. After half an hour, he succeeded in pushing one of the animals down the bank, with the help of two of his fellows. The sheep plunged into the water and swam across the torrent. Following the example, the rest of the sheep, one after another, jumped into the torrent, and in a few minutes all had reached the opposite bank of the stream and could easily access the summer quarters.

In Europe, a medallion from seventeenth century Germany depicts the scene of sheep crossing a river (Henckel and Schöne 1967: 528; see Figure 6.1). A large ram with a bell hanging under its neck enters the river ahead of the flock and the other sheep follow behind. One is even leaping down into the river from a bridge. In the accompanying commentary, we learn that the medallion is to illustrate the ideal relationship between a leader and his faithful followers, according to the allegory of the bellwether. This bellwether is known as a kind of herd guide, castrated and instructed by the shepherd.

Figure 6.1 Group of ewes guided by a herd guide-wether as a leader/follower allegory

Sheep become timid when faced with a gap or stream or any dangerous obstacle: when the leading group stops, the followers, jostling with each other, begin to flow sideways like a stream of water that has been intercepted. On such occasions, the flock sometimes divides into two, or changes direction and does not follow the course intended by the shepherd. A flock is usually accompanied and guided by only two shepherds. For them, such splitting of the flock or deviating from the planned course ought to be avoided, as restoring order consumes time and energy. The shepherd expects, in general, a flock on the move to advance smoothly. It is thus convenient for the shepherd to have an individual animal to lead the flock, especially when they stall in front of some obstacle or when, during herding time or seasonal migration, the shepherd occasionally requires his flock to turn back, halt or change direction. On such occasions, too, it is convenient for the shepherd to have a leader that will respond to his vocal orders and that will, in turn, induce the rest of the flock to follow him.

Of course, this technique is not indispensable for herding control. The Bakharwal, who do not use a guide-wether, have a basic repertoire of herding techniques to keep their large flocks under control. Using a guide-wether is but one of the elaborated techniques.

A guide-wether was trained and used by transhumant shepherds in the Abruzzo region of Central Italy, where I carried out fieldwork in 1970. Abruzzo shepherds cull most male yearlings except for a number retained for reproductive purposes. In the second year, they choose one of them and castrate it to train as a guide-wether. After castration, the shepherd puts a short woollen rope around the wether's neck and walks along with it as if he were walking a dog. When the wether becomes used to him, the shepherd begins to instruct him to respond to his vocal commands. In order to teach the meaning of each vocal command, the shepherd shouts the command and at the same time pulls the rope in such a way as to make the wether learn how to react. At the next stage, after the castrated ram has mastered responding to vocal commands, the shepherd replaces the short rope around the neck with a longer one and places the ram in the midst of the flock in the grazing field where he continues to train it until it behaves obediently when in the flock. Having completed the training he removes the rope. Now, without any physical control, the trained wether goes ahead or returns at the shepherd's vocal commands, even from a long distance (Tani, 1977: 155–7).

The shepherd generally calls the guide-wether *manziero* or *guidarello* and gives it a special personified name (for example, Generale, Mussolini etc.). He places great value on the guide-wether as his faithful follower, and the theft of such a precious animal can start a vendetta. The shepherd makes use of the guide-wether not only when the flock has to cross a river during seasonal migration or to change the direction the flock is moving in. In winter, when the sheep must move through snow, the wether also makes a path advancing in front of the flock. The Bakharwal shepherds who did not know of the use of the guide-wether wasted a lot of time in getting their flock across the river. Indeed, the utility of the guide-wether is considerable.

Guide-wether and eunuch: Positional homology between them

Apart from the real value of the guide-wether in terms of flock control, this technique is based on the following three items of practical ethological knowledge.
1. Sheep and goats are predisposed to follow a preceding fellow.
2. Human beings can control the behaviour of domesticated animals by means of vocal signals taught in the context of a bond of intimacy between man

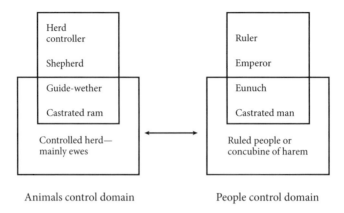

Figure 6.2 Homology of the roles of herd guide-wether and eunuch

and animal. The guide-wether is even given a proper name and instructed to follow the shepherd's vocal commands.

3. Castration makes rams become obedient.

These elements are common knowledge to shepherds everywhere. Though their simple combination does not necessarily lead to the invention of the guide-wether, it nevertheless suggests the following idea. In order to control a flock on the move that does not understand human vocal orders, you may rear an individual that is tamed and instructed to respond to these commands. By controlling the instructed individual, you can, in turn, control the rest of the flock, because sheep are disposed to following. From the interesting combination of these two pieces of knowledge, we can understand how elaborate this herd guiding technique using a guide-wether is. It is worth enquiring into how people arrived at such an idea.

The guide-wether holds a unique position in terms of the relationship between human beings and domestic animals. Establishing a special relationship with the shepherd that the other flock members do not have, the guide-wether acts as an agent for the shepherd and is positioned on the shepherd's dominant side. At the same time, of course, it remains a member of the flock that is dominated by him. It is a castrated male and therefore is alienated from the flock's reproductive process; it plays the role of mediator between the dominator (shepherd) and the dominated (flock). As most of the flock is comprised of females, it can also be regarded as a

The Domesticated Animal as Serf: Herd Guide-Wethers and Eunuchs

Photo 6.1 Eunuch in the period of Sargon the second

guardian of the females. In this context, the guide-wether plays a role functionally analogous to that of the eunuch (see Figure 6.2).

Aristotle defined the eunuch as the mediator between the emperor and the people and the transmitter of the emperor's commands to them. Being castrated, the eunuch was also the guardian of females in the harem. Because of his biological inability to have descendants, he was in a position to win the emperor's trust and was raised to become the emperor's confidante. The eunuch's position in the imperial world corresponds to that of the castrated male guide-wether in the pastoral world. Very similar techniques of management are employed in the two domains: control of domestic animals and of human subordinates. We know that eunuchs were already widely adopted in the Achaemenides Dynasty of the ancient Near East before they appeared in the Chinese imperial court in the Han dynasty (Watanabe, 1992: 357–369; Mitamura, 1963) (See Photo 6.1).

Of course, the functional similarity between the herd guide-wether and eunuchs could be coincidental. Alternatively, we may suppose that either of them worked as the model for metaphorical extension to the other; from herd guide-wether to eunuch or the reverse. In this chapter, I first demonstrate various simpler and more rudimental herd guide techniques discovered during my extensive surveys in the Middle East and the Mediterranean. This suggests that the herd guide-wether was the final product in the course of elaboration of preceding more rudimental herd guide techniques, without any reference to eunuchs. Moreover, after having demonstrated that the geographical distribution of herd guide-wethers and ancient eunuchs overlap in the Middle East, I suggest that the following unique perspective of the large household chiefs in the ancient Near East facilitated the metaphorical extension from herd guide-wether to eunuchs—their domesticated animals and their subordinated serfs and slaves belong to the same category as living movable property.

Geographical distribution of three types of caprid herd guides

When I first became interested in the cultural implications of the guide-wether and its geographical distribution, I could find little historical or ethnographic data on this topic outside the European region. In order to clarify the geographical distribution, I had to collect information by making extensive visits to various pastoral groups, starting in Abruzzo, Italy where I first observed the guide-wether in use.

Moreover, while I was visiting various pastoral peoples in order to pinpoint geographical distribution, I was surprised to find other herd control techniques simpler than the guide-wether and with more restricted functions than those covered by it. This suggests that there were some rudimentary techniques preceding the adoption of the guide-wether that can be regarded as a more complex final result in the development of herd control techniques.

Beginning from the more simple methods, I now describe all the herd guiding techniques and their respective geographical distribution and attempt to clarify how and under what kind of precursors the guide-wether flock control technique was developed.

Incidentally, as shepherds utilise either goats or sheep in herd control, I will show the respective methods with the distinctive sign: G for goats and S for sheep.

G series-inducement by goats
Capricious and active goats promptly react to any external stimuli. Even if they often deviate from the main flock, they easily respond to the shepherd's chasing

and move ahead in front of the flock. Especially in the morning when it is time to set out for daily herding and sheep are stuck inside the enclosure, goats begin to move out first and by doing so they induce the sheep to follow.

Simple method by goats (Gn)
The simplest method using goats is just to mix several goats, males or females indifferently, with the flock of sheep. In this method, only the goats' natural behavioural characteristic of easily reacting to stimuli is utilised. I will call this method Gn (Goat nature). There is evidence of mixing goats in a sheep flock in the tablet records of flocks entrusted to shepherds in the Old Babylonian period, so we may suppose that this method had already been adopted in the earlier stages of pastoralism (Van de Mieroop, 1993: 178–9). As I observed this practice among various pastoralists from the Mediterranean area to Afghanistan, I can affirm that its geographical distribution is very wide.

Castrated male goat (Gcm)
Usually not only billy goats but also nanny goats are kept in mixed herds. Since males tend to become excited among females and disturb the flock order, it is better to castrate them except for the breeding candidates. In 1979, I found such castrated billy goats among the Durrani Pashtun, Arabi and Uzbeck shepherds in Northeastern Afghanistan (details in Tani, Matsui and Omar, 1980 and Tani, 1997: 154–5). Beck, who carried out a very detailed survey of the Qashqa'i tribesmen in Iran, reports that billy goats in a sheep flock are castrated after maturity (Beck, 1991: 312). I will refer to these castrated bucks as Gcm (goat castrated male).

Instructed castrated male goat (Gcim)
When I visited the Baxtyâri shepherds in the mountain area not far from Masjed-Soleyman in Iran (February, 1993), I was able to confirm that they mixed four to five billy goats in the sheep flock to use them for herd control. They said that they would castrate them at the yearling stage in winter and train them to obey the shepherd's command by call signals and sticks. They distinguished the castrated ones from other goats in the flock by calling them *sahi* and defined their function as herd guides. Being castrated and instructed to respond to human signals, they are the goat version of a guide-wether. I will refer to this category as 'Gcim' (goat castrated instructed male).

Both the above-mentioned Iranian Qashqa'i and the groups in Afghanistan mix goats in their flock and castrate them, but they do not give them any instruction.

In the Middle East, I was able to find these castrated and instructed male goats (Gcim) only among the Kurdish and Baxtyâri shepherds. On the other hand, shepherds of Crete in the Mediterranean area who usually utilise sheep guide-wethers sometimes use a castrated instructed male goat instead. This means that both are interchangeable and have equal status in terms of flock control techniques.

The above-cited herd guiding animals are goats and are different species to the predominant sheep flock. Conversely, I have counted several kinds of methods of guiding sheep herds aside from a sheep guide-wether. I now demonstrate these in order from simplest to most complex.

S series-inducement by sheep

Use of mother-offspring bond (Snbmo)

I observed this method at the campsite of the Marwari shepherds in Rajasthan in 1993. In the morning, before departure for daily herding, one shepherd clapped his hands and made chasing sounds to try to make the flock, lying in the enclosure, begin to move. The flock, however, did not start to move out of the enclosure. Presently, another shepherd picked up from a pen the newborn of a mother ewe standing near the exit and began to walk out of the enclosure, showing it to its mother. At once the mother stood up and began to follow it and in turn the rest of the flock started moving out of the enclosure. Ensuring that all the flock had begun to follow in a long row, the shepherd handed the newborn to a young shepherd who carried it back to the campsite while he walked in front of the flock to take them to the herding field.

I encountered this simple herd guiding method that used the mother-offspring bond for the first time when I was in the final stage of my extensive survey on herding techniques, so I was unable to ascertain as to whether other pastoralists I had visited also adopted this method. Therefore, I can exemplify only this case in Rajasthan.

I will refer to the above method as 'Snbmo' (sheep natural bond between mother and offspring). Actually, during daily herding in the fields, this method cannot be used because newborns are kept in a pen at the campsite. For this reason its use is restricted to the time of departure for daily herding.

In all the flock control methods using either goats or a newborn lamb mentioned above, natural behavioural properties are utilised. Below I discuss the methods in which a personal relationship artificially established between a shepherd and a specific animal is employed to instigate the initial move.

Use of a provisioned ram or ewe (Sm/fp)

When I visited the Sarakatsani shepherds in Epirus, Greece (1980), I observed the following method. Several male and female lambs were selected in the early period after delivery, kept in a pen and given milk from a milking bottle or skin bag instead of letting them suckle from their mother ewes. Shepherds took care of them and even caressed them as if they were pets. They gave them a special proper name, calling them repeatedly by it and gave them grain after weaning in order to get them to come running to their call. Once they had grown up and joined the main adult flock, the shepherds continued to give them grain when they drew near upon the shepherd's call. On returning to the campsite too, shepherds gave them grain so that they would hurry home to get their reward. By providing such a prize, they became obedient to the human voice and mediators between human intentions and the rest of the flock.

The Sarakatsanis call the provisioned male *manari* and the female *manara*. These terms do not designate a 'leading individual', but only a 'provisioned and intimate individual'. Even though they are given proper names, their relationship with shepherds is established through the giving of grain: the motivation for approaching the shepherd is to be fed grain. In this sense, they differ from the individuals that understand and follow the shepherd's command that I will mention next. The range of available opportunities is limited to initially induce the rest of the flock to follow them on departure or return to the campsite or when a shepherd wants to make the flock move smoothly forward.

I will call this type of technique using a provisioned male/female 'Sm/fp' (sheep male/female provisioned). In addition to the Sarakatsani, I observed this method among Cretan shepherds in Greece and Marwari nomadic shepherds in Rajasthan (in the neighbourhood of Jaipur, India). We can say that its geographical distribution seems to be quite extensive.

Differently from herd guiding techniques, if shepherds can use individuals that not only react when enticed by grain, but also obediently respond to the shepherd's vocal and physical commands to go ahead, stop and go back, the range of availability might be widened. In fact, the guide-wether is not the only animal with these capabilities. In Romania, for the first time, I encountered another technique that uses several ewes instructed to obey the shepherd's command.

Use of plural instructed ewes (Splif)

During the summer of 1978, I stayed at the summer camp of the villagers of Ardan in the province of Bistrița-Nasaud in Northern Romania.

I had already observed the use of the guide-wether, locally called *batal* by the shepherds of Tilişca in the province of Sibiu, Central Romania, and I wanted to confirm if it was used in the northern part of Romania too, so I visited the shepherds of Ardan. First I asked one of the Ardan shepherds if they usually adopted the guide-wether called *batal*. He replied that he knew that in some southern parts of Romania they adopted *batal*, but that they did not make use of it here. He said, 'We utilise another kind of herd guide called *fruntaşa*'. In order to know what kind of guiding individual he was referring to, I further asked him to actually indicate *fruntaşa* in his flock. To my surprise, he indicated seven to eight individuals, saying, 'this one, that one and that one, etc.'. Until then I had thought that the number of guiding individuals must be at maximum two or three. Then, in order to reconfirm it, I asked another fellow shepherd the same question. He indicated five individuals that were unexpectedly quite different from the *fruntaşa* indicated by the former shepherd. If *fruntaşa* literally means 'individual that goes in front of the group' and 'innate leader', it seems unimaginable to keep numerous leading individuals as herd guides, because univocal guiding to move on cannot be realised. Moreover, each shepherd indicated different female individuals in the same flock as *fruntaşa*. After exchanging several questions and answers, I finally learned what *fruntaşa* actually were. Shepherds choose several female lambs among newborns and begin to call them by their respective names according to classificatory terminologies based on the colour pattern of the fleece. After weaning, they establish intimacy with them by daily providing them with *mamaliga* (a ball of boiled corn). Confirming that each of the animals memorised its name and responded to its call, they began to instruct them in vocal commands with different meanings, i.e. 'stop', 'come back', 'go ahead', emitting special whistles accompanied by touch. *Fruntaşa* therefore did not denote an innate leader of the flock as I had first thought, but individuals specially instructed to understand the meanings of the shepherd's vocal commands and obey, inducing the rest of the flock to follow. In this sense, the *fruntaşa* method is a kind of plural female version of the guide-wether.

Later, in the herding field, I asked a shepherd to actually order *fruntaşa* to come back by calling them. He blew an acute whistle towards his flock that was about 100 meters from him and loudly called out several classificatory names of colour patterning corresponding to several *fruntaşa*: *neagra*, *oaciçe* etc. Soon after his calls, I could see the named individuals stop and move towards him. He repeated the acute whistle and some of them began to run and their moves in turn, as in a domino effect, induced the whole flock to follow. Watching such a scene, I understood why they produce so many *fruntașa*: the more *fruntașas* that respond to the shepherd's command, the more stimuli to induce movement can be produced creating a wave in the rest of the flock and therefore setting off a march more quickly.

Besides the case of Northern Romania, I confirmed the use of *fruntașas* in the following areas. I found this system in use in the villages in the area of Tilișca of Central Romania where they also use *batal* (guide-wether) and in the Romanian-speaking people of Aromani in Thessaly of Northern Greece, too. Instead, the Greek-speaking shepherds, the Sarakatsani in Epirus and Cretan shepherds did not adopt the *fruntașa* system. I did not have the chance to carry out my survey further north than the northern frontier of Romania, in the Russian territory. To the east, instead, I was able to verify that Turkish and Kurdish pastoralists were unaware of the *fruntașa* herd guiding technique. From this data, we may conclude that the herd guiding technique by plural instructed females is distributed towards the north from the northern parts of Greece to Romania, i.e. among Romanian-speaking pastoralists.

I will also call this type 'Splif' (sheep plural instructed females). The *fruntașa* method, of course, is very similar to the guide-wether, which is our topic here. If there is any difference between them, what functions distinguish them? To answer this question, I compare the two, recalling the herd guiding technique of the guide-wether.

Guide-wether (Scim)

I have already illustrated how the guide-wether was born, using the example of Central Italy, but I need to describe it again briefly. The shepherd, choosing amongst the breeding candidates, castrates a ram. Later on with a short rope around the wether's neck, he always walks with it in tow and when the wether becomes accustomed to him, the shepherd begins to instruct it on how to respond to vocal commands. The shepherd will only remove the rope after completing this training, at which point the trained wether will go ahead or come back upon receiving the shepherd's vocal commands without any physical coercion, even from a long distance.

As for instruction by vocalised commands, there is no difference between *fruntașas* and guide-wethers. The key difference here is that the latter is male and castrated. If it was not castrated, it would mate with ewes throughout the year and as a result, the prolonged delivery period would make it impossible to achieve the collective management of milking. During the mating season, sexually excited rams are not likely to obey human commands, even when instructed. In these two senses, the castration of the guide-wether is important and assures his availability all year long. On the other hand, the female guides are not available in all seasons, because in autumn, the mating season, the shepherds put breeding rams into the flock. *Fruntașas*, too, will be chased by these rams and become less obedient to the shepherd's command. Being male, a guide-wether is more daring and goes ahead courageously in front of obstacles and can march ahead even in deep snow. Such ability cannot be expected of female *fruntașas*. To conclude, even if both of the techniques were to be elaborated and found to be similar in their method, the latter is effective throughout the year and can be used in a wider range of herding situations.

Now, leaving aside the techniques using goats, I sum up the four examples of the sheep series as shown in Figure 6.3. Here I locate them in order according to the degree of availability and efficiency: the use of 1) natural property, 2) a provisioned individual that draws near at the shepherd's call, 3) plural instructed female individuals that respond to the shepherd's commands and 4) castrated and instructed male individuals (guide-wethers) that not only obediently respond to the shepherd's commands in any situation, but also dare to go ahead when faced with obstacles.

Alternatively, in the goat series, there were only three types: the use of 1) common goats, 2) a castrated male individual and 3) a castrated and instructed male goat. There are several grades in development similar to the sheep series and the last one is the corresponding goat version of the sheep guide-wether, even if we cannot determine which was invented first.

After examining all these types of herd guiding techniques, we may say that the guide-wether is the most developed, has the widest range of uses and can be esteemed as the pinnacle in the development of herd guiding techniques.

Moreover, I pointed out above that the guide-wether plays the role of mediator between the 'dominating shepherd' and the 'dominated flock', somehow corresponding to the eunuch's role as mediator between the 'dominating emperor' and the 'dominated people'. Of course, even if there is a certain homology in the role and function between them, we cannot neglect the possibility that they were independently invented, but we may also suppose the possibility that either came first and became the model for the other. In this case, either 1) the human control technique 'eunuch' was invented following the 'guide-wether' model or 2) the animal control technique 'guide-wether' was invented following the 'eunuch'

The Domesticated Animal as Serf: Herd Guide-Wethers and Eunuhs

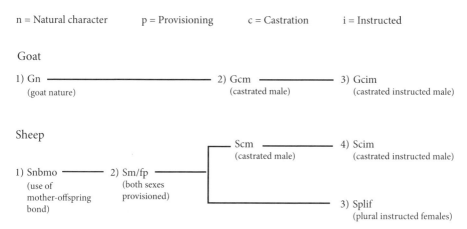

Figure 6.3 Various types of herd guide and the hypothetical process of their elaboration

model. After examining various herd guiding techniques, however, I have learnt that there are several techniques less developed than the guide-wether, which can be considered as the final result of the elaboration. This suggests that the guide-wether was invented and came into use as the last stage in the development process, independently from the 'eunuch'. Then, case 2) can be regarded as less probable and case 1) remains more possible as far as modelling can be considered. The more probable hypothesis is that 'eunuch' was introduced following the 'guide-wether' as a model.

Before giving credit to that hypothesis, however, we must check the following possibilities linked to the geographical distribution of each technique. Theoretically speaking, there are two possibilities. Either 1) the geographical distribution of the 'guide-wether' overlaps that of 'eunuch' at least in a certain area, or 2) overlapping is not present at all. In the second case, there would be no possibility of borrowing the model and we should suppose that both developed independently. Only if the spread of both techniques coincides in a certain area, it becomes probable that the eunuch idea was invented there from the 'guide-wether' model. Of course, in that case, we must not forget that in ancient times the distribution of 'eunuch' covered a very wide area, from the Near East to China in East Asia. Given this fact, if the geographical spread of the 'guide-wether' covers all of these areas, we cannot determine the place where 'eunuch' had been invented following the 'guide-wether' model. On the contrary, if the guide-wether is present in a limited area inside the distribution of 'eunuchs', this area could be the place where the eunuch method was supposedly copied from the guide-wether model. So, we must check the geographical distribution of the 'guide-wether'.

Distribution of guide-wether: Identifying the origin of eunuchs

I described how Bakharwal shepherds, who do not use the guide-wether herd guiding technique, wasted considerable time getting their flock across a torrent to arrive at their summer quarters in Kashmir. On the other hand, from a German medallion we learned that shepherds in Northern Europe used this technique, as shepherds continue to do in Central Italy. This means that the herd guiding technique was adopted both in Northern Europe and the Mediterranean area. Between these two areas, western India and Europe, there should be a geographical boundary delineating the presence and absence of that technique.

Among the Sarakatsani shepherds of Epirus and Thessaly in Greece, I was able to ascertain the use of guide-wethers (in the summer of 1980 and in the winter of 1993), which they called *kliari ghissemia* (Campbell, 1984: 19; Tani, 1982: 14 and 1987b: 20). The Vlach and Aromani groups also used it as did groups in Crete, even if they sometimes substituted it with the castrated and instructed goat (Gcim). However, in all the above-mentioned places the training method was mostly the same as that used by the Italian shepherds.

Towards the east, the Yöluk of Turkey (Turkish nomads who migrated there from Central Asia in the Middle Ages) did not adopt the guide-wether approach. They have probably maintained the herd guiding technique of their place of origin.

Going further east, I observed the guide-wether method again, used by Kurdish shepherds in the neighbourhood of Hakkari in Eastern Turkey. They said that they sometimes use a castrated and instructed billy goat (Gcim) instead of a castrated ram and put only one in each flock (Tani, 1989a: 189). The method of training is almost the same as that used by the Italian shepherds. The Baxtyâri shepherds in the area adjacent to Masjed-Soleyman in Iran also use the castrated and instructed goat (*sahi*) instead of the sheep guide-wether, and even though Kurds and Baxtyâris adopt goats instead of sheep, the method of training is exactly the same (direct observation in 1993). Baqqāara shepherds in Northeastern Syria adopt the sheep guide-wether (Oral report of Dr. M. Hirata of the University of Obihiro Chikusan).

Further east, among the Pashtun, Arab and Uzbeck pastoralists in Northeastern Afghanistan, they castrate goats as herd guides, but they do not instruct them to respond to vocalised commands. In India, among the Marwari shepherds who camped at Shobhasar near Bikaner and at Karoli near Jaipur, I was unable to find any sheep or goats castrated and instructed for herd guiding, and found the same with the Bakharwal in Indian Kashmir. To sum up, the distribution of the herd guiding technique by guide-wethers ends at the eastern part of the so-called Fertile Crescent area where the domestication of sheep/goats originally took place and does not spread further east.

On the other hand, going north from the Mediterranean, I have no data for ex-Yugoslavia, but I was able to ascertain that in Romania the transhumant shepherds at Topalu in Dobrogea province adopt the guide-wether, calling it *batal*. The situation was the same for the province of Sibiu in Central Romania, while further north in Romania in the province of Bistrița-Nasaud, they do not use this method. This indicates that the distribution does not go further north than Central Romania. As an aside, the guide-wether is commonly called *batal* in Central and Southern Romania, which probably derives from the Greek *batallos* that designates a castrated ram (Hasdeu, 1976). Observing that the guide-wether is not present in the north, but only in Southern and Central Romania, we may infer that this herd guiding technique spread towards the north from Greece.

Now I shift my attention to the far distant northeastern areas of Central Asia, Tibet and Mongolia.

From a documentary report I saw that some Kirghiz nomads, when trying to get their flock to cross a river, would get one shepherd to carry a sheep under his arm in order to make the rest of the flock follow it. They did not use a guide-wether. In Ladakh I was able to confirm that Tibetan shepherds did not know the guide-wether method (either with sheep or goats) (Tani, in August 1985), neither do the shepherds of Amdo-Doma and Kailash in Central Tibet (oral report by Matsubara, 1985) nor do Mongolian nomads surveyed by Konagaya (Konagaya, 1991 and 1996).

I should collect full information on the geographical distribution across Eurasia, however, from the above-mentioned information, we may approximately determine the geographical distribution of the guide-wether within a long horizontal belt: northern Europe, Italy and Greece to the west, Southern and Central Romania to the north and mountainous regions of the Fertile Crescent to the east (Kurds of Levant and Baxtyâri in the area of Zagros in Iran). It neither extends further north, nor further east from the belt, nor to Central Asia, Tibet and Mongolia (see areas outlined by the black line in Figures 6.4 and 6.5).

Supposing the possibility that the guide-wether as an animal control technique was a model for the eunuch human control technique and not the reverse, I posed the following questions. Where was the place of origin of the adoption of

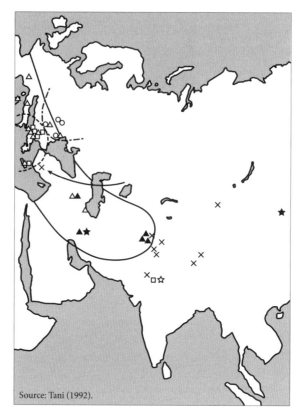

★ Mixing of goats   ☆ Use of mother-offspring bond   ◻ Sheep: both sexes provisioned
○ Plural instructed ewes   △ Castrated ram   ▲ He-goat instructed   × Absence of any herd guide

Figure 6.4 Geographical distribution of various herd guiding techniques

eunuchs? Was it in the ancient Near East or in ancient China where its use was equally attested from ancient times? Of course, if the guide-wether is diffused in both areas, we cannot univocally determine the original birthplace of the eunuch. On the other hand, if it is distributed only in one of the two areas, we may conclude that the eunuch method was invented in the area where the use of the guide-wether can be attested.

Now, after having demonstrated the geographical distribution of the guide-wether herd guiding technique, we can say that East Asia, including China, is out of its distribution. So, as far as we can presume the possibility of an analogical

The Domesticated Animal as Serf: Herd Guide-Wethers and Eunuhs

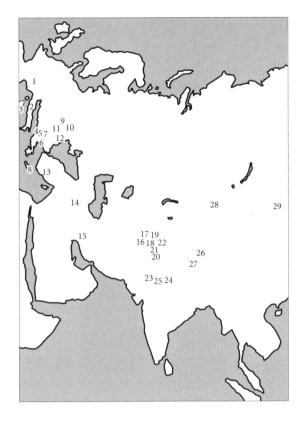

1 Nevache, Hautes Alpes, France (Delamarre, 1975).
2* Abruzzo, Central Italy (1969).
3 Sardinia, Italy (Ledda, 1975).
4* Sarakatsani, Epirus, Greece (1978).
5* Sarakatsani, Thessaly, Greece (1982).
6* Vlach, Thessaly, Greece (1982).
7* Aromani, Thessaly, Greece (1982).
8* Crete, Greece (1982).
9* Ardan, Bistriţa-Năsăud, Romania (1978).
10* Şebis, Bistriţa-Năsăud, Romania (1980).
11* Tilişca, Sibiu, Romania (1982).
12* Topalu, Constanţa, Romania (1980).
13 Yöluk, Burdur, Turkey (1979) (Matsubara, 1983).
14* Kurds, Hakkâri, Turkey (1980).
15* Bâxtyari, Masjed-Soleyman, Iran (1980).
16* Durrani Pashtun, Badakhshan, Afghanistan (1978).
17* Uzbeck, Badakhshan, Afghanistan (1978).
18* Arabi, Badakhshan, Afghanistan (1978).
19* Tajik-Shagni, Badakhshan, Afghanistan (1978).
20* Bakharwal, Jammu-Kashmir, India (1987).
21* Kashmiri, Kashmir, India (1987).
22* Tibetan Zanskar, Ladakh, India (1985).
23* Marwari, Bikaner, Rajasthan, India (1987).
24* Marwari, Karoli, Jaipur, India (1989).
25* Marwari, East of Jaipur, India (1992).
26 Amdo Doma, Tibet (1985) (Matsubara, oral report).
27 Kantisshan, Tibet (1985) (Matsubara, oral report).
28 Southern part of Altai range, Shinkyan (1990) (Matsubara, oral report).
29 Sirin Hoto, Mongolia (1987) (Konagaya, oral report).

Note. * = places that have been visited and confirmed by the author.

Figure 6.5 Data collecting locations of various herd guides

extension of the guide-wether to the domain of people control, we may conclude that the people control technique of the eunuch was not originally invented in China, but in the Near East or in the Mediterranean areas where ancient civilisation flourished.

Before accepting this as fact, we ought to test the following question.

Thus far, I have carried out my discussion under the presumption that, starting from the functional homology between guide-wether and eunuch, either of these two was the model for a metaphorical extension into the other domain. Of course, even if the metaphor has some objective background, as Lakoff and Johnson (1980) say, there are no *a priori* guidelines for its occurrence. It is true, however, that metaphorical and analogical extensions are often guided according to categorical proximity unique to the cultural area concerned. In our case, i.e. in the ancient Near East and the Mediterranean, was there any categorical proximity between the domestic animal domain and the human domain? If there were not, the possibility of metaphorical extension becomes low and we should accept that the eunuch was invented in the context of human control independently from the animal control technique and that a similar functional homology happened by chance. We must check, therefore, if in the ancient Near East and the Mediterranean area there was a certain categorical proximity between the two domains as a cultural fact.

The viewpoint of the household chief

It may be opportune to recall the following remark of Émile Benveniste in *Le Vocabulaires des Institutions Indo-Européenes* (1966). He paid attention to the terms *paśu* in the ancient Vedic texts and *pasu* in the texts of Avesta. These terms have been understood as a collective term to designate domesticated animals in general. Benveniste, against common interpretation, pointed out that these terms were used in antithesis (i.e. as pairs) in the following way, 'quadripedal *paśu* and bipedal *pasu*'. There is no doubt that 'bipedal' means 'human' and 'quadripedal' means 'animal'. Moreover, in a text of Avesta, the term *pasu vira* appears as a customary term and is used to indicate 'house serf' or 'slave'. From these uses of *pasu*, Benveniste concluded that the terms *paśu* and *pasu* designate not only domestic animals, but also men subordinated to the household chief (Benveniste 1966: 48). If Benveniste's interpretation is correct, in the ancient Indo-Iranian linguistic world, members of the two different semantic domains, domestic animals and subordinated domestic serfs or slaves, were classified in the same category under the term *pasu*. In this mode of categorisation, we can discern the eyes of the dominator-owner who identifies both domesticated animals and serfs as movable living property belonging to him.

This perspective is *dominus* centric and under such a categorical identification, it might be easy to extensively apply the management techniques for domestic animals to the human domain.

I now show that such a viewpoint can also be confirmed in the ancient Sumerian world.

Maekawa, a leading specialist on the Sumerian temple economy, has analysed certain groups of economic tablets from the Sumerian temple-state of Lagash in the third millennium B.C. In his paper, he examines two different groups of economic texts: one is the records of the periodic supply of captured female slaves in the weaver's camp and the other is the records of cattle kept in the training centre to supply ploughing oxen to farmers under the temple economy (Maekawa, 1979, 1980, 1982).

From the former text, Maekawa reveals the following fact. Even if captured female slaves who engaged in weaving were generally not allowed to marry, they often had their own children. Among these children, the daughters, after growing up, were recruited into their mother's weaving group in order to make them work as weavers too. On the other hand, the sons were castrated and left their mother's group to work as labour-slaves, for example pulling boats up the river. These sons were called *amarKud*, the meaning of which I will explain later. We can find here two different life paths according to sex distinction: daughters remain in their mother's group, whereas sons, after castration, leave the group in order to be used for physical labour.

The other set of records of the training centre for supplying ploughing oxen show that male calves, annually brought into the centre from local cattle breeders as a tribute to the temple, were first castrated, then trained for ploughing and distributed to the temple farmers. Maekawa points out that it was this castrated ploughing ox that was originally called *amarKud* (= bull cut), and the term was metaphorically applied to the weaver's castrated sons.

It was preferable for cattle breeders to offer male calves to the temple as tribute, since it was important to retain female calves in order to secure the reproduction of the herd and future milk suppliers. On the other hand, male calves, except for a few kept for breeding, were superfluous, and in the Mediterranean and the Middle Eastern regions, they were castrated and either slaughtered for meat or used for transport or ploughing. Thus there were two different courses of life for these animals according to sex: the females remained in the maternal group, the males, castrated, leaving it. This pattern was not unique to the Sumerian world, but was also a customary feature of pastoral flock management throughout the Mediterranean and the Middle East. Note that the same pattern is attested among the children of the captured female slaves in the Sumerian camps: daughters remain in the maternal group, while sons, after being castrated, leave it. While in the case of *pasu* its usage shows an example of semantic identification between domesticated animals and subordinated serfs and slaves, the sons of the captured weavers here are not only called by the term for the castrated bull *amarKud* as a metaphorical extension, but they are also practically treated in the same way as bulls (Maekawa, 1979 and 1982).

Maekawa, as well as Benveniste, provides us with very important supporting evidence to our discussion: in the ancient Indo-Iranian and Sumerian worlds, there was a perspective that identified both the domestic animals and serfs (slaves) owned and controlled by a household chief as the same kind of movable living property.

What kinds of people were they who identified their subordinates with their owned and controlled domesticates? There is no doubt that they were large household chiefs (according to Weber's terminology) of the temple city-states in the ancient Near East who kept large numbers of domesticates and serfs in their households. If these large household chiefs regarded both their human subordinates and domesticated animals under close categorical proximity, that increases the probability that the model of the guide-wether previously invented was transferred to human control techniques that lead to the invention of the 'eunuch' method. As the distribution of guide-wethers overlaps that of eunuchs in the ancient Near East and the Mediterranean, this fact increases the possibility that the eunuch as a human control technique was invented under the political chiefs of the ancient Oriental states in the Near East who were acquainted with guide-wethers.

After answering the question as to the origin of the eunuch starting from the functional homology between guide-wether and eunuch, let us return to the guide-wether as flock control technique and discuss its distinctiveness.

The guide-wether is an individual animal selected by the shepherd, given a proper name and trained to obediently respond to the shepherd's vocal commands in order to induce the rest of the flock to follow. His sexual instinct is extinguished by castration in order to allow him to well observe the shepherd's command and to carry out his role as leader of the flock. He cannot be substituted by other common sheep in the flock, as his ability depends on a 'personal' specific command-obedience relationship established between him and the shepherd. Even though this herding technique aims at guiding the flock as a whole during herding and can be classified as 'collective bio-control', there is a kind of 'personal bio-control' at its base in the sense that it is effected only by establishing an unsubstitutable personal tie between the shepherd and the guide-wether.

Now let us compare it with other 'individual bio-control' techniques described in the previous chapter.

At suckling time a shepherd assists a newborn that is unable to encounter its mother in the crowd of adults, or he gives an orphan the chance to suckle from a different ewe making use of her offspring as a decoy. Shepherds can achieve these nursing acts through memorising which offspring belongs to which mother ewe. This kind of assistance was also defined as a form of 'personal bio-control', however, the focus is centred upon the mother-offspring bond as a natural fact. Here the shepherd attends to the unsubstitutable mother-offspring bond with 'affection' towards a newborn that would otherwise die of starvation. On the other hand, in the herd guiding technique of the guide-wether, a shepherd controls the whole flock through his personal bond with the animal artificially established through naming and instruction. The shepherd depends on a 'strong trust' in the guide-wether's faithful assistance with flock control. In the ancient Near East they were able to find an effective measure of 'collective bio-control' over the flock through the 'personal bio-control' of a trained faithful assistant.

Now, before ending this chapter on a idiosyncratic cultural aspect of the intervention techniques in the Near East, I would like to add a fact concerning the influence of the 'guide-wether' model in the creation of 'eunuchs': the relationship 'human ruling chief (emperor) → eunuch → dominated people' emerged in parallel with the relationship 'animal ruling chief (shepherd) → guide-wether → dominated flock'. With this practical metaphor, the view that considered domesticated animals and subordinate serfs and slaves as the movable living property of the household chief must have been present. If we look at this fact from the serfs' point of view, they are identified in the same category as domesticated animals. Conversely, from the domesticated animals' point of view, they are identified in the same category as the subordinated men. Under such categorisation, both the serfs and the animals come to completely belong to the household chief, i.e. *dominus*.

Now, I would like to recollect once more the practice of the Mongolian shepherds who regard a special individual in their flock as responsible for the whole herd's reproduction and for that reason do not slaughter it but let it die a natural death.

They believe that by killing it the reproduction mechanism in the flock will be damaged. Even if this practice derived from Siberian hunters, it is supposed to have been maintained even after the beginning of pastoralism in Mongolia and is based on the belief that the flock maintains its own innate reproductive mechanism which belongs to an inviolable natural domain and cannot fully fall under artificial human control.

Instead in the Near Eastern attitude that categorised domesticated animals with subordinated serfs as movable living property, dominated men and domestic animals come under full human control. In such a view, there is no room for the animal's own life process independent from and beyond human control.

Interestingly, the discourse concerning animals in the Old Testament seems to be in accordance with this background view. In the well-known passage of Genesis 1:27–29, God entrusts man with the control of all animals created by Him, because he was created in similitude to God. In this statement, we cannot recognise any inviolable and independent animal domain for their life preservation as we have seen with Mongolian shepherds. How did such a view that considers animals as objects of human control emerge in the ancient Near East? I think that the key to unlocking this question could be in the fact that professional shepherds in that area had achieved not only collective and classificatory bio-control, but also individual bio-control of mother-offspring pairs through their nursing assistance, as I explained in Chapter Four. However, if only this kind of bio-control were relevant to the genesis of such a view, all the pastoralists who adopted the same intervention techniques in other areas could have developed the same view towards animals, which is not the case. We must find out the reason why such a view was taken for granted and was peculiar to the ancient Near Eastern world. Even if I suggested that large household chiefs in that world regarded their domesticated animals and their subordinated serfs as the same living movable property, we need more knowledge about them. In the next chapter, I will analyse extant tablet texts revealing the relationship between large household chiefs and the entrusted shepherds in the large temple city-states of the ancient Near East in order to understand the sociocultural background of the message in the Old Testament: 'man is worthy of being master of all animals because he has been created in similitude to God'.

7 Relationship Between Temple Cities and Pastoral Groups in the Ancient Near East

'Civilisation resides in the city and nomads on the borderlands are the destroyers of civilisation'. Such duality has been maintained as a paradigmatic idea since historians began to describe the alternation of dynasties in the ancient Near East. However, the relationship between nomads and the city cannot be described by such a simplistic oppositional framework. There has always been a tight political and economic relationship between them, especially in the context of providing animal food for the cities. The relationship between temple city-states and nomadic pastoralists in ancient Mesopotamia is no exception. In this chapter, referring to the materials published by researchers who have deciphered the texts on excavated tablets and shed light on the relationship and providing my own critical analysis, I describe the general aspect of providing animal food to urban dwellers and the relationship between the large urban herd owners and the entrusted shepherds under contract. By such work, I hope to be able not only to demonstrate in more detail the actual status of the urban animal proprietors as large household chiefs who considered domestic animals and house servants as belonging to the same category, as noted in the previous chapter, but also to provide a clue to understanding the background of the famous proposition 'Man is worthy of being master of animals because of his similitude to God' and other statements related to the God-man-animal relationships in the Old Testament.

Feeding cities

On the relationship between the ancient Mesopotamian cities and the shepherd groups, Zeder published an interesting volume entitled *Feeding Cities* (1991). In her book, having analysed the excavated bones of domestic animals in a primordial city that emerged in the second half of the fourth millennium B.C., the author demonstrates how the city was provided with animal food from outer areas and how meat was distributed among the people. Through her detailed analysis, we have

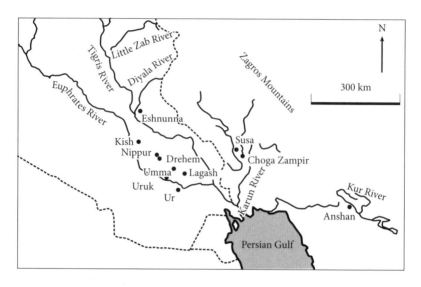

Figure 7.1 Major Mesopotamian cities around the third millennium B.C.

come to learn the oldest facts about the relationship between the city and pastoral groups in the ancient Near East (see Figure 7.1).

The archaeological site excavated by Zeder is a dwelling site at Tal-e Malyan (later called the city of Anshan) in the basin of the Kur river in the southern part of the Zagros mountain range situated at the same latitude as the river mouth of Tigris-Euphrates (about 300 km east of the river mouth). The excavated periods of the site range from the seventh to the second millennium B.C. In the dwelling site from 6000 B.C. to 4500 B.C., people lived in a primordial village and engaged in simple irrigation agriculture and goat herding, relying also on the hunting of gazelles and onagers. Later, it developed into a pottery-producing site and, reinforcing its function as a trading centre, it began to develop into a primordial city and strengthen its economic ties with adjacent villages (4500 B.C. to 3900 B.C.). By the last half of the fourth millennium B.C., it was surrounded by walls and had come to be topographically divided into different residential districts according to the social stratification between the upper ruling and middle administrative class and the specialised professional working class.

Zeder at first analysed the excavated animal bones consumed in each chronological layer. Especially for the periods after the fourth millennium B.C., she classified them into the Banesh stage (3300–2800 B.C.) and the

Table 7.1 Age distribution of consumed bones in primordial villages

Age class	Mohammad Jaffar (6000–5600 B.C.)	Ali Kosh (6750–6000 B.C.)	Bus Mordeh (7500–6750 B.C.)
A: 10 months	92	89	70
B: 16 months	73	75	76
C: 24 months	76	67	50
D: 28 months	69	59	45
E: 36 months	44	41	30
F: 42 months	36	43	34

Source: Zeder (1991: 148).
Note: Expressed in percentages of animals surviving beyond each age class (data from Hole, Flannery, et al., 1969: 289).

Kaftari stage (2400–1800 B.C.). Analysing the bones excavated in each district belonging to different social classes, she revealed very interesting facts related to each period.

At first in the Banesh stage, she distinguished the residential zones between the upper elite class (ABC) and the specialised craftsmen class (TUV), and after identifying the age of the animal bones across each district she pointed out the general tendency in terms of their slaughtering age (most of the animals consumed were sheep and goats, but in the earlier period goats were more prevalent).

There are several differences between the two districts. In the district of the upper class there were no examples of yearling consumption and the bone count of two to three year olds was distinctively high, while in the specialised craftsmen district many examples of yearlings were found, even though two to three year olds were consumed as well.

Zeder compares these facts with the pattern of animal consumption in the older primordial villages (Mohammad Jaffar 6000–5600 B.C., Ali Kosh 6000–5600 B.C. and Bus Mordeh 7500–6750 B.C., see Table 7.1). She points out that the difference in the consumption pattern between the primordial village stage and the Banesh stage is generally larger than that between the different classes in the urbanised Banesh stage. In the primordial village, except for the fact that the consumption of yearlings of ten months to one year old is rather high, no remarkable difference was found between two to three year olds and older animals. On the other hand, in the urbanised Banesh stage, animals older than one year, especially the two and three year olds, were abundantly consumed not only in the upper class district, but also in that of the lower class. Zeder interprets the meaning of this distinction between the primordial village stage and the Banesh stage as follows.

In any period, after the beginning of milking, shepherds must have equally adopted the following culling strategies: the females that every year delivered lambs and provided milk over the following months were to be kept alive as far as they maintained lambing potentiality and were later consumed after the delivery pause, while the males, except for breeding candidates, were to be culled early after reaching maturity as they would consume grass without increasing their meat-mass. This strategy must have been in general use as far as shepherds' management strategies are concerned.

In the samples from a primordial village in the seventh millennium B.C., the number of consumed bones of ten month to one year olds accounts for a relatively high percentage, while no distinct concentration of a special age group among the older individuals has been attested. This fact is a direct reflection of the above-mentioned shepherd's management strategy in the age pattern of consumption. In the primordial village stage, the relationship between consumers and meat providing shepherds must have been rather direct. People at the place of consumption must have passively received the meat of young culled males and the tough meat of females that had lost the capacity to deliver offspring and provide milk, following the shepherds' management strategy. Alternatively, the primordial village people may have kept their own herds and consumed them according to their general culling strategy as pastoralists.

Conversely, the residential sites in the Banesh stage were already urbanised. In the residential district of the upper class, consumption of yearlings was scanty and most of the remaining bones were of two to three year olds. There the consumption pattern in the primordial village that clearly reflects the shepherds' culling strategy can no longer be found. In this fact, Zeder reads a transition of the meat supply mechanism from the primordial village pattern to the primordial city pattern. In this new stage, the urban consumers no longer passively accepted the products brought about by the shepherds' management strategy, but must have begun to concentrate and consume meat according to their own selective preference for animals of a certain age. Of course in residential districts of the lower class living in peripheral areas of the city, many examples of yearlings were found, differing from those found in the upper class. Zeder supposes that in the district of the lower class the previous direct relationship with the surrounding shepherds was maintained or the dwellers themselves possibly continued to keep their own herds.

Moreover, Zeder pays attention to what parts of the body were mainly consumed in each district. She demonstrated that in the upper class district the bones of tender parts of the hind legs were dominant, whereas in the lower class district most of the bones excavated were of frontal legs that are full of tendons. This suggests that the animals brought into the city were divided into pieces and different parts were distributed according to social class.

Zeder applied the same analysis to the bone materials in the Kaftari stage (2400–1800 B.C.). In that period, the city had expanded and its urban territory of about 200 hectares was surrounded by walls. It is confirmed that the city had established strong economic relationships with seventy-three neighbouring towns and villages, which must have supplied food for the non-agricultural population in the city. This suggests that the economic relationship between the shepherds as meat suppliers and the urban consumers had become less direct.

Topographically, the city in this period can be divided into two groups of districts: those of various artisan groups including metal manufacturers (FX106) and those of the upper classes including the merchant group who had probably traded in finished goods (GHI). In the upper class districts, most of the consumed bones were from one year and four months to three year olds, which accounted for sixty percent of all bone samples. Particularly the bones from one year and four months to two years and four months covered fifty-three percent of the total. On the contrary, in the lower class districts the percentage of the bones of six to eight year olds, probably females, was rather high in contrast with that of the upper class districts, even if some bones from ten months to one year and four months were found as well.

As for the consumed parts of bones in the respective districts, Zeder found the same distributional tendency as that of the Banesh stage, which reflects the meat distribution principle of the city authority. At the same time, she pays attention to the fact that many individuals of six to eight years old were found in the lower class districts and wonders about the reason. In this regard, we know that the ewes that had ceased milk production and were no longer useful to the pastoralists must have been successively discharged into the meat circulation route, so most of the animals of six to eight years consumed in the lower class districts must have been these old ewes. We can find here a reflection of the pastoralist's culling strategies. Zeder supposes rather direct meat supply routes to the people of the lower class, even though it is not clear whether there was direct contact with the shepherds or not.

Moreover, from the analysis of cultivated plant fossils excavated in the agricultural fields of the Kaftari stage, we are informed that wheat was probably already cultivated in the irrigable fields of the adjacent areas and the barley used for feeding domestic animals was grown in the non-irrigable fields with rainfall agriculture. With the increasing urban population, not only the irrigated wheat fields were enlarged, but also the fields of barley for animals had largely expanded towards areas distant from the city. This suggests that animal breeding in the adjacent villages had developed to satisfy urban demands. In order to explain the reason why the reflection of the shepherd's culling strategies can be again attested in the lower class districts of the Kaftari stage, Zeder supposes that at that stage the meat supply routes from the adjacent villages where barley cultivation and animal breeding had developed were established in response to the demands from the more populated cities.

Of course, before Zeder's laborious work, many specialists who dedicated themselves to deciphering the excavated tablets had shown that in the Sumerian temple cities after the third millennium B.C., a great number of domestic animals kept and fattened by temple administrators were consumed as the temple's sacrificial victims and distributed as food to the city dwellers (Durand and Charpin, 1980: 131–156; Maekawa, 1983: 81–111). They called it the 'Drehem system'. Many herds owned by the temples had been entrusted to shepherds in order to produce wool for the temple's textile manufacturing. Moreover, even in the later period of the second millennium B.C., they showed that people of the upper classes had received the tender parts of meat from the temple, while those of the lower classes had been provided with the tougher parts with bone and tendons (MacEwan, 1983). In this sense, Zeder's work which shed light on the city authority's meat distribution system should not surprise us as a new discovery. However, she not only archaeologically reconfirmed the facts suggested by the specialists of cuneiform tablets by means of a detailed comparative analysis of the consumed bones between socially differentiated districts, but also verified that the meat distribution system in the city had already developed in earlier periods preceding the third millennium B.C.

Zeder's contributions can be summarised as follows. She comparatively analysed the bones consumed in different archaeological periods in which the development from villages to the primordial city had gradually occurred. She identified the period the transition from a feeding pattern in which the shepherd's culling strategies directly reflected the meat supply pattern to one in which the deliberate selective consumption of animals of two to three years old occurred.

Confronting the analytical results of the consumed bones excavated in the city districts of different social classes, she showed that different cuts of meat were distributed to different social classes: the more tender parts were for the upper class and the tougher ones for the lower class. Until then, this distributive system had been noted as a fact later than the third millennium B.C. and has been called the 'Drehem system'. She confirmed the same system was already initiated in the primordial city stage of the fourth millennium B.C.

Now, after learning that the city supply pattern had shifted into the stage that no longer reflected the shepherd's culling strategies, the following question emerges: even if the meat supply pattern of the city changed into indirect procurement, the pastoral groups in the fields must have maintained their own basic culling strategies. We cannot help but hypothesise that a certain change must have occurred in the relationship between city dwellers as consumers and shepherds as meat suppliers. We must therefore now ask what kind of change had actually occurred in the process of meat procurement and consumption.

To this question, there is no evidence from the materials of the excavated consumed bones that Zeder analysed. Even if it were possible to identify the age of the bones, it is not easy to judge their gender. The data on the culling age without gender identification cannot provide sufficient information in order to judge whether the shepherds' culling pattern was no longer reflected in the meat supply pattern. In such a situation, if there are written materials providing relevant information, it is better to rely on these leaving aside archaeological data.

We know that specialists on cuneiform tablets have published their analytical results on the procurement of meat animals and herd management in the ancient Oriental temple cities of Mesopotamia, which can be used to understand the relationship between the city and the shepherds.

I first introduce their work on materials concerning the management of the sheep/goat herds owned by the temple of the Sumerian city of Lagash in the third millennium B.C. From these materials we will be informed not only of what kind of sheep/goats were kept, fattened by temple administrators and consumed for temple festivities, but we will also learn that these animals had been brought into the temple cities as tributes from the shepherds' groups under the temple's political rule.

Secondly, we know that besides the temples' herds kept for fattening, the temples and the rich citizens owned large numbers of sheep/goats and entrusted them to hired shepherds for herding care in the fields. The available documents are the accounting tablets recorded on the occasion of contract renewal. Moreover, these entrusted men were not always shepherds who directly engaged in herding, but were sometimes middlemen who sub-contracted the herds to shepherds. In fact, these documents do not necessarily provide sufficient actual knowledge on the management strategies of the shepherds. However, from trivial facts deciphered in the accounting texts, we can obtain much information not only on the contractual relationships between the urban large herd owners and the entrusted shepherds, but also on the extent of the suspicion and fraud that occurred between them. The herd owners lived too far from the herding fields to witness the entrusted shepherds' actual management. The shepherds thus had space to fabricate facts during the contract period. In order to know about the real relationship between the urban large herd owners and the entrusted shepherds, we can refer to recently published materials from the Old and Neo-Babylonian periods.

I now present these relevant documents and their analyses, some of which I judge to be not always sufficient and correct, and I show the actual system of meat and wool procurement in the temple cities and the interesting relationship between the large urban herd owners and the entrusted shepherds.

Rams fattened in the city: Examples from a Sumerian city, Ur

In the Mesopotamia of the second half of the third millennium B.C., many Sumerian territorial city-states had developed such as Nippur in the north and Lagash in the south. In these archaeological city sites, a great number of tablets were found among which were quite a number of records on herd management in the city. A summary of this information is as follows.

1. There were records on grain supplied for the sheep/goat herds maintained and fattened under the temple's administrators in the city.
2. Among the herds owned by the temple, some were kept to obtain wool for the temple's textile manufacturing. They were entrusted to shepherds and were annually counted at contract renewals to check the number of animals in the respective age groups. From these accounting texts, we can learn how these herds were managed.
3. Royal families and rich citizens privately owned their herds and entrusted them to shepherds in order to increase their size. From the annual accounting texts of these herds, we can sometimes learn how the same herds were successively developed and how many of the newborns were secured by the owner as his possessions.

As for the first category of records, Durand and Charpin (1980) have analysed the texts dealing with grain supplied to fatten the herds in the city of Ur, third dynasty. They note that these herds were kept and fattened for the temple's sacrificial use and for supplying the citizens. However, they failed to shed sufficient light on the following question. According to which principles were these animals managed? Maekawa, not only newly analysing the materials used by Durand and Charpin but also adding other materials, has cast light on some interesting facts as I will illustrate below (Maekawa, 1983 and 1994).

The materials analysed by Maekawa were mainly records on the grain provided monthly for the sheep herds owned by the temple and kept in the so-called 'internally retained enclosure' next to the temple. He paid attention to the fact that these sheep were differently categorised according to the different amount of grain provided daily per head, which increases according to age. The total quantity of grain provided monthly to each age category is successively written: the total amount of grain provided to a category group in a certain month should be the fixed daily quantity provided to each head multiplied by thirty times the number of head in the corresponding group. So, if we divide the total amount of grain provided monthly to the group by thirty and by the daily quantity of grain provided per head, we can ascertain how many head were kept in the enclosure of each category in a certain month. It is self-evident that, as time passes, an individual from the younger group which was provided with smaller amounts of grain grows and must be transferred into the next age group and fed with a larger quantity of grain, so the number of head in the respective group changes month by month. Paying attention to the monthly decrease in the number in the younger group and the corresponding increase in the older group, Maekawa has reconstructed how these animals were managed.

The most interesting fact among his findings is as follows. Individuals in the category groups to which the largest and second largest amount of grain was provided and must have been more than twenty months old, were transferred to a different enclosure twice per year in the periods corresponding to the temple's annual festivals. A more interesting fact is that after such output from the original enclosure, a certain number of weaned sheep and goats were regularly added to these groups and most of the sheep and goats kept there for fattening were male.

For example, in the herd records kept in the internally retained enclosure, the total number of sheep/goats in a certain month was 3,032. Among them were ninety-two ewes, four female lambs and six female kids, while all the rest were male. In the same records, moreover, Maekawa found that the lambs born in this enclosure in that year were only twenty: they may have been born from some of the ninety-two ewes mentioned above. The number of delivery ewes is rather small if we compare it to the number of ewes. In fact, the ewes must have been kept for milk production. Considering the fact that only a small number of lambs had been born in the enclosure, Maekawa checked the total amount of grain provided to the juvenile group in the year: for this juvenile group an amount of grain far larger than the amount necessary for the twenty juveniles born there was annotated. This indicates that besides those who were born there, a large number of yearlings were brought into this enclosure. Moreover, incidentally, in this enclosure males greatly outnumber females. The sex composition in this herd is quite different from that usually found in a herd under a shepherd's management, in which males were culled early and females kept alive. Here a question arises: from where were these males procured? We cannot help but think that their origin was from outside of the enclosure.

From his findings, Maekawa judges that the animals administered under the temple were used for fattening in order to prepare well-grown sheep and goats of about twenty months for consumption at the temple's festivals. The internally retained enclosure was, so to speak, a temporary waiting room where young sheep and goats destined for the city were annually brought in from somewhere, were fattened by grain and culled in order to be consumed during the temple's festivals.

It is important to note that these sheep and goats destined to be consumed were already adult individuals of more than twenty months old. As mentioned above, Zeder pointed out that the city selectively consumed animals of two to three years old. The fact attested in the urban enclosure coincides with Zeder's results. On the other hand, from Zeder's analysis of the excavated bones, it was difficult to judge the gender composition of the consumed animals in the city. Maekawa's finding that most of the fattened animals in the urban enclosure were males is worth considering.

The materials used by Maekawa, however, are the records of the monthly amounts of grain provided to the herds retained in the urban enclosure. These records do not tell us the origin of these animals. Fortunately, the latest studies suggest that yearling males must have been periodically brought in as tributes by shepherds in the surrounding peripheral areas under the temple's power.

It is common knowledge that for shepherds who own their own herds, it is important to maintain and grow the herd size. They want to keep as many females as possible alive for delivery and milking, while except for a minimum number as breeding candidates, they prefer to cull or discharge males from the herd after maturation. Conversely, in the city that was the centre of meat consumption, except for the case of animals that they kept for themselves, there was no preference for the meat of males or females because the taste does not change significantly. For the needs of urban consumption, the temple authorities may have demanded from the subordinated shepherds only superfluous young males as tributes in order to not violate the shepherds' need to keep females for breeding. After keeping and fattening these males brought into the urban enclosures, they slaughtered them for consumption when they reached two to three years of age. The temple's demands for male animals as tributes can be understood as an expression of appropriate authoritative strategies in order to facilitate meat acquisition as tributes from shepherds. From the cuneiform tablets recording the monthly grain supply for the herds in the temple's enclosure, we can infer a very important aspect of the relationship between city authority and shepherd groups living at a distance. And, as I discuss below, the same concentration of juvenile males in the city as seen in Ur in the second half of the third millennium B.C. was maintained even in the later Babylonian periods.

As I pointed out above, the analyses of the tablet records in Ur in the third dynasty on grain supplied for the temple's enclosure suggests that shepherds' superfluous males were concentrated as tributes for the temple city. However, besides these tablet records, we have other accounting records that show 1) when the temple administrators renewed the annual contract for wool with the entrusted shepherds and 2) when the private large herd owners in the city renewed their contracts for herding care. Among them, several important accounting records of the temple's herds entrusted to shepherds have been recently published by several cuneiform researchers, even though they are records from the second millennium B.C. From these accounting texts, we come to know very interesting facts concerning the relationship between urban large herd owners and entrusted shepherds.

I now begin analysing the tablets excavated at Ur of the Old Babylonian period.

Wool herds entrusted to private shepherds: Old Babylonian

The documents to be first examined here are the two archives excavated at Ur, the largest city in Old Babylonia in the period at the beginning of the second millennium B.C., which Van de Mieroop once deciphered and analysed (1993: 161–182). One group of these archives, derived from illicit excavation, covers the period from 1845 B.C. to 1825 B.C. and deals with the herds of the Nanna-Ningal temple complex. The other archive found during Wooly's excavation in the house named No.1 Broad Street covers 1836 to 1811 B.C. In both cases, several common shepherd names can be found. So, these two archives must have belonged to the same temple complex. The tablets can be classified into two categories.

The first deals with the accounting of sheep and goats when the flock was brought to the temple's administrator by the entrusted private shepherds on the occasion of annual shearing. It concerns the number of shorn sheep/goats, the quantity of wool and the number of animals lost through accident or disease during the year.

The second category of data are the periodical accounting texts of the animals brought in as tributes and entrusted to the temple's shepherds. Between them there are some differences in contents, but they provide us with a clue as to how the temple's herd management was carried out.

Now, let's examine the accounting texts concerning the herds entrusted to external private shepherds recorded on the occasion of annual shearing.

From the date of the texts we learn that the accounting would be done in February–March after shearing. Administrators took notes on the numbers in each group classified according to gender and shearing history, noting if they were sheared for the first time or had already been sheared in previous years (kir11-aš-ur4 = first shearing female, sila4-aš-ur4 = first shearing male, u8 = mature ewe, udu-nita = mature ram). However, from other related texts we can learn that there are other categories including suckling female lamb (kir11-ga), suckling male lamb (sila4-ga), weaned female (kir11-gub) and weaned male (sila4-gub). These groups are clearly distinguished from the former categories counted on the occasion of shearing. With this regard, 'suckling lambs' are too young to be sheared, and so must not have been brought to the accounting place to be sheared. Instead, theoretically speaking, the 'weaned' may include not only the individuals weaned in that year, but also those weaned in the previous year coming to be shorn for the first time. However, as Van de Mieroop suggests, the denomination 'weaned' designates only the individuals just weaned in the current year. The lambing season in general covers the end of autumn and early winter, and weaning must be completed in two to three months after delivery. This means that there were individuals born in the previous autumn or winter and weaned just before the shearing season of February or March. These were too young to be sheared, as were the 'suckling lambs', and therefore must not have been brought to the shearing place. This may be the reason why the numbers in these juvenile groups were not recorded in the accounting text after shearing.

Presupposing the above, we may interpret that the 'first shearing' group in a current year is made up of the individuals counted as 'suckling lambs' and 'weaned' in the previous year. They must have already been thirteen to seventeen months old with fleece grown well enough to be sheared. On the other hand, the individuals categorised as 'mature ram/ewe' must be those that had already been shorn more than once in the previous years, namely all those more than three years old.

The accounting is related to each herd entrusted to each shepherd. The herd size ranges from one hundred to one thousand. In the case of a large herd of a thousand head, it must have been impossible to be managed by one shepherd alone. Among the denominations of entrusted people, we can find different grades of status, from 'shepherd' who directly took care of the flock to 'head of shepherds' who was probably the entrusted middleman of a higher level. The latter 'head of shepherds' to whom a large herd was entrusted must have sub-divided the herd into smaller units and sub-assigned them to shepherds of a lower level.

In the accounting records of a certain year, we can find that the number of persons entrusted for herding care reached ninety-one. Considering herd sizes, ranging from 100 to 1,000 head, we can presume that the temple owned great numbers of sheep/goats for wool production.

The next table (Table 7.2) is based on several years of accounting texts taken after shearing.

For convenience, a serial number is given to each entrusted herd cited here. There are seventy-six recurring cases in total, even though the years of accounting are different. From such a text in which only the respective numbers of each category group are written for a herd of a certain year, we are unable to follow how the herd size increased over the years. Nevertheless, comparing the proportional numbers of each group (mature males/females and first shearing males/females), we can see a general tendency towards herd composition and management strategy as follows.

In the chart, the 'first shearing' females and males are respectively written as ♀2 and ♂2. On the other hand, 'mature' ewes/rams are respectively shown as ♀E and ♂R. The number of the former 'first shearing' represents the number of individuals shorn for the first time that year, while the number of the 'mature' must be the total amount of individuals counted as 'mature' in the previous year plus those counted as 'first shearing' in the previous year. In fact, the individuals categorised as 'first shearing' in a year must have been transferred into the 'mature' category in the following year and this can be shown by the fact that the number of the latter 'mature rams/ewes' always largely outnumbers that of the former 'first shearing' males/females.

Another characteristic feature in the chart is that in most cases the mature rams (♂R) outnumber the mature ewes (♀E), as Van de Mieroop points out. But when we compare this proportional difference between sexes in the 'mature' category

Table 7.2 Age and sex composition of entrusted herds for wool production at annual shearing owned by the temple in the old Babylonian city of Ur

	Sheep					Goats				
Series no.	Adult ewe ♀E	First shearing female ♀2	Adult ram ♂R	First shearing male ♂2	Total	Adult doe ♀D	Weaned young doe ♀1	Adult buck ♂B	Weaned young buck ♂1	Total
1*	150	85?	200	65	500	–	–	–	–	–
2*	374	176	674	130 ⎫		–	–	7	– ⎫	
3*	30	24	40	16 ⎭	1,464	11	–	6	3 ⎭	27
4*	50	33	130	27	240	–	–	2	–	2
5*	250	115	650	105	1,120	–	–	4	–	4
6	75	27	65	20	187	4	–	3	–	7
7	346	138	334	118	936	–	–	5	–	5
8*	338	135	421	108	1,002	2	–	2	–	4
9*	178	86	318	80	662	3	–	5	–	8
10*	74	58	96	40	248	7	5	8	5	25
11	290?	84?	340	95	809	–	–	11	–	11
12	70	20	61	9	160	–	–	–	–	–
13	320?	187	308?	130	945	–	–	6	–	6
14	349	113	402	116	979	2	–	3	–	5
15*	200	90	345	61	696	2	–	2	–	4
16*	92	25	142	15	274	1	–	2	–	3
17*	233	90	253	47	623	6	2	5	2	15
18*	131	64	164	22	381	[8]	2	5	2	17
19*	350	162	586	124	1,222	4	–	4	–	8
20	45	24	30	18	117	–	–	1	–	1
21*	122	55	140	44	361	2	–	3	–	5
22*	130	80	220	63	[493]	2	–	4	–	6
23	[]	18	[]	[]	208	–	–	–	–	–
24*	66	36	[93]	10	205	–	–	–	–	–
25*	306	160	466	75	1,007	–	–	5	–	5
26	67	20	110	[21]	218	–	–	2	–	2
27*	70	23	84	20	197	–	–	2	–	2
28*	236	104	282	83	705	–	–	4	–	4
29*	140	61	147	52	400	–	–	2	–	2
30*	123	50	170	45	388	5	–	5	–	10
31*	88	20	148	14 ⎫	–	–	–	–	–	–
32	50	20	40	14 ⎭	394	–	–	–	–	–
33*	61	29	80	20	190	10	–	10	–	20
34*	34	13	36	10	93	10	–	4	–	14
35*	77	30	121	23	252	–	–	2	–	2
36*	28	26	80	15	149	–	–	2	–	2
37*	51	20	58	14	143	–	–	2	–	2
38*	56	20	80	16	172	–	–	2	–	2
39*	59	12	80	8	159	–	–	1	–	1

40*	58	30	78	22	188	–	–	3	–	3
41*	174	131	387	96	788	–	–	5	–	5
42*	30	21	51	19	121	–	–	2	–	2
43	101	40	100	31	272	–	–	4	–	4
44*	47	30	107	20	204	4	–	6	–	10
45*	47	20	48	11	126	–	–	2	–	2
46*	64	35	77	30	206	–	–	1	–	1
47*	41	16	87	15	159	–	–	1	–	1
48*	165	80	319	70	634	–	–	3	–	3
49*	123	44	132	40	339	–	–	2	–	2
50*	50	20	94	15	179	–	–	2	–	2
51*	92	40	139	37	308	–	–	2	–	2
52*	106	39	124	30	–	–	–	–	–	–
53*	58	18	61	12	448	–	–	2	–	2
54	89	55	193	55	392	–	–	[]	–	–
55*	447	188	618	132	1,385	–	–	–	–	–
56	30	12	52	12	106	–	–	–	–	–
57*	110	48	160	43	361	5	–	8	–	13
58*	40	16	49	15	120	–	–	–	–	–
59	124	42	122	[30]	318	–	–	5	–	5
60*	134	50	[170]	46	400	–	–	5	–	5
61*	32	14	58?	13	117	–	–	1	–	1
62*	313	112	335	111	871	–	–	5	–	5
63*	90	26	101	25	242	–	–	3	–	3
64	55	14	100	[15]	184	–	–	–	–	–
65	96	32	120?	[40]?	288	[]	–	17	–	[]?
66	[]	26	120?	[]	252	–	–	–	–	–
67	149	29	140	–	318	–	–	–	–	–
68	219	40	–	54	313	–	–	–	–	–
69	75	16	68	–	179	–	–	–	–	–
70	99	52	54	–	217	–	–	–	–	–
71	178	87	[]	[]	624	2	–	[1]	–	3
72	15	4	14	3	36	3	–	–	–	3
73*	100	58	160	36	406	4	–	2	–	6
74*	200	76	276	50	602	–	–	3	–	3
75*	49	23	112	13	–	8	–	7	–	–
76	20	15	10	5	247	10	–	8	–	33

Source: Constructed from Van de Mieroop (1993: 178–179).

Notes:

1. In each herd they counted the number of adults (more than three years old) and the number of first shearing individuals ♀ (two years old) according to sex.

2. Series numbers correspond to the order of herds listed in the chart by Van de Mieroop based on accounting texts (1993: 178–179).

3. Asterisks indicate cases in which a reversal of sex distribution occurred between the first shearing group and the adult group from ♂2 < ♀2 to ♂R > ♀E. In these cases the males were supplemented from outside.

($♂R > ♀E$) with that generally found between 'first shearing males' and 'first shearing females', we can find the following interesting fact disregarded by Van de Mieroop.

Now, let's look at the chart again and compare the number of first shearing males ($♂2$) and first shearing females ($♀2$) in each case of accounting. Except for the cases in which there is a lack of numbers due to tablets being damaged, in the seventy-three accounting texts we can compare the numbers and in sixty-five cases the females outnumber the males, while in only six cases the males are more numerous than the females. Summing up the total numbers from all the cases, the male numbers were only seventy-five percent of that of the females. Let's call this fact a general tendency: 'first shearing' males are fewer than 'first shearing' females ($♂2 < ♀2$). After pointing out this fact, let's compare this proportional difference with the abovementioned proportional difference between the sexes in the 'mature' groups. Surprisingly, the sex proportion is reversed in the transition from the 'first shearing' stage to the 'mature' stage ($♂2 < ♀2 \Rightarrow ♂R > ♀E$).

As to the reason why in most cases the number of 'first shearing' males are fewer than 'first shearing' females, we can make three suppositions. Firstly, the general custom of slaughtering yearling males for sacrificial offerings to the temple; secondly, their use for meat consumption; and thirdly, a contractual custom for the entrusted shepherds to receive more young male than female lambs as rewards.

While we have confirmed a general fact that in the first shearing stage males are fewer than females, we cannot forget that all those in the 'first shearing' category were to be transferred into the 'mature' category in the following year. If so, the proportion of sexes in the first shearing stage ($♂2 < ♀2$) ought to be the same in the 'mature' stage as well. Instead, after the transition it is reversed: 'mature' males outnumber 'mature' females ($♂R > ♀E$). In the chart I have put an asterisk in each case where the reversal can be found. In fifty-two of the sixty-five cases where 'first shearing' males are fewer than 'first shearing' females, males outnumber females in the 'mature' stage.

Females are necessarily important for herd reproduction and they should have been kept alive even after reaching maturity, and the same numerical proportion between males and females in the 'first shearing' stage ($♂ < ♀$) should have been found even in the 'mature' stage. Nevertheless, if the numerical proportion is unexpectedly reversed ($♂ > ♀$), we cannot help but think that not a small number of the adult males had been supplemented from somewhere during the transitional period from the first shearing stage (thirteen to seventeen months old) to the second shearing stage (more than three years old), even though the texts do not mention anything about it.

The herds owned by the temple were kept to obtain wool for the temple's textile industry. Now, the wool of males, especially after castration, is better than that of females, so we can suppose that by the temple's interest in wool for its textile industry the males were supplemented in order to get the best quality wool. To satisfy this need for textile use, there must have been some external supply routes, probably either directly from the herd managed by the entrusted shepherds or in the form of tributes from those subordinated to the temple.

With regard to this fact, we know that even at the present time in Iran and in the neighbouring areas there are large herd owners who obtain males put into circulation routes by shepherds and assign them to entrusted shepherds in order to sell them after fattening or to collect wool for urban textile manufacture (Beck, 1991: 104). We can define such herds as 'secondary herds' to distinguish them from those owned and managed by common shepherds. The above-mentioned Old Babylonian shearing texts provide us with evidence that in order to obtain wool for textile manufacturing, such a management system was already present in the temple economy in this period. We have learned that already in the Sumerian city-states of the third millennium B.C., young males kept by shepherds in the neighbouring areas were taken into the temple city-states as tributes and were consumed in the city after fattening. Now, we have learned that the males discharged by the shepherds were destined to be brought to the city also for wool production.

It is not only in the Sumerian and Old Babylonian world that a great number of males kept for wool production were collected for the temple's textile industry. As for the Micaenean period of Crete, Killen points out that males outnumber females in most of the herds kept for wool production in the temple (Killen, 1964: 1–15). Also, from the text of the Neo-Babylonian temple's contract for herds for wool production that I discuss later, we shall learn that the temple demanded the entrusted shepherds deliver the same number of newborn males as newborn females. By the shepherd's original management strategy mentioned above, most of the males were likely to be culled or discharged into the market. On the other hand, males were in demand for the textile industry of the city temple and supplied from outside to herds owned by the temple. The former wanted to discharge the males, while the latter wanted to gather them. Under such complementary economic interests, the males were likely to be further put into circulation in order to satisfy both of their different needs.

Incidentally, I have pointed out that in the above-cited accounting texts there is no mention of male/female 'suckling lambs' or male/female 'weaned' sheep, aside from 'first shearing' and 'mature' ones. I have suggested that these categories too young to be shorn might not have been brought in for the annual accounting check on the occasion of shearing. As far as they were not brought to the place of contract renewal, the owner could not have any information on how many lambs were born. Does this mean that the temple owner had no interest in confirming how many lambs had been born or how many lambs had died by accident each year? Perhaps not. Actually, as I will mention below, there are scores of tablets in which the number of skins of the dead is accounted for. The owner was keen to know how many animals in his entrusted herd had died in each contractual period and to check the shepherd's quality of herding care. Even though the temple's administrator could not have any means of checking the number of newborns in the current year because of the absence of yearlings on the occasion of accounting, they could get to know at least the number of 'first shearing' males and females born in the previous year that would have grown into two year olds. If their total number was too small in comparison to the number of 'mature' breeding ewes, the temple's administrator could demand compensation for the shepherd's insufficient care in the previous year.

Moreover, from the tags attached to the basket where the tablets were kept, we learn that three kinds of accounting checks were carried out annually.

1. The number of individuals respectively kept for a wool-producing career: 'mature' and 'first shearing' males/females.
2. The number of individuals consumed in the form of offerings to the temples on the occasion of the harvest feast.
3. The number of animal skins brought in by the entrusted shepherds as evidence of accidental deaths.

Regarding the last issue, of course, it was not possible for the administrator of the temple to confirm if all the skins handed in were necessarily those from their entrusted herds. The administrator of the temple's herds lived far from the herding fields, thus could not witness what happened on the pastureland. There always remained room for the entrusted shepherd to manipulate the actual facts: the shepherds could deceptively mix the skins of the consumed and/or diseased sheep of their own. What the owner could do at a maximum must have been only to impose the obligation of bringing as many skins of the animals as prescribed by contract as the maximum loss allowance in order to prevent excessive loss in the entrusted herd.

Even if in the temple's accounting records on shearing occasions there is no written contractual prescription regarding the maximum allowance for loss, we can learn from the texts of other temples that the shepherd had to assure eighty live lambs per 100 breeding ewes. Yearlings were prone to becoming ill and the death rate could be rather high. The loss allowance of twenty percent is quite normal. So we may suppose that more or less the same proportion might have been fixed in the contracts concerned here. If we remember that the temple could check the number of two year old 'first shearing' males and females, then by comparing this number to that of 'mature' ewes, the owners must have been able to more or less understand if the shepherds had taken good care of their herd or not. In addition, with the obligation of bringing in the skins of the dead animals, they could prevent the excessive decrease of their entrusted herd caused either by the shepherd's insufficient care or fraudulent manipulation.

To sum up, from the accounting records of the Old Babylonian temple at Ur in 1800 B.C. we can learn the following facts:

1. The temple entrusted its own herds of various sizes to private shepherds. Among the entrusted herds many were too large to be managed by only one shepherd. In such cases, the entrusted persons must have been middlemen who divided the herd into smaller units and sub-assigned them to several shepherds. There must have been a kind of multilayered contractual relationship between the entrustors and the entrustees.

2. The sex proportion: in the 'mature' group this is reversed ($♂R > ♀E$) in comparison to the 'first shearing' group ($♂2 < ♀2$). If the 'mature' group was composed only of grown 'first shearing' individuals born in the original flock, the sex proportion seen in the 'first sharing' group should have been maintained in the 'mature' group. This reversal of sex proportion suggests that at this stage many adult males were supplemented from outside. These supplied males might have been provided by shepherds who discharged superfluous males according to their management strategies.

3. The place where the entrusted shepherds took care of the herds and delivery occurred were fields far from the city temple. The temple was therefore not able to directly witness the actual herding care of shepherds or check the number of newborns during the year. There must always have been the potential for shepherds to manipulate the figures. Moreover, in relation to point (1), I would like to underline the presence of intermediaries between the temple and the entrusted shepherds who sub-assigned the herds to the shepherds. This suggests a further distance between owner and shepherds. The owners

could not help but satisfy their interest only with post facto data obtained by counting the number of grown first shearing males/females, and in order to compensate the shortage of information they could only impose the duty of bringing in and displaying the skins of the dead animals. However, this measure still leaves room for the shepherds to manipulate and deceive.

Herd owner/entrusted shepherd relationship: Neo-Babylonian

We can consult the extant texts of contracts between urban large herd owners and entrusted shepherds in the Neo-Babylonian period. Van Driel analysed some of these texts and found out very interesting facts (Van Driel, 1993: 219–258). His analysis, however, seems to need a closer examination to decipher revised new facts. I would like to do this by reading the materials in detail.

Van Driel analysed the tablet texts of temples Erbach of Sippar and Eanna of Uruk. From these materials we learn of the kinds of interests the temple's administrators had and the form of economic relationship they kept with the shepherds. The texts contain not only the accounting records on the herds owned by the temples, but also those privately owned by a wealthy city dweller. There are different ways of management according to temple or private ownership. Interestingly, the last tablet of the private owner is a compilation of successive annual accounting records of the same herd entrusted to the same shepherd from which we learn the process of increasing a herd through the years. Of course there are differences between the Sippar texts and the Uruk texts in their contents, which cannot be disregarded. However, from the common features found in both, we can get a general idea of the herd management in a city of this period.

General facts

Among the materials analysed by Van Driel, there is a group of accounting texts on the temple's herds entrusted to private shepherds. They document contract renewal after the annual shearing: the number of individuals according to sex and age of sheep and goats are respectively annotated. From several comments regarding the entrusted person's name, we can understand that there were intermediaries who sub-assigned a large herd to several shepherds under their own responsibility. This means that there were multilayered relationships between entrustor and entrustee (Van Driel, 1993: 221). Some animals of the herd were sometimes transferred into a group destined for offering to the temple and to be consumed by the temple workers. Van Driel calls this group 'internal' herds in order to distinguish it from the external herds entrusted to external herdsmen (Van Driel, 1993: 222–224).

Regarding the contract for external herds with the middlemen, even if there are some differences between the Sippar and Uruk texts, the contents are similar in principle, as I will show below (Van Driel, 1993: 222–223).

1. Per annum, per 100 breeding ewes, sixty-six, i.e. two-thirds of lambs belonging to the owner were to be secured as his share.
2. Per annum, per 100 breeding goats, sixty-six, i.e. two-thirds of young goats belonging to the owner were to be secured as his share.
3. Without distinction between males and females, per ram and ewe one half *mina* (unit of weight) of wool was due to the owner.
4. Without distinction between males and females, per goat five-sixths *mina* of goats hair were due to the owner.
5. Without distinction between sheep and goats or males and females, ten head lost through death per 100 animals was allowed, provided that for each lost animal its skin and two half shekel of tendon were to be handed over to the owner.

(1) and (2) establish that newborn individuals that correspond to two-thirds of the breeding ewes are to be secured for the owner independently from any actual variation in the annual birth rate. The ten percent allowance for death by accident or disease seems rather high, but newborns are likely to be ill and older rams and ewes may also die one after the other. Taking into account these losses, the ten percent allowance is not very high. In the text the shepherd's possible fraud is mentioned. The obligation for the shepherds to deliver the skins of the dead animals might be derived from the owner's interest in preventing the shepherd's fraudulent reports on the actual death rate rather than from the owners' economic interest in the skins. In any case, from these prescriptions we can learn that the owners' side secured a fixed proportional number of newborns as their gain independently from the real birth rate that might have been low or high in the year in question.

Most of the people entrusted for herding care documented in the texts were not the actual shepherds who directly engaged in herding, but entrepreneurs as middlemen. These intermediaries must have sub-assigned the herds subdivided among shepherds, but must also have taken the role of collecting the wool and skins to be delivered to the owner. Especially in the texts of Sippar, we can read that the renewal of the contract after shearing was done at a certain centre far from the city where the temple's administrator responsible for tax collection resided.

Van Driel supposes that the delivery of wool and the accounting inspection took place at this centre, and also that the documentation on tablets for the renewal of contracts was carried out in the presence of both the temple's administrator and the entrepreneur in spring when the shepherds would begin their seasonal migration to the south for herding (Van Driel, 1993: 225–226). Van Driel points out another interesting fact: some of the entrepreneurs received herding fields in trust from the temple that also contained arable land. In one text, an entrepreneur who owned 2,000 head of sheep and 500 head of goats promised to deliver a certain amount of grain and a certain number of unblemished animals to the temple. Therefore, he was proprietor of a large herd and must have entrusted the herding care to several shepherds. This text shows that middlemen could not only earn intermediary profits as a private entrepreneur, but also by allotting the rented herding fields to shepherds they could subordinate the shepherds under their economic and political power.

Historically such a phenomenon was not rare. We know that a century ago in the Abruzzi region in Central Italy, the entrepreneurs who obtained monopolised rights on herding fields from large landowners in the lowlands allotted the fields to shepherds. Even nowadays among the Qashqa'i of Iran (Beck, 1991: 87) and the Kashmir Bakharwal in India (Tani, 1989b: 83–85), the powerful clan heads who monopolise herding rights from local powers allot the herding fields to subordinate shepherds. The conditions of these allotted herding fields vary depending on the location. I observed once in Kashmir that one of the clan heads allotted good land to his relatives or collaborative shepherds and less productive land was given to shepherds who were poor or relatively distant from him (Tani, 1989b: 83–84). These subordinated shepherds not only paid for the usufruct of the allotted herding field, but were also obliged to engage in the work of shearing the chief's herds and to carry out other work at his request. Among the poor shepherds there were some who could not help but work as hired shepherds, even though they belonged to the same clan group. The hierarchical differentiation is likely to progress upon acquisition of monopolised herding rights from local powers. Disputes over the usufruct right to herding fields between different clans arise after local power transitions under politically unstable situations.

The entrusted external herds were taken back to the herding field by entrusted shepherds after the renewal of contracts on the occasion of annual shearing. From these contract texts we can learn not only the general relationships between the owner and the entrusted shepherds, but also how many newborn lambs had been actually delivered to the owner in proportion to the number

Table 7.3 Composition of herds owned by Prince Arsham

	Case number								
	1	2	3	4	5	6	7	8	9
Adult rams ♂ R	85	9	[34]	13	21	39	22	25	106
Two year old males ♂ 2	36	27	36	27	23	36	36?	22	72
Newborn males ♂ 1	58	37	64?	40	42	?	63	34	152
Adult ewes ♀ E	229	144	247	152	166	200	255	144	603
Newborn females ♀ 1	58	38	64	40?	41	41	63	34	163?
Total	466	255	445	272	293	?	439	259	1,096

Source: Van Driel (1993: 253).

Notes: newborn males (♂ 1) = newborn females (♀ 1); adult ewes (♀ E) x 1/2 = newborn males (♂ 1) + females (♀ 1).

of breeding ewes. Moreover, where the annually successive accounting records are included in the texts, we can see what kinds of animals were culled and/or removed from the herd. From this information we have a clue as to the owner's management strategies.

Share secured by the owner (case 1): Herds of Prince Arsham

Van Driel shows nine accounting records concerning the herds owned by Prince Arsham. As seen in Table 7.3, these records carry the numbers of yearlings and adults according to their sex. Especially for rams, they carry respectively the number of two year olds and older animals.

From these records, the first fact to note is that the number of males begins to diminish when they reach two years old. Taking a general view of the texts, even though the number of breeding ewes in respective years varies, we observe that the number of two year old males (♂2) generally decreased to sixty percent or less compared to that of male yearlings (♂1). In half of the cases, the number of adult rams (♂R) is smaller than that of the two year old males (♂2). The general decreasing tendency suggests that the young males were probably delivered to the entrusted shepherds as their share and/or culled after fattening. On the other hand, the average number of ewes is about twice that of male and female yearlings in all cases. We can conclude that females must have been kept alive without culling. From these texts we are unable to learn the destination of the missing males. The fact that the adult ewes outnumbered the adult rams

(♀E > ♂R) shows a striking contrast to the above discussed Old Babylonian herds where the rams outnumbered the ewes because of males supplemented from outside (♂R > ♀E). In the case of the Old Babylonian herds mentioned above, the temple side supplemented more males in order to get more good wool for their textile manufacturing. On the contrary, in this case the younger males were discharged from herds they were born into. In this contrast, we can see two opposite destinations for males. However, in both cases we can confirm the same general tendency: males flow in the outer circulation routes leaving their original herds, while females remain in the herds where they were born.

Another fact worth noting is that in most cases the number of male yearlings is the same as that of female yearlings. Does this only show the biological fact that the birth sex rate is almost the same? It is better to presume that the owner secured the same proportional number of individuals from newborn males as from newborn females. I cannot be sure if Van Driel was aware of the following fact that the total of male and female yearlings to be delivered to the owner corresponds approximately to half the number of adult ewes (♂1 + ♀1 = half of ♀E). The rate of half of the breeding ewes is found not only in this case, but also in the contract text of the privately owned herd I will discuss below. Even though this rate (half of the number of adult ewes) differs from that seen in the contract prescription mentioned above (two-thirds of the breeding ewes), it is not exceptional as it is seen in other cases too (Snell, 1986: 138–135). To sum up: the newborns secured by the owner were as many as half the number of breeding ewes and the proportion of newborn males and females to be secured was equal (♂1 = 1/4♀E. ♀1 = 1/4♀E).

Now, let's again compare the number of two year old males with that of male yearlings. The number of two year old males, as noted above, is much smaller than that of male yearlings (smaller than sixty percent). Even if the number of adult breeding ewes varies each year, the remarkably small number of two year old males compared to that of male yearlings seems unnatural. We cannot help but think that a certain percentage of male yearlings were discharged or culled after maturation. In this regard, Van Driel, examining other texts, points out that male yearlings must have been transferred into an 'internally retained herd' for fattening and been used as offerings to the temple or for the temple's subordinate's consumption. He points out that on the occasion of this transfer, the animal changes its denomination. He supposes that this denomination change occurred because of their status change into animals for fattening and probably for castration (Van Driel, 1993: 238).

Moreover, regarding these males transferred into an internally retained herd, we have several interesting records in the excavated texts at the temple of Anna of Uruk, in the Neo-Babylonian period. In these texts these males were killed to be offered to the temple and their meat was distributed to subordinate temple officials. MacEwan, after analysing these texts, points out the following facts: these animals were at first administered by a responsible person (*satammu*) and were destined to be successively offered to the temple and to be consumed (MacEwan, 1983). Which parts of and to whom the slaughtered animals were distributed are clearly stated in the texts. Among the people to whom the meat was distributed, we find not only royal family members and temple priests, but also administrators responsible for the internal herds and other professional people subordinated to the temple. The list begins from the soft parts of the meats (shoulder and rump) and successively downgrades to the less valuable parts. The more valuable parts were to be assigned to the people of higher status (royal family and priests), while the less valuable parts, head, neck, legs and intestines, were distributed in the order of clerical scribe, administration chief of the internal herds, orators, singers, bread-makers, special shepherds, rowers, cooks and eventually animal slaughterers. I have already mentioned that by comparing the consumed bones of animals found in different residential districts, Zeder has demonstrated that in a primordial urban centre in 4000 B.C. the valuable parts of the meat were consumed by people of higher status and the less valuable parts were consumed by those of lower status. The meat distribution system which had already been confirmed in the early stage of urbanisation is observed in this Neo-Babylonian period as well. In conclusion, the male yearlings in the externally entrusted herd that were secured by the temple owner were removed from their original group after maturation and, together with the juvenile males collected as tributes under temple power, were consumed after being fattened in the internally retained herd.

Share secured by the owner (case 2): Herds of a private owner

Another text Van Driel analysed is one in which the annual accounting records of a privately owned herd were successively compiled for several years. From it we can learn of a high incremental rate of herd size. For example, at the beginning of the year of recording, the herd size was 134 head. After eleven years it had grown to 888 head. Through his analysis, Van Driel clarified several facts regarding the owner's management strategy and the relationship between the owner and the entrusted shepherd, but his analysis leaves space for further observation. From this text, we learn that the owner secured fewer male yearlings than females, while in the herds owned by Prince Arsham the same number of male and female yearlings were secured by the owner and consumed during the temple's festivals. Moreover, we may find that the entrusted shepherd reserved the possibility of manipulating the actual facts to gain a larger share of animals for himself.

I now show the number of sheep documented in the accounting records, omitting the number of goats and the quantity of wool delivered for simplification (see Table 7.4).

In Table 7.4 the following items are successively shown along the horizontal line: 1) the year of accounting, 2) the rams (♂R), 3) the ewes (♀E), 4) the newborn males (♂l), 5) the newborn females (♀l), and 6) the total number of individuals in the herd.

Vertically in the frame of the respective year, several items are repeatedly written: a) the first line is the total number of the owner's share counted at the contract renewal, b) the second line is the number of animals lost by accident or disease, c) the third line is the number of animals given to the shepherd as a premium and d) the fourth line is the number of animals eventually diminished after the contract.

For our better understanding, let us examine one of these cases. In the third year, Nbk II 38 (B.C. 567), there are: 2-a) thirty rams in the herd as the owner's share (♂R); 3-a) 119 ewes (♀E); 2-b) three lost rams; 3-b) twelve lost ewes; 2-c) one ram given to the shepherd as a premium; and 3-c) three ewes given to the shepherd as a premium.

Looking vertically down at items 6-a where the total number of the owner's share in the last year is written (888 head), we can learn how the herd size increased over the course of ten years. In the year Nbk II 43 (B.C. 561), 101 head were supplemented. Taking aside this external supplementation in this year, the total number of the herd increases rapidly each year. This annual increase is the result of the annual entry of the previous year's newborns into the adult group. These lambs can be regarded as the owner's gain according to his proportional share of the newborns provided by the breeding ewes, i.e. the original capital. After a continuous entry of newborns over ten years, the herd size increased from the initial number of 134 to the final count of 888; i.e. more than six times the original size. As a capitalistic enterprise, we can say that this profit rate is conspicuously high.

Looking in detail at the table, we can find several general facts as follows.

At first, we can confirm that the number of rams (♂R) or ewes (♀E) in the respective year exactly corresponds to A + B − C.

A: the number of rams (♂R) or ewes (♀E) in the previous year (y-1), that is the amount of capital carried forward to the next accounting year.

B: the number of newborn males (♂1) or newborn females (♀1) in the previous year (y-1), i.e. income.

C: the total number of individuals lost by death and/or disease (b) + the individuals given to the shepherd as a premium (c) + the individuals diminished after the contract in the previous year (y-1) (d), i.e. expenses.

In any year, we can find the exact consistency without errors according to this way of accounting as if we were looking at an annual balance sheet of the present day.

The number of adults lost in each year corresponds to one-tenth of the total number of rams and ewes (♂R + ♀E), omitting the decimal points. The number of lost newborn females (lost ♀1) also corresponds to one-tenth of the number of newborns secured by the owner (♀1), omitting the decimal points. This proportional allowance of loss coincides with prescription 5) in the contract of Uruk cited above (page 135): 'without distinction between sheep and goats or between males and females, ten losses by death per 100 animals are allowed'. However, as for newborn males, the number of lost head and the premium always remained zero. In this zero fact, Van Driel reads the owner's inclination to secure more males for himself (Van Driel, 1992: 235), but I have a different interpretation that I will explain later.

As for the proportional share of newborn lambs to be taken by the owner, the contract of Uruk prescribed that 'per annum per 100 breeding ewes, sixty-six and two-thirds of lambs belong to the owner', without any reference to the proportion between males and females. The lambs assigned to the owner should be two-thirds of the total number of breeding ewes. Van Driel says that in this text, too, the same proportional share of two-thirds is secured by the owner. However, leaving aside how he read the chart, we must presume that the total number of male and female lambs taken by the owner does not correspond to two-thirds of the breeding ewes, but reaches only half of them in every accounting year.

How was it possible for Van Driel to reach such a different conclusion? He seems to have compared only the number of female lambs secured by the owner with that of breeding ewes. The number of female lambs secured by the owner is in fact one-third of the number of breeding ewes. Doubling the number of female lambs, he must have arrived at the conclusion that the owner's share of the male and female lambs is two-thirds of the breeding ewes. He writes as follows:

> Only about two out of three ewes would have had a lamb per annum. Whether this indicates real productivity or a withdrawal of female lambs from the herd remains undecided, but it possibly reflects the contract between owner and herdsman. Optimistically we might reason that this two out of three represents the sixty-six

Table 7.4 Compiled tablet of the successive annual accounting of the entrusted herd of a private herd owner, Naab Aha Heshurrim, from 569 B.C. to 559 B.C.

		1. Year	2. Adult male ♂R	3. Adult female ♀E	4. Newborn male ♂1	5. Newborn female ♀1	6. Total
		Nbk II 36 (B.C. 569)					
a.	Mother group		7	90	12	25	134
b.	Loss		1	9	0	2	12
c.	Premium		0	3	0	1	4
		Nbk II 37 (B.C. 568)					
a.	Owner's share		18	101	16	36	171
b.	Loss		2	10	0	3	15
c.	Premium		0	3	0	2	5
d.	Diminution after contract renewal		—	—	2	—	—
		Nbk II 38 (B.C. 567)					
a.	Owner's share		30	119	18	40	207
b.	Loss		3	12	0	4	19
c.	Premium		1	3	0	2	6
d.	Diminution after contract renewal		—	—	2	—	—
		Nbk II 39 (B.C. 566)					
a.	Owner's share		40	138	23	45	246
b.	Loss		3	14	0	4	21
c.	Premium		1	4	0	3	8
d.	Diminution after contract renewal		—	—	2	—	—
		Nbk II 40 (B.C. 565)					
a.	Owner's share		54	158	27	53	292
b.	Loss		5	16	0	5	26
c.	Premium		2	5	0	3	10
d.	Diminution after contract renewal		—	—	6	—	—
		Nbk II 41 (B.C. 564)					
a.	Owner's share		68	182	31	60	341
b.	Loss		7	18	0	6	31
c.	Premium		2	5	0	3	10
d.	Diminution after contract renewal		—	—	1	1	—

Relationship Between Temple Cities and Pastoral Groups in the Ancient Near East 143

		Nbk II 42 (B.C. 563)					
a.	Owner's share		89	209	40	65	403
b.	Loss		8	21	0	6	35
c.	Premium		3	6	0	4	13
d.	Diminution after contract renewal		—	—	7	—	—
		Nbk II 43 (B.C. 562)					
a.	Owner's share		111	237	41	80	469
b.	Loss		10	23	0	8	41
c.	Premium		4	7	0	4	15
d.	Diminution after contract renewal		—	—	7	—	—
		AW, M1 (B.C. 561)					
a.	Owner's share		131	275	48	90	544
e.	Supplement from outside		5	68	8	20	101
d.	Diminution after contract renewal		—	—	5	—	—
a.	Mother group		136	343	56	110	640
b.	Loss		13	34	0	11	58
c.	Premium		4	11	0	7	22
		AW, M2 (B.C. 560)					
a.	Owner's share		170	390	66	133	759
b.	Loss		16	39	0	13	68
c.	Premium		6	11	0	7	24
d.	Diminution after contract renewal		—	—	5	—	—
		AW, M3 (B.C. 559)					
a.	Owner's share		209	453	80	146	888
e.	Diminution after contract renewal		—	—	11	—	—

Source: Compiled from Van Driel (1993: 258).

percent due to the owner according to the contracts, the other one third being the herdman's share. (Van Driel, 1993: 235)

As mentioned above, in the contracts of the temples of Sippar and Uruk in the Neo-Babylonian period the prescription 'per annum, per 100 breeding ewes, sixty-six, i.e. two-thirds of lambs belong to the owner to be secured as his share' was written without specification of the respective sex proportion. In his interpretation of the private owner's accounting text, was Van Driel inclined to read it so that it coincided with the common rate found in the contract texts of temples Erbach of Sippar and Eanna of Uruk? If we want to know not the total number of lambs secured by the owner, but the minimum number of lambs actually born indifferently from sex distinction, we can get it by doubling the number of female newborns secured which is always larger than male newborns, because the birth rate must be mostly the same based on sex. However, what is interesting is the proportional rate of lambs secured by the owner compared to the number of breeding ewes. If the proportional rate to be secured by the owner is different depending on sex, the total number of lambs secured by the owner cannot be obtained by doubling the number of the female lambs secured. In fact, the number of female lambs secured corresponds to one-third of the breeding ewes, while the number of male lambs secured is always less than that of female lambs. And, as seen in Table 7.5, the number of male lambs secured by the owner regularly corresponds to half of the female lambs secured.

Now, let's confirm that the number of female lambs secured by the owner corresponds to one-third of the breeding ewes ($♀1 = 1/3♀E$), as Van Driel correctly pointed out, and the number of male lambs secured corresponds to half of the female lambs secured ($♂1 = $ half$♀1$). This means that the male lambs secured is one-sixth of the breeding ewes ($♂1 = 1/3♀E \times $ half $= 1/6♀E$). After finding this general regularity in the text, let's add the number of male lambs secured and the number of female lambs secured, which must be the total number of lambs secured by the owner indifferently from sex distinction—it becomes half of the number of breeding ewes ($1/3♀E + 1/6♀E = 3/6♀E = $ half$♀E$). Even though there is a plus or minus discrepancy from the number of half of the breeding ewes, the actual numbers in the text correspond to this principle.

With regard to this fact, we are reminded that also in the Arsham texts (page 138) the number of newborns to be secured by the owner was half that of breeding ewes. In this sense, the principle of half of the breeding ewes found here is not exceptional, even though there is a difference between them: in the Arsham texts the proportion between male lambs and female lambs to be secured was one-to-one, while in the current private text the male lambs correspond to half the female lambs: one-to-two. This difference may depend on different management motivations: the Arsham herd was managed by the temple where the males had to be guaranteed for sacrificial offering, while in the current privately owned

Table 7.5 *Number of breeding ewes, newborn females and newborn males secured by the owner*

	\multicolumn{11}{c}{Year}
	1	2	3	4	5	6	7	8	9	10	11
Breeding ewes ♀E	90	101	119	138	158	182	209	237	275	390	453
Newborn females ♀1	<u>25</u>	36	40	45	53	60	<u>65</u>	80	90	133	<u>146</u>
Newborn males ♂1	12	16	18	23	27	31	<u>40</u>	41	48	66	<u>80</u>
Total newborns ♀1 + ♂1	<u>37</u>	52	58	68	80	91	105	121	138	199	226

Note. See that in most cases the number of newborn males is half that of newborn females, and the number of newborn females is one-third of the breeding ewes aside from the cases underlined in which this principle is not observed.

herd there was no such need to reserve males for ritual use. The private herd owner must have been inclined to increase his herd size by keeping the more productive females. Especially at the first stage of management, having only a small number of ewes (ninety), the effort to get more breeding ewes must have been considerable.

After my revised analysis, I can assume that Van Driel, placing too much attention on the proportional rate between breeding ewes and female lambs secured by the owner (♀1 = 1/3 ♀E), did not take into consideration the actual number of male lambs delivered to the owner—that is half of the female lambs secured (♂1 = half♀1 = half × 1/3♀E)—and could not decipher that the total number of male and female lambs secured by the owner was half that of the breeding ewes (♀1 + ♂1 = 1/3♀E + 1/6♀E = half♀E).

Now, based on the revised results, let's think about their implications. First, the total number of male and female lambs in a year (♂1 + ♀1) ought to be always smaller than that of adult breeding ewes (♀E), because the birth rate cannot always be 100 percent. The owner who was far from the herding fields could not know the actual birth rate. He could not help but mechanically prescribe his proportional share of the newborns as half of the number of adult ewes. I will define this mechanical prescription as 'the principle of the owner's right to secure as many newborns as half of the number of adult ewes'. This principle to mechanically fix the owner's proportional share without taking into consideration the actual number of newborn lambs was also observable in the temple contract. However, in the case of the temple's herd, the share was two-thirds of the breeding ewes, while in the case of a private herd the rate was half. At first glance, this latter rate looks quite low and the owner seems to have left half of the newborns to the entrusted shepherd as his share. However, the birth rate must have always been much smaller than 100 percent. If the birth rate was eighty percent of the hundred adult ewes and male and female lambs were born in equal proportion (forty-to-forty), the owner could secure 33.3 female lambs and 16.6 male lambs, while the entrusted shepherd could receive 6.7 female lambs and 23.4 male lambs as the remainder. The owner could regularly secure more newborns than the entrusted shepherd.

Second, the proportion of female lambs and male lambs to be guaranteed to the owner is two-to-one. I will define it as 'the owner's right to more female than male lambs', which is different from the case of the Arsham herd where the same number of male and female lambs were guaranteed to the temple.

There is a corollary to this principle: the entrusted shepherd always gets more male than female lambs. I will define it as 'a de facto procedure in getting more male than female lambs for the entrusted shepherd'.

According to principles (1) and (2), I attempt to mechanically calculate respectively how many male and female lambs were secured by the owner, on the basis of two cases: the starting year when the herd size was small, about 100 head, and the final year when the size had grown to about 700 head. The number of male and female lambs left to the shepherd varies according to the actual birth rate, while the owner's share remains invariable, because independently from the actual birth rate he can demand a fixed number of male and female lambs automatically calculated on the basis of the number of breeding ewes and the share rate prescribed to each sex. From Table 7.6 we can see the numbers of male and female lambs respectively kept by the owner and the shepherd, supposing three different birth rates: three-fifths, two-thirds and four-fifths of breeding ewes.

In the case of a herd size of 100 head and a birth rate of three-fifths, the owner could demand 16.7 males and 33.3 females, while the shepherd would get 13.3 males and –3.3 females.

In the case of a birth rate of two-thirds, the owner secures 16.7 males and 33.3 females, while the shepherd would get 16.5 males and zero females.

In the case of a birth rate of four-fifths, the owner could invariably get the same number of males (16.5) and females (33.3), but the shepherd would secure 23.3 males and seven females.

Unless the birth rate was more than two-thirds, no female lambs would remain with the shepherd, and even worse, if the birth rate was lower than two-thirds, the share of the shepherd became negative as seen in case of a birth rate of three-

Table 7.6 Experimental supposition of the owner's share and the entrusted shepherd's share of the newborn female and male lambs according to the variable birth rate (3/5, 2/3 and 4/5 of the breeding ewes) in the early stage (breeding ewes = 100) and the last stage (breeding ewes = 390)

	Owner's lambs		Shepherd's lambs	
	Male	Female	Male	Female
Breeding ewes: 100				
Birth rate				
3/5 (lamb nos.: m.30, f.30)	16.7	33.3	13.3	−3.3
2/3 (lamb nos.: m.33.3, f.33.3)	16.7	33.3	16.5	0
4/5 (lamb nos.: m.40, f.40)	16.7	33.3	23.3	7
Breeding ewes: 390				
Birth rate				
3/5 (lamb nos.: m.117, f.117)	65	130	52	−13
3/5 (lamb nos.: m.130, f.130)	65	130	65	0
3/5 (lamb nos.: m.156, f.156)	65	130	91	26

Note. m = male, f = female.

fifths (−3.3). Even in such a case, must the shepherd invariably deliver to the owner as many female lambs as one-third of the breeding ewes (33.3), i.e. more than the actual newborn females (thirty)? If this is true, it probably occurred, but we have no evidence for cases where the shepherd supplemented the shortage from his own female lambs.

To conclude: the owner could secure a great number of female lambs as his share despite the actual birth rate, while the shepherd would get fewer female lambs. As for male lambs, the shepherd could obtain many male lambs from the outset. In fact, his share of male lambs became larger than the owner's, provided that the birth rate was higher than two-thirds, and when the number of breeding ewes reached 390 ten years later, the shepherd could get an even greater number of male lambs. In the case of a birth rate of two-thirds this figure was sixty-five male lambs and with a birth rate of four-fifths it was ninety-one male lambs.

Generally speaking, among the adult females some were old and infertile, therefore the birth rate reduced according to their presence in a herd. Let's suppose an average birth rate of between two-thirds and four-fifths. If two-thirds, no female lambs remained on the shepherd's side. Therefore, in order to grow his own herd size, he must have felt the need to raise the birth rate and reduce the loss or death by accident or disease through his good herding care.

Until now, I have not discussed the number of losses by disease or accident or the number of the premium given to the shepherd. From the tablet text, for rams and ewes we can see that the loss number is approximately one-tenth of that for newborn female lambs. Instead, for male lambs, the loss number is always zero. As for the premium, approximately one-thirtieth of the number of rams/ewes and half the number of female lambs secured by the owner are given to the shepherd. Instead, no male lambs are given as premium. What was the reason behind the zero fact in both cases of loss and premium?

Given the owner's demand for more female lambs due to their management strategy of securing productive females, he would have kept their loss allowance at a lower rate than male lambs. Nevertheless, it seems that the owner allows a loss of female lambs as great as one-tenth of the number of female lambs secured, while he does not allow for any loss of male lambs. In the same way, as for the premium, the owner gives the shepherd as many as half the number of female lambs secured, while he does not give any male lambs. To explain this fact, Van Driel assumed that the owner had some need to secure more male lambs (1993: 235). However, if the owner had such a need, he could prescribe a larger proportional rate as his share: for example one male lamb to one female lamb as the sex proportion of his share, as we have seen in the case of Arsham, instead of one-to-two as in this case. Nevertheless, the owner demanded female lambs as many as twice the number of male lambs. Van Driel supposed that 'the owner attached importance to male lambs'. But such an attachment could not be found on the owner's side, as shown by the ratio of one male lamb to two female lambs. Moreover, the number of male lambs consumed after the annual accounting was not large. It would have been sufficient to keep male lambs at a ratio of one-sixth of breeding ewes. In this respect, too, Van Driel's assumption that the owner attached importance to males is not plausible. It is better to look for another reason as to why the male lamb loss allowance and premium to the shepherd were always zero.

First, as for the zero premium, let's underline the fact that the shepherd could keep male lambs at a rate of one-sixth of the breeding ewes. Even in the case of 100 breeding ewes in the period at the beginning of the contract and in the case of a birth rate of two-thirds, the shepherd could already obtain 16.5 male lambs, and zero female lambs. In the later years when the herd size had grown and the ewes had increased to 390, the share of male lambs for the shepherd arrived at sixty-five, even if the birth rate is estimated low at two-thirds. The higher the birth rate, the higher the number of male lambs the shepherd could obtain, becoming even larger than the owner's share. Under such circumstances, did the shepherd think the gift of male lambs more meaningful and rewarding? This is the reason why the premium of male lambs for the shepherd is always zero, in contrast to that of female lambs.

On the other hand, in the chart we can see that in any year a certain number of female lambs is reported as a loss, while the loss of male lambs is zero. This imbalance seems unnatural, because the death rate must have been approximately the same. Therefore, the number of male lambs marked as lost must not represent the actual facts. What is hidden behind such an imbalance?

In order to explain the zero fact, we can for the time being assume that the total sum of lost lambs was recorded in the space for female lamb loss without sex distinction, because it was difficult to distinguish the sex from the skin. However, this assumption does not seem right. Now, if the loss allowance rate of one-tenth had been equally applied to male and female lambs and the number in both categories had been jointly written in the space for lost female lambs, the number must have been as great as one-tenth of the total number of male and female lambs secured by the owner. But the loss number written in the space is always the same—one-tenth of the number of female lambs secured as the loss allowance to rams or ewes. The assumption of joint recording is not acceptable. We cannot help but assume that the owner did not demand that the shepherd report the loss number of male lambs, or had no interest in confirming it. If this is the case, why?

In this respect, we have seen above that the owner demanded the shepherd deliver as many male lambs as half the number of female lambs secured. Supposing less interest in obtaining more male lambs, we can for the moment imagine that the owner did not find any great significance in knowing how many male lambs had died. Such an explanation seems plausible, but insufficient. I would like to suggest another reason hidden in the relationship between owner and entrusted shepherd.

Once per year, during the inventory, the owner or his administrator could actually count the individuals of each respective category: rams, ewes, male and female lambs brought to the accounting place. Being far from the herding fields, however, they did not have any means to confirm how many lambs had been born or how many individuals had died. They could not help but impose on the shepherd the obligation to bring in the skins of the dead animals as evidence.

Here, it is important to examine how the number of lost animals was recorded in the text. In the case of adults as well as female lambs, the respective loss precisely coincides with the arithmetically calculated result by the fixed rate of one-tenth of the corresponding number secured by the owner, even if the real loss must have fluctuated year by year. We cannot help but put forward the possibility that the owner one-sidedly fixed the loss allowance without any consideration of the actual loss and imposed on the shepherd the requirement that he bring as many skins as required to satisfy the number calculated mechanically. As for female lambs, the owner in fact secured them at a rate as high as one-third of the breeding ewes and allowed a loss number calculated according to the allowable maximum death rate of one-tenth of the secured female lambs. The shepherd had to bring the number of skins allowed by the owner independently from the actual number of dead female lambs, which fluctuates yearly.

Under such a situation, let's now try to imagine the possible strategies of the shepherd. When the actual death rate was higher than one-tenth, he must have delivered some of his own living females to his detriment. On the other hand, if the actual death rate had fortunately been lower than one-tenth, he would have been short of skins to take as evidence. In such a case, he could have mixed the skins of his own dead lambs to account for the shortage and retain the corresponding number of the owner's living female lambs. But the question remains: why was the loss number of male lambs always zero and why did the shepherd not have the duty to take the skins as evidence in the case of the death of male lambs? To this question, we may give the answer already mentioned above, that he was not particularly interested in having more male lambs and checking the loss, because the owner could already secure male lambs at a rate of one-sixth of the breeding ewes. However, I do not think that this was the only reason.

In this regard, it seems appropriate here to refer to the interesting story told in Genesis of the Old Testament about the herd owner Laban and the entrusted shepherd Jacob. There we can find a relevant clue to answer the zero puzzle of male lambs.

'I have never eaten a male sheep', said Jacob

The story developed as follows.

Young Jacob married a daughter of his uncle, Laban, and took charge of Laban's own herd as payment of the bride price.

After several years, the contract came to an end and as a result of Jacob's good care, the herd size had much increased. Laban offered Jacob a reward for this achievement.

To this proposal, Jacob asked for Laban's black spotted sheep and goats as a reward and for the renewal of the contract. As his demand was accepted, Jacob promised that he would care separately for Laban's herd and his black spotted herd without mixing them. By keeping the herds separated, the possibility of cross-mating could be avoided and the subsequent disputes as to whom newborns belong would not occur. Such a promise served to reassure the owner Laban, who was probably suspicious of the shepherd's management.

After obtaining Laban's trust, Jacob applied a kind of magical means to Laban's breeding ewes on the occasion of mating in order to have them deliver black spotted lambs. Moreover, he also applied this magical means to the best pairs who could bring about strong and healthy newborns. With these tricks, he could obtain the healthy black spotted lambs born in Laban's herd and leave the plain-coloured and weak ones to Laban. This story suggests how it was possible for the shepherd to manipulate information and deceive the owner, who resided far from the herding place.

Jacob's own herd was increased and he became the owner of a large herd. He could acquire transport animals (donkeys and camels) and even succeeded in owning slaves. This suggests the possibility for a shepherd to become a large herd owner and finally to become a small household chief with several slaves.

After his success by means of manipulation and fraud, the time came for Jacob to leave Laban. At his departure, he stole an important sacred object from Laban and fled. As soon as Laban noticed the disappearance of the sacred object, he chased Jacob. After catching up with him, Laban began enquiring about the matter, but Jacob, in order to make Laban believe that he was not a thief, insisted on his diligent work in caring for Laban's herd. He said, 'In all the twenty years I was under you, your ewes and your she-goats never miscarried and I never ate rams from your herd. Those mauled I never brought back to you, but bore the loss myself. You demanded compensation from me, whether the animals were stolen in daylight or at night' (Genesis, 31:38–42).

In this dispute, in order to avoid Laban's suspicion and accusation, he stresses not only his competence in terms of herding care, but also emphasises his honesty and faithfulness as a reliable shepherd, as Laban will never be able to obtain proof or evidence of the fraud. We can recognise here the so-called information gap between herd owner and entrusted shepherd. Taking advantage of this gap, Jacob succeeded in cunningly manipulating the facts and hiding them from Laban.

Generally speaking, someone who needs to evade suspicion and must defend themself tries to do so by insisting they have acted correctly by enumerating items that should rather raise suspicion and need to be checked. By Jacob's statement, 'In all the twenty years I was under you, your ewes and your she-goats never miscarried, and I never ate rams from your flock', he tries to make Laban believe in his herding care ability and his honesty. In addition, he affirms 'Those mauled I never brought back to you, but bore the loss myself. You demanded compensation from me, whether the animals were stolen in daylight or at night'. Here he stresses that he had supplemented the numerical shortage caused by accident by providing his own living animals without asking for any compensation for the loss from Laban's herd. The first part of the talk can be described as emphasising the positive aspects of his responsible observance of his duties as an entrusted shepherd, while the second part can be described as highlighting the good intentions of a faithful shepherd.

Jacob made two kinds of performative acts of speech. One is a boasting display of his excellent ability in lamb delivering care—'your ewes and your she-goats have never miscarried'—and the other is an anticipated defensive rhetoric in order to evade the owner's suspicion of fraud—'I never ate rams from your flock'. Both concern matters the owner cannot witness and would be most interested to check. However, in order to evade suspicion, why did he mention never eating rams, as if this act was one of the shepherd's typical acts of fraud.

Before proposing an answer to the question, I would like to return to the discussion on the shepherd's strategies on the occasion of accounting.

Birth and death rates are not constant and may fluctuate year by year. The owner who was far from the herding place imposed a fixed rate in order to secure his share independently from the actual birth and death rates. From the accounting texts, we learned how the delivery of newborns and of skins of the dead was achieved arithmetically according to these rates. In such a situation, however, the shepherd must have reserved some room to manipulate reality. If the actual birth rate had been lower than the owner's share, the shepherd had to provide his own lambs at his sacrifice, but sometimes it happened that the birth rate was higher than the fixed rate for the owner. On these occasions the shepherd could keep superfluous lambs for himself. When the actual losses were fewer than the number allowed, the shepherd could bring enough skins to account for the rate of one-tenth of either rams or ewes or female lambs secured by including the skins of his own dead animals to satisfy the shortage, pretending that they were the owner's. Now, let's call this strategy the 'substitution strategy'. In the same way, he could adopt the same substitution strategy by bringing his own dead male lambs to satisfy the shortage. Why then is the loss of male lambs always zero in contrast to that of female lambs, which is always reported? It is true that the owner's main interest was to have more female lambs because of their importance for future reproduction. So, we may conclude that the owner did not care about the loss of male lambs. However, I asked above, was that the only reason?

We can imagine another strategy to satisfy the shortage of dead lamb skins when the actual losses were fewer than the number allowed. The simplest way would be to kill a number of the owner's lambs to meet the shortage. Of course, it is unthinkable that a shepherd might kill the owner's female lambs to satisfy the shortage of skins. In such a case, he could satisfy the shortage with the skins of his own dead lambs so as to keep as many of the owner's living female lambs as the number of substitution. But as for the lost male lambs, did he take the same substitution strategy so as to keep as many of the owner's living male lambs? The shepherd already received large numbers of male lambs. He must thus have been less interested in gaining more of the owner's living male lambs. The best way must have been to kill a number of the owner's male lambs to account for the shortage and to bring in their skins, pretending that the skins were those of individuals who had died by accident. Doing it this way, he could, moreover, enjoy eating the meat of the owner's slaughtered male lambs. He could apply this strategy not only to male lambs, but also to rams.

Now, let's return to Jacob's anticipatory self-defensive rhetoric in which he denied eating the owner's males in order to insist on his honesty. In the custom of reporting losses by skins, the owner can neither judge whether the skin is from one of his own animals or from the shepherd's, nor whether it is the skin of a male who died by accident or of males deliberately killed by the shepherd. It must have been a rather frequent occurrence among entrusted shepherds to kill and eat the owner's males and to bring their skins in order to satisfy the shortage, in addition to the substitution strategy. Behind Jacob's words, 'I never ate rams from your flock', can we suppose such deceptive strategy would be commonly shared among entrusted shepherds? Jacob must have deliberately negated his act of eating the owner's males as anticipated self-defence against the owner's suspicion.

Now, returning to the analysis of the Neo-Babylonian private herd owner's accounting text, I presumed that there was room for the shepherd to manipulate and conceal the real facts. I left open the answer to the question as to why the loss number of male lambs is always zero. Of course it is unimaginable that the de facto accidental death rate of male lambs was always zero. Behind the zero fact, I supposed a certain special hidden reason and tried to find it. Above I have cited the story of Jacob and Laban in the Old Testament, where Jacob anticipated his self-defence by highlighting his honesty and denying eating the owner's males. This story suggests that it was a common strategy for entrusted shepherds to kill and eat the owner's male lambs, later handing over skins pretending that they were those of male lambs who had died by accident. When faced with such strategy, could it be considered important for the owner to impose the duty of bringing the skins of dead male lambs as evidence. Instead, it would be better for the owner to secure the full prescribed share of male lambs by contract, without leaving the possibility of subtracting the losses from his share. In the regularly zero fact of male lamb losses, we can glimpse the information gap between owner and entrusted shepherd and the shepherd's room to manipulate the actual facts. Being unable to verify the truth, the owner's option was to secure, in any case, his prescribed share, while the entrusted shepherd profiting from the situation obtained more advantage and at the same time apparently observed the contractual obligations. The accounting text reflects the relationship between them characterised by deception and suspicion.

In such a situation, what countermeasures were available to the owner? One may have been to represent an ideal image of a good shepherd in order to appeal to his moral sense and to recompense good behaviour with special rewards. Another measure may have been to threaten him with possible dismissal if any hidden fraud came to light. One more effective way to prevent such fraud must be to allude to an omniscient God, who had the power to see through deception. It is worth noting Jacob's psychology when, in anticipation of any suspicion regarding his work, he denied the issue even before Laban alluded to it. He had adopted many strategies in manipulating the mating in order to make the ewes deliver healthy black spotted lambs, nevertheless he pretended to have done nothing, describing himself as an honest shepherd. He was certainly aware of the consequences if his dishonesty was revealed. Between the lines of this defensive performance, we can view the intersection of the other's notions of deception/suspicion and reveal the tense relationship between owner and entrusted shepherd.

The entrustor-entrustee relationship cannot be described simply as a peaceful mutual agreement. At the inventory they must have met as one who acts as the good shepherd concealing any kind of manipulation and one who suspects and tries to see through the falsification to the point of threatening discharge, both trying to protect their own interests. With a thorough analysis of the Neo-

Babylonian private owner's accounting text and referring to Jacob's story in the Old Testament, we could obtain some more detailed knowledge on the hidden relationship between the herd owner and the entrusted shepherd.

Shepherd as labour resource: Structure of the pastoral world

We have been able to catch a glimpse of the characteristics of the relationship between the temple and the shepherds tied to the domestic animals as mobile property. One aspect was a power relationship between dominator and dominated evident in the levy of young males as tributes, the other was the multilayered relationship bound in the contract between entrustor and entrustee—the household chiefs who entrusted their domestic animals as mobile property, the entrusted middlemen and the reassigned shepherds—but how did such an entrustor-entrustee relationship come into being?

The first motivations must of course have been the need for the temple to manage their large herds to satisfy the meat demand in the highly populated city and the wool demand for urban textile production whose products, incidentally, served as exchange goods in trading to obtain precious goods from outside. Such demands could not have been steadily met unless one assumes a constant need on the shepherd's part to enter into a submissive contractual relationship to provide herding care. In other words, it would not have been necessary for the shepherds to seek such servile employment if they were able to continue their own independent pastoral management and realise their self-sufficient livelihood roving far from the cities.

Regarding these conditions, Beck who referred not only to her survey on the Qashqa'i nomads, but also to the literature on other shepherds in the same areas, suggests that in the Middle East there is a latent structural mechanism at play that constantly reproduces young men aspiring to be hired shepherds (1980: 327–351).

Let me examine the sustainability of the labour force in a family through the life history of a shepherd. We will see that he cannot always provide necessary labour alone, because herding care is carried out by at least two shepherds. At a certain age he will get married and begin to maintain his family. He will have sons. However, in the first period until his son is seven to eight years old, he will not be able to expect any assistance from him. In such a situation the problem is usually resolved by forming a joint herding team with another family in the same situation, but if he had inherited a large herd, the labour shortage could not be resolved. It would become necessary to employ assistant shepherds from outside his family. In the next stage when his child was old enough to help him, he could manage without employing anybody, but his son would eventually marry and become independent. Later, arriving at the age when his physical strength weakened, he would again find himself short of herding labour. Looking at the whole life history of a shepherd, we can see that he must resolve the labour shortage twice by employing an assistant from outside his family. Requests for shepherd assistants are constantly found within pastoral groups.

On the other hand, there is the problem of the sustainability of a shepherd's family from the perspective of the expected economic income from their own herd. Sustainability is not constant throughout a shepherd's life. While still young and helping his father care for the herd, he can rely on him, but when he arrives at the age of marriage, he cannot always inherit a herd with a sufficient number of sheep from his father to maintain his future family. In fact, if there are several brothers then the father cannot provide him with a sufficient number of sheep to live on. In such a case, he must try to increase his own small herd in some way in order to pay the bride price and sustain his future family. The only way to increase the sustainability of his family's livelihood is to work as a hired labourer. In that case the best option is to work under a herd owner because he can simultaneously take care of his own small herd, mixing it with the owner's entrusted herd in the employer's field.

Before taking into consideration the demand for hired shepherds by the large urban herd owners, let me say that within the pastoral world there were always latent offers of employment for assistant shepherds as well as demands from the young to be employed. Of course, the most important thing for the employer is to have a reliable shepherd, so it would be preferable to employ him from the same tribe and better yet from his own clan rather than hiring a shepherd from another tribal group. In the case of close relatives, though, it may be difficult to impose stringent demands on them.

This is why it became rather common for an employer to hire shepherds from families not too close to the same pastoral group. When young shepherds finally increase their herd enough to sustain their family, they gain their independence. Eventually some could even become owners of a large herd, employ several hired shepherds and enjoy freedom from daily herding care in the fields. Such upward mobility has become a common goal in the pastoral world.

Latent requests are always present within pastoral groups. They are the result of a structural mechanism inside that world and must have been reproduced through the millennia in Middle Eastern pastoral culture. In the story of Jacob and Laban in the

Old Testament, Jacob was a member of the same group to which Laban belonged and finally succeeded in having a large herd and subordinated servants. Jacob provides us with the typical success story of the cunning hired shepherd.

Given such a structural mechanism within the pastoral world, what happened when the city-states as large consumption centres developed and it became a necessity for large urban herd owners to hire shepherds? A successful person such as Jacob, for example, may have become a middleman entrepreneur in order to satisfy the needs of an urban owner and may have assigned the entrusted animals as well as his own animals to subordinated shepherds. For these middlemen there must have been opportunities to settle in the city and to subsequently even become urban household chiefs. The multilayered entrustor-entrustee relationship mentioned earlier must have developed extensively. The large herd owners in the city as well as the middlemen must have been able to take advantage of competition among those aspiring to be entrusted shepherds. They could take a privileged position in contracts to the point of threatening discharge and would check the shepherd's herding care in the annual inventory with suspicion. Conversely, the entrusted shepherd had countermeasures to manipulate his position: for example he could shift his own unhealthy individuals into the owner's herd, mix the skins of his own dead females with those of the owners and bring skins of the owner's killed male lambs after eating them. The accounting records on tablets on the occasions of contract renewal provide not only the opportunity to confirm the share of gain between entrustor and entrustee, to check the animals were well managed as the owner's economic capital and to decide the renewal of the contract, but they also reflect the moment where the interests of both sides meet. The owner's intention was to see through the actual facts on the births and deaths of his animals and to appeal to the hired shepherd's honesty or threaten him, and the entrusted shepherd's aim was to conceal the manipulation of herd management and pretend to be a good and honest shepherd.

Summary

I have analysed several materials relating to herd management in the Sumerian temple cities of the third millennium B.C. and in the Old and Neo-Babylonian cities, based on specialists' readings of the tablets concerned. By complementing their reading with my revised interpretations of these materials, I have been able to depict the general characteristics of the relationship between the temple cities and the pastoral groups.

To sum up: there were several different owners of sheep/goats, either the temple, the kings and their relatives or high officials in the temple. These animals were entrusted to shepherds for herding care and were periodically checked by the administrator in charge. Judging from the records, the herds can be classified into two categories: 'internally retained herds' and 'externally entrusted herds'.

The first category, 'internally retained herds', were either for the temple's ritual use or for common consumption in the city and kept in a place adjacent to the city. From there a certain number of head were occasionally taken for use. Such diminution of the herd must have been constantly supplemented from outside. From the tablet records of Ur in the third dynasty in which the supplying of an amount of grain corresponding to each animal's age group was recorded, we are able to see that a great many young males were supplied from outside, and as a supply source the animals brought as tributes from local pastoralists were taken into account. The fact that young males were mainly supplemented from outside corresponds to the common strategy of shepherds of keeping reproductive females for themselves and discharging males as surplus. We can observe here the general principle that young males were collected in cities as a kind of circulating goods.

Besides the 'internally retained herds', the 'externally entrusted herds', including the herds that produced wool for urban textile manufacturing, were under the temple's ownership or the private ownership of high officials. They were entrusted to middle entrepreneurs or directly to shepherds. These herds were accounted for after the annual shearing in spring in order to check the owner's share established by contract. They would detract the number of losses confirmed using the skins as evidence and renew the contract for the following year after recording everything on tablets.

Quite often the entrustees were middlemen who would take charge of management and would sub-assign the herding care to other shepherds. There must have been a multilayered structure in the entrustor-entrustee relationships beginning from the urban herd owner as the centre of the contractual relationship. The middlemen would obtain the usufruct right to the herding fields from the urban authority. They must have had room to wield contractual power over the sub-assigned shepherds by means of their arbitrary rights to allocate herding fields.

By entrusting his herd to the shepherds, the owner could annually obtain a certain number of male and female newborns as his share. Even though the percentage of this share varied on a case-by-case basis, the number of newborns to be secured was generally established by contract at two-thirds or half the number of breeding ewes independently from the actual birth rate. However, the respective percentage of female and male lambs to be secured varied according to the purpose of herd management. In a herd for wool production or for the temple's consumption for rituals, the percentage of male lambs tended to increase. On the other hand, when increasing the herd size was the main goal, the proportional rate of female lambs became higher.

Generally speaking, the herd owner tended to keep female lambs as reproductive capital at his disposal and transfer the superfluous male lambs as consumable goods to be put into circulation.

In the case of wool production, the lambs born in the herd were kept and the males in circulation were often supplemented from outside.

Even though the rate of the owner's share was unilaterally and mechanically established independently from the actual birth rate, there remained room for the entrusted shepherd to conceal the actual loss by disease and accident. One trick was to mix the skins of his own dead female lambs with those of the owner's dead lambs, allowing the shepherd to obtain as many living female lambs from the owner as the number of the skins he mixed. Another cunning way was to kill and eat some of the owner's male lambs, but deliver the skins to the owner pretending they were lost by disease or accident. Under such circumstances, a tense relationship between the cheating shepherd and the suspicious owner was unavoidable. In the shepherd's strict duty to satisfy the owner's share and to bring the skins of the dead as evidence, we can read the owner's principle that the lives of the entrusted animals belonged to him. The loss of animals by the shepherd's carelessness or intentional slaughtering must be compensated as a violation of the contract. By demonstrating the ideal image of the good shepherd, the owner could implicitly impose on the entrusted shepherd non-contractual moral rules and could threaten him with the definitive punishment of discharge.

At the beginning of this chapter, I said that my aim was to clarify the relationships between large household chiefs in the city and pastoral groups, but at the same time with reference to this knowledge, I hoped to elucidate the background of the following subjects: 1) the socioeconomic position of household chiefs in the city who identified their domestic servants with domestic animals, which I discussed in the last chapter, and 2) the unique views in the Old Testament concerning the relationship between God, man and domestic animals such as that represented in Genesis 1:26 which can be summarised as follows—'man is worthy of being master of all animals because of his similitude to God'.

With regard to the first subject, in the last chapter the homology between the guide-wether and the eunuch was pointed out. In this context I demonstrated that herd control techniques using a guide-wether must have been invented as a development of more elemental herd control techniques and suggested that it was in turn applied as a means to control people, i.e. the utilisation of eunuchs. As a precondition that had made it easy to apply these techniques to people, I noticed that the household chiefs in the ancient Oriental world identified their domestic serfs and slaves as living mobile property along with domestic animals (see page 110). By way of example, I pointed out that the captured slave women were obliged to work in a collective location as weavers and their children were treated according to the same sex management strategy found in the management of domestic animals (see pages 111, 112). The view that identifies domestic servants with domestic animals as mobile property was latent in the *forma mentis* of the large household chiefs who owned serfs and herds. However, even if in the last chapter I outlined the necessary conditions for the metaphorical extension of herd control techniques to the domain of human control techniques, I did not discuss the possibility of household chiefs being acquainted with such techniques.

In this regard, what we have learned in this chapter is that these household chiefs as large herd owners met annually with the entrusted shepherds for contract renewal, collected the superfluous males annually brought by the pastoralist groups as tributes and consumed them after fattening in internally retained enclosures. They must have had the chance to become well acquainted not only with the castration of male sheep/goats, but also its effect: the castrated ram becomes obedient and can be utilised as a faithful transmitter of the shepherd's orders to other animals. Moreover, the royal families who were the large household chiefs not only managed the agricultural land by entrusting it to subordinated farmers, but also managed their textile or craft industries, keeping many subordinated serfs and slaves under their control. It must have been quite natural that through such authoritative power they began to see these subordinated people as the same movable property as their domesticated animals and came upon the idea to apply the guide-wether herd control technique to the human control domain. Even though the use of eunuchs as a political control technique spread when the historical situation matured, the promoting conditions were present among the ruling class of the temple cities in the ancient Near East.

The second theme proposed at the beginning of this book was the underlying historical background of the well-known message in Genesis—'Man is worthy of being master of animals because of his similitude to God'—and of the basic notions in the Old Testament on the relationship between 'God, man and domestic animals' that have been generally taken for granted in the Judeo-Christian world.

I have already examined the relationship between the rulers of the temple city-states as large household chiefs and pastoral groups in the ancient Oriental world surrounding the Israelites. Household chiefs with their temple authority controlled enormous agricultural fields and owned very large herds of domestic animals. They not only collected animals as tributes from the shepherds, but also entrusted their own large herds to the shepherds through middlemen.

With this basic knowledge it may be interesting to ask how in the Old Testament the syllogism 'Man is worthy of being master of animals because of his similitude to God' was accepted as a taken for granted proposition, because such a proposition does not seem to be taken for granted in any other cultural environment. In fact, if we try to attribute this premise, 'man is similar to God', to the peoples in Southeast and Far East Asia who have animistic cosmologies, they would have difficulty in understanding it. Instead, in the ancient Near Eastern world, gods were anthropomorphically represented by human figures. What is positivistically true is not the 'similitude of man to God', but the 'similitude of thus represented God to man'. Anyhow, from this premise the conclusion 'man is worthy of being master of the animals' cannot be directly drawn. There is a logical gap. In this regard, it is opportune to return to the reality where the household chiefs with their temple authority used to entrust the management of their animals to the subordinated shepherds as God entrusted control of animals to man. Taking such a reality into consideration, let us now try to replace the figure of the 'temple's large household chief' with God and the 'entrusted shepherd' with 'man'. The proposition in the Old Testament can be obtained. The logical gap is complemented with reference to the actual reality and the proposition obtains its plausibility.

Not only in the above proposition in Genesis, but also in many other passages of the Old Testament mentioning the relationship between God, man and animals, we can find reflections of the relationship between the ruling household chiefs (*dominus*) and the entrusted shepherds. In the last paragraph of Noah's story, God openly allows man to eat any animal meat prohibited until then.

However, on this occasion, God allows it with the caveat that man must not eat animal meat containing blood, that being a symbol of life, lest he revenge on them demanding atonement. In other words, the act of eating animal meat without pouring sacrificial blood is considered usurpation of life that belongs only to God, and breaking this rule reserves Him the right to revenge. Besides, in the passages of Leviticus that describe the ritualistic procedures of animal sacrifice, the duty to pour the blood of sacrifice on God's altar is repeatedly prescribed (Leviticus 17:14). In the sentences that prohibit eating meat with blood and express God's right to revenge for its violation as usurpation, we can find the claim of the absolute belongingness of the animal's life to God. In this claim can we read the reflection of the large herd owner's claim to the absolute belongingness of the animals to him in the presence of his entrusted shepherd?

Under the conditions of the contract that we have so far analysed, it must have been natural for herd owners to prohibit the entrusted shepherd to conceal the act of eating the meat of animals that belonged to him. If they ate them, they ought to correctly report each case to the chief himself. If it came to light that they had failed to observe this entrusted duty, they would be punished. In this light, we can better understand the passages in the Old Testament where God shows the same attitude of strictly controlling against violations and claiming retribution from the entrusted man. In God's severe accounting claim against man's usurpation of life, even after having entrusted the right to control animals to man, we can find a precise reflection of the household chief's strict accounting claim to the entrusted shepherd. In ancient West Asia, preceding the idea of 'the contract with God' in the Old Testament, was the idea of 'the contract with the herd owner' that should be strictly observed by the entrusted shepherd.

In connection with the exclusive belongingness of all animals to God, Konagaya, who researched the representational world of Mongolian shepherds, reports the following findings, as discussed above: the Mongolian shepherds choose an individual in the herd that will not be killed but will be left to die a natural death. They charge it with the symbolic responsibility of the reproduction and growth of the herd. Here is the idea that the herd can reproduce and increase as long as they do not kill the representative individual, even if they kill and consume as many other members as they want. Konagaya suggests that this idea must be an extension of a Siberian hunters' custom (Konagaya, 1994) according to which they never kill the most handsome and largest animal and they regard it as the head, particularly responsible for the reproduction of the group they hunt

(Lot-Falk, 1953). Behind this custom, we can find the notion that in any animal group there is an individual that represents and guarantees the reproduction of the group itself. This idea recalls the contemporary idea of reproduction by cloning. At the same time we can identify the following premise: the incremental and reproductive mechanism in a living group is inherent in the group itself, and it can be realised by a representative individual. This presupposes the idea of the autonomy of the preservation of the life of a species or population. On the contrary, what we have seen in the passage of the Old Testament is the idea of the absolute belonging of individual life to a transcendental singular God. In other words, there is attention to individuality in living beings owned by a transcendental chief who assures the continuity of life.

As Konagaya says, we can ascribe the origin of the Mongolian idea of not killing a special animal to the Siberian hunters' tradition. The hunters do not keep wild animals under their control; the births assuring continuation of the animal group are realised within the group itself out of the hunters' hands. Taking into consideration such an idea in the relationship between the hunters and the objects of hunting, the belief that 'the increment and reproductive mechanism of the group is inherent in the group itself, and that reproduction is realised by a representative member in the group' seems natural. On the contrary, the idea of attributing the ownership of animal lives to a superior transcendental chief is a direct transposition from the pastoralistic reality where animal reproduction is under human control. In this sense, I find Ingold's definition on the transition from hunting to herding as 'from trust to domination' appropriate (Ingold, 1994).

However, as evident in the cases of the Mongolian shepherds, not everywhere in the world do shepherds commonly share the view of human domination over domesticated animals. Why, then, was the idea of considering animal lives as belonging to a transcendental God particularly born in the ancient Near East and why in the Book of Genesis in the Old Testament did God entrust the care of animals to man in his similitude to Himself? Our thought turns naturally back to the urban large herd owners who entrusted herding care to the subordinate shepherds and strictly controlled their animals' lives and deaths on the basis of the temple's religious authority.

Of course, we cannot ignore the fact that the writers of the Old Testament described the Israelites as wandering herders of small domesticates and as people who always tried to separate themselves from the powerful urban temple authorities in the ancient Near East. If they wanted to clearly separate themselves from the urban temple authority, they could have avoided describing their relationship with God, which clearly mirrors the relationship between God, man and domestic animals found in the antagonistic temple states. In the next chapter where the dietary regulations on the edible and non-edible animals in Leviticus of the Old Testament are to be analysed, I will find the answer to this question.

8 Mode Analysis of Dietary Narratives in the Pentateuch

Preface

The Pentateuch in the Old Testament contains mythical-historical narratives of events perceived as significant in the course of the transmission of the Israelites' oral tradition. These narratives were edited by testament writers on the assumption that they actually occurred and were relevant to the history of the Israelites. The Pentateuch deals with intervention into human affairs by Yahweh from motivations that can be described as legislative-religious.

Leaving aside the question of how the narratives were orally transmitted and finally edited into the final written version, here we can find God's prescriptive proclamations on dietary principles that are not only relevant to dietary life, but also to the ritualistic and ethical life of the Israelites. Interestingly, these prescriptions on food are successively reported at three different stages in the historical narratives, each being quite distinct in terms of propositional content and even contradicting the others. Moreover, the final proclamations (Leviticus 11:1–47) prescribe the purity and impurity of animal species with reference to their habitat, mode of locomotion and morphology in order to distinguish between edible and inedible species. We know that Jewish food restrictions have been based on these rules since those times.

It may be because of their historical importance that the rules found in Leviticus have aroused the interest of biblical commentators and lay-scholars, stimulating attempts to identify the guiding principles behind these dietary regulations. In the second half of the twentieth century, cultural anthropologists too have tried to identify certain hidden yet coherent principles that are supposed to have generated such prescriptions.

Among all cultural anthropological approaches, Mary Douglas' study is most well known. She was a symbolic anthropologist who in *Purity and Danger* analysed dietary rules to find supportive evidence for her theoretical hypothesis on taboos (1966: 41–57), even though she later withdrew her interpretation and provided a different view that I disagree with (Douglas, 1999). In her analysis of taboos, she regarded the inedibility of an animal defined as 'impure' or 'abominable' as an issue of its anomalous taxonomic status: something that is a violation in relation to a system of categorisation. She claimed that the inedible animals described as abominable or unclean are imperfect and/or deviated members from the classes defined in their respective folk classification.

Starting from Mary Douglas' formal analysis of dietary rules, cognitive anthropologist Eugene Hunn goes further to show the relevance of the empirical environment in relation to the categorisation process (1979: 103–116). His fundamental notion is that a symbolic system does not exist in an empirical vacuum, but takes its form on the basis of a frequently perceived pattern in the empirical world. With reference to the fauna of the Middle East, he demonstrates that the animals prescribed as edible take a central position in terms of the frequency of behavioural and morphological traits. Reviewing the natural homeland where the symbolic system and dietary rules were formulated, he concluded that the animals prescribed as unclean and inedible are anomalous because of the infrequency of their trait complex in the animal world.

In *Purity and Danger*, Mary Douglas suggested that the fact that an animal was clean (edible) or unclean (inedible) is an issue of truth function depending on a culturally given cognitive and classification system. In this sense, she was an idealist, emphasising the independence of the human categorisation process from external and empirical constraints. Hunn, instead coming from a materialistic standpoint, elucidates the significance of the external empirical world or the empirical-perceptive process, while at the same time acknowledges a cognitive requirement to attain logical consistency or orderliness within a symbolic system by excluding cognitive ambivalence in order to avoid equivocality in human communication.

However, even though the explanatory (deductive) principles supposed by Douglas and Hunn could explain many ethnographic facts of the taboo phenomenon, we must not forget that the dietary regulations of Leviticus were reported as God's final proclamations on the subject and were particularly addressed to the Israelites. They can be considered as a set of performative speeches with the intention of producing a special message in the Israelites' minds rather than as statements formally deducted from the abstract 'principle to exclude deviators from a given cognitive classificatory system'. In fact, in an article where I examined Douglas's and Hunn's analyses on dietary regulations, I pointed out that the actual prescriptions do not always coincide with their interpretation principles (Tani, 1989c: 314–353). For example, some animal species classified in a well-defined group of beasts are judged abominable and unclean. God's dietary discourse in Leviticus seems to have been uttered to implicitly convey a certain message from God to the Israelites by arranging each prescriptive phrase in a special order. If the guiding principles pointed out by Douglas and Hunn cannot fully account for the generation of the actual regulations, we must reinterpret these dietary narratives in order to find other covert motivations creating such proclamations by examining the mode of utterance and deciphering the intended message.

Moreover, Douglas and Hunn did not take into account the contextual position of God's dietary regulations in Leviticus. In fact, the dietary rules in Leviticus are God's last discourse on the topic after his two preceding proclamations on food habits in the Eden and Noah periods. These two previous proclamations are addressed to humanity in general, while the last ones are addressed exclusively to the Israelites in order to underline and attain their holiness as a chosen people. Because of this, these regulations are even now culturally valid and have been observed through the ages by the Jews as rules governing their food habits as outlined in the Old Testament. It is important to note that these dietary rules were written as reports with the intention of generating legislative-religious power. In order to understand the real meaning of God's final proclamations on dietary regulations, we ought to look at them in their proper place in the successive food narratives and try to read between the lines in God's and the testament writers' intentions, by taking their context into account. We know that this kind of tentative interpretation has been carried out by Soler on the dietary rules of Leviticus from the perspective of the successive stages of dietary narratives (1973: 943–955). However, sufficient attention was not paid to the mode of utterance relevant to the speaker's underlying intention.

In this chapter, examining the modes of utterance and the contextual position of the last dietary discourse in Leviticus, I attempt to infer God's intentions and those of the Testament writers' who arranged His phrases as if they had been actually uttered by Him. This constitutes a cautious analysis of the dietary rules of Leviticus in order to decipher the performative force (in the sense of Austin, 1962) of the narratives on food in the Pentateuch that induced the Israelites to eventually observe the regulative prescriptions on edible and inedible animals.

Now, before beginning my analysis of the mode of utterance in the third and last dietary regulations in Leviticus, I provide an overview of God's former proclamations on food in the Eden and Noah stages in order to understand the contextual significance of those in Leviticus.

Dietary principles in the age of Eden

In the first part of Genesis, after creating man and giving him special status among living creatures, God's first proclamation on man's food is as follows[1].

> God said, 'let us make man in our own image, in the likeness of ourselves, and let them be masters of the fish of the sea, the birds of heaven, the cattle, all the wild beasts and all the reptiles that crawl upon the earth'. God created man in the image of himself, in the image of God he created him, male and female he created them. (Gen. 1:26–27)

> 'Be fruitful, multiply, fill the earth and conquer it. Be master of the fish of the sea, the birds of heaven and all living animals on the earth'. God said, 'See, I give you all the seed-bearing plants that are upon the whole earth, and all the trees with seed-bearing fruit; this shall be your food. To all wild beasts, all birds of heaven and all living reptiles on the earth I give all the foliage of plants for food'. (Gen. 1:28–30)

In the former proclamation, it is said that man is gifted with the qualification to govern all animals because he is created in the image of God. After giving man a superior status over animals, God in the following proclamation orders man to eat only seed bearing plants and fruits, and prescribes animals to eat the foliage of plants. That means that in the paradise of Eden both animals and human beings were vegetarians, not carnivorous.

Incidentally, the former statement which can be summarised as 'man is worthy of being master of animals because man is created in the image of God' may sound a little alien to Eastern and Southeastern Asian people who inhabit an animistic world. In terms of interpretation, in Chapter Seven I suggested this was a reflection of the actual relationship between ruling household chiefs in the temple city-states and the entrusted shepherds in the ancient Near East.

However, as for the second part of the statement, the following question must be raised: why did God give man only plants as food, even though He gave him the right to rule over animals and to be their master? In the ancient Near East, people had maintained their subsistence economy through pastoralism and had eaten animals since the prehistoric ages, contrary to the phytophagean people of

Southeast Asia. If man in the original Eden stage was described as vegetarian, it was to depict him in an ideal sense. Such idealisation of primordial man is a rather common feature in cosmologies, even though we can find creation myths in which man could enjoy consuming an abundance of plants and animals. Presupposing such an idealised life of man who avoids the bloodshed of animals, this story drastically marks a transition from a toil-free and clean life in a primordial world when killing was unnecessary, to a subsequent sinful life of hardships.

The following narration in Genesis tells the story of the expulsion of Adam and Eve from the Garden of Eden. After the expulsion, man was obliged to obtain food by toiling through the exhausting cultivation of plants, to wander in wastelands and to accept death as his destiny for punishment. In the following story of Cain and Abel, Cain, the farmer, murdered the shepherd Abel motivated by jealousy, as God preferred Abel's offerings of sheep to Cain's offerings of grain. Leaving aside the reason why God preferred a shepherd's gift to a farmer's, after the story of Cain and Abel the descendants of man degenerated morally and murder prevailed. The subsequent story of the flood is narrated as God's punishment for the wickedness of human beings, and at the end of the story God's changing view on dietary principles is outlined.

Dietary regulations in the era of Noah

In the narration of events, after the waters receded from the earth and Noah descended from the ark, we can find the following passages.

> Noah built an altar for Yahweh, and choosing from all the clean animals and all the clean birds he offered burnt offerings on the altar. Yahweh smelt the appeasing fragrance and said to himself, 'Never again will I curse the earth because of man, because his heart contrives from his infancy. Never again will I strike down every living thing as I have done. As long as the earth lasts, sowing and reaping, cold and heat, summer and winter, day and night shall cease no more'. (Gen. 8:20–22)

> God blessed Noah and his sons, saying to them, 'Be fruitful, multiply and fill the earth. Be the terror and the dread of all the wild beasts and all the birds of heaven, of everything that crawls on the ground and all the fish of the sea; they are handed over to you. Every living and crawling thing shall provide food for you, no less than the foliage of plants. I give you everything, with this exception: you must not eat flesh

with life, that is to say blood, in it. I will demand an account of your lifeblood. I will demand an account from every beast and from man. I will demand an account of every man's life from his fellow man. He who sheds man's blood, shall have his blood shed by man, for in the image of God man was made. As for you, be fruitful, multiply, teem over the earth and be lord of it'. God spoke to Noah and his sons, 'See, I establish my Covenant with you, and with your descendants after you; also with every living creature to be found with you, birds, cattle and every wild beast with you: everything that came out of the ark, everything that lives on the earth. I establish my Covenant with you: nothing of flesh shall be swept away again by the waters of the flood. There shall be no flood to destroy the earth again'. (Gen. 9:1-11)

It should be first mentioned that the paragraphs cited above, (8:20-22) and (9:1-11), belong to different source materials (Habel, 1988). On the basis of analytical studies of Genesis, the former is now ascribed to the source called Yahwist's versions and the latter to the Priestley writer's versions, and, even though they deal with the same event, we can find differences in terms of description.

In the former Yahwist version, a binary distinction between clean and unclean animals can be identified. This distinction appears for the first time in the beginning section of the flood story (Gen. 7:2-3), when Noah brought the animals onto the ark. Upon landing, at Noah's ritualistic burnt offering of clean animals and clean birds, God was pleased by the appeasing fragrance of the smoke and dissolved His curse on the earth that had lasted since the expulsion from Eden. Even if the burnt offerings was a direct motivation for the dissolution of His curse, it is important to note that the curse was removed as a concession from God's resignation in the face of the original wickedness of man's nature: in His words, 'because his (man's) heart contrives from his infancy'. Incidentally, God is depicted in an anthropomorphic way in this Yahwist version, as can be attested in the phrase, 'Yahweh smelt the appeasing fragrance'.

Conversely, the Priestley writer's version emphasises a different aspect of God. In his account, God formulated a decree and made a covenant with man without expressing any emotion, and it is in this version that God's change of mind regarding dietary principles is narrated (Habel, 1988). Up to that point, man had been allowed only vegetable food, now God permits him to eat all kinds of animals. It is interesting to note here that at the beginning of both passages we can find the same commanding phrase 'Be fruitful, multiply and fill the earth', as uttered in Genesis 1:28-30, when God at the Eden stage gave man seed-bearing plants and fruit trees as food. This concordant repetition undoubtedly serves to highlight the clear contrast in the dietary principles and God's change of mind between the Eden stage and the post-Noah stage.

However, it must remembered that God did not approve of man eating the meat of all animals without reservation, as evident in the phrases cited above: 'I give you everything, with this exception: you must not eat flesh with life, that is to say blood, in it. I will demand an account of your lifeblood. I will demand an account from every beast and from man. I will demand an account of every man's life from his fellow man'. Of course, consuming flesh is unimaginable without taking life. Adding this reservation, a kind of redemptive act of compensation is demanded. It may not be without reason that in the final part of the flood narratives the writers placed the Yahwist version before the Priestley version. Locating the Priestley version after the Yahwist version, where God's withdrawal of the curse was conceded from God's resignation, God's total approval of eating flesh, which had not been tolerated until then, through the prescription to observe a redemptive act, could be interpreted as a concession by God resigning in the face of the wickedness of human nature. Of course, even if the approval was given as a concession, this does not clear God's conviction on the original sinfulness of man. On the contrary, as far as the concession was given through resignation, God's conviction of man's wickedness and sinfulness must have remained unchanged and readers, from a sense of guilt, must have felt indebted to God's approval. The narrative of God's approval of eating flesh obtains a perlocutionary force to induce readers to faithfully observe a redemptive prescription to abstain from eating flesh with blood, provoking some self-reflection on their original sinfulness. God's demand not to eat flesh with blood serves as an anaphoric narrative for the redemptive sacrificial ritual prescribed later in Leviticus.

Incidentally, we know that the flood myth is narrated not only in the Old Testament, but also in the records of different neighbouring peoples in the ancient world of the Near East. Between them, we can observe a common plot: a dove is sent out to verify the presence of land, offerings are burned at the altar after emerging from the ark, a covenant is made between God and man, etc. These myths are said to have been handed down from a Sumerian prototype and later developed in parallel to take their own unique forms (Hämmerly-Dupuy, 1968; Frymer-Kensky, 1977; Follansbee, 1939). Interestingly enough, the story of the approval of eating flesh is absent in the Assyrian and Sumerian flood myths. We may say that the story of the approval of eating flesh was an important and indispensable element in the narrative about Noah seen from the Old Testament writers' perspective.

Having mentioned these differences, God's discourse in the last part of Noah's story in which He withdraws His preceding vegetarian principles can be regarded as a fundamental point marking a new era in dietary rules. As long as a procedure to avoid the consumption of blood was observed, the consumption of any animals was approved. However, God's prescriptions on dietary regulations do not end here with Noah, but continue in Leviticus where we can find further regulations on the edibility and inedibility of animals. Here God classifies them as clean or unclean, restricting the range of edibility and declaring those who observe these restrictive regulations by eating only clean animals to be holy (Leviticus 11:1–47). We know that these final prescriptions in Leviticus were one-sidedly addressed to the Israelites and became the foundation that determined their dietary customs.

To sum up, by outlining the dietary narratives, we know that God, who did not permit eating flesh at the stage of Eden, tolerated the consumption of all living animals in the Noah stage. Thereafter, the same God comes to restrict the range of edibility at the stage of Leviticus, as if He had changed the principle of total tolerance. God's discourse in Leviticus restricting the range of edibility is God's final address to the Israelites. In front of God's new rules underlying the distinction between clean and unclean animals, I cannot help but examine and ask what the last proclamations on dietary regulations mean. Of course, when I try to identify their meaning, the preceding narratives on the dietary rules in the Eden and Noah stages must be taken into account as anaphoric narratives ('former stories') to be referred to.

Moreover, in my attempt to decipher the meaning of God's last proclamation, it is important to keep in mind the following fact. The Pentateuch is the final version of the transmitted stories edited by the Priestley writers. It is a report, not only on the historical events the writers took as having 'truly happened', but also the report they arranged so that Israelite readers would receive them as truth and take special messages from them. The narrative on God's proclamations on dietary rules is a report of 'utterances by God addressed to the Israelites', i.e. a report of someone else's words.

Generally speaking, in order to understand the meaning of a report of another's words, we must take into account two levels of meaning as speech acts. For example, given a report by B of A's utterance, 'A said U (utterance)', at first level, we must identify what perlocutionary meaning the original speaker A intended to produce by his utterance (U), and then we must decipher what perlocutionary meaning the reporter B intended to produce by their act of reporting. Of course, the performative force of B's report depends on the contents of A's utterance. If A's utterance has a meaning that is favourable to the recipient, he will willingly accept B's report and be inclined to believe A's utterance. If unfavourable, he will reject the credibility of A's utterance, eventually questioning B's intention in reporting. Reporter B can arrange A's utterances as he pleases; for example, by managing his report in order to produce a special perlocutionary force by means of some figurative comments. Even if the reporter B is a mediator between the original speaker and the final recipient of the original talk, the intentionality of reporter B does not necessarily coincide with that of original speaker A.

In my work to find out the meaning of dietary prescriptions in Leviticus, too, we must decipher the respective intentions of God and of the Rabbinic writers, distinguishing them into different levels as follows: 1) the level of God's speech acts and 2) the level of the Rabbinic writers' reporting acts.

In order to tackle the first task, i.e. to decipher the intentions of God's proclamations in Leviticus, it is necessary to refer to the preceding dietary discourses of God in the Eden and Noah stages that can be regarded as anaphoric. God's preceding discourses are easy to understand, while on the contrary, the last discourse in Leviticus is rather complicated, as I will explain below. First, I would like to analyse precisely what is said in God's last discourse and examine the mode of utterance with which such rules are prescribed. Having clarified them, I subsequently identify God's intention in the last dietary regulations in Leviticus with reference to the preceding ones.

My discussion will be carried out according to the following order:

1. a) Formal analysis of the mode of utterance in the dietary regulations on the edibility/inedibility of animals in Leviticus. b) Identification of what kind of message God intended to produce in the Israelite's minds by His last utterances in Leviticus that constitute the final rules following His preceding ones.
2. Identification of the intention of the Rabbinic writers as reporters of God's words.

Dietary rules in Leviticus: Restrictions on edible animals

For convenience, all the passages of God's utterances will be shown below divided into segments. In fact, on a primary level they can be classified into four segments and the first two segments can be further subdivided according to subject matter.

Yahweh spoke to Moses and to Aaron and said to them, 'Speak to the sons of Israel and say:

A.1) Of all the beasts on the earth, 1) these are the animals you may eat: You may eat any animal that has a cloven hoof, divided into two parts, and that is a ruminant. 2) The following, which either chew the cud or have a cloven hoof are the ones that you may not eat: the camel must be held unclean, because though it is a ruminant, it has not a cloven hoof; the hyrax must be held unclean, because though it is a ruminant, it has not a cloven hoof; the hare must be held unclean, because though it is a ruminant, it has not a cloven hoof; 3) the pig must be held unclean, because though it has a cloven hoof, divided into two parts, it is not a ruminant. You must not eat the meat of such animals nor touch their dead bodies; you must hold them unclean'. (Levit. 11:1–8)

A.2) 'Of all that lives in water, these you may eat: Anything that has fins and scales, and lives in water, whether in the sea or river, you may eat. But anything in the sea or river that has not fins or scales, of all the small water creatures and all the living things found there must be held detestable. You must hold them detestable; you are not to eat their flesh and you must avoid their carcasses. Anything that lives in water, but has no fins and scales, is to be held detestable'. (Levit. 11:9–12)

A.3) 'Among the birds there are those you must hold detestable; they may not be eaten, they are detestable: The tawny vulture, the griffin, the osprey, the kite, the several kinds of buzzard, all kinds of raven, the ostrich, the screech owl, the seagull, the several kinds of hawk, horned owl, night owl, cormorant, barn owl, ibis, pelican, white vulture, stork, the several kinds of heron, hoopoe and bat'. (Levit. 11:13–19)

A.4 'All winged insects that move on four feet you must hold detestable. Of all these winged insects you may eat only the following: those that have legs above their feet so that they can leap over the ground. These are the ones you may eat: the several kinds of migratory locust, solham, hargol and hagab locusts in their several kinds. But all winged insects on four feet you are to hold detestable'. (Levit. 11:20–23)

B.1) 'By these you will be made unclean. Anyone who touches the carcass of one will be unclean until evening. Anyone who picks up their carcasses must wash his clothing and will be unclean until evening. (1) Animals that have hooves, but not cloven, and that are non-ruminant, you are to hold unclean; anyone who touches them will be unclean. (2) Those four-footed animals which walk on the flat of their foot must be held unclean; anyone who touches their carcasses will be unclean until evening, and anyone who picks up their carcasses must wash his clothing and will be unclean until evening. You are to hold them unclean'. (Levit. 11:24–28)

B.2) 'These are all the small beasts crawling on the ground that you are to hold unclean: the mole, the rat, the several kinds of lizards: gecko, koah, chameleon and tinshameth'. (Levit. 11:29–30)

B.3) 'Any small beast that crawls on the ground is detestable; you must not eat it. Anything that moves on its belly, anything that moves on four legs or more—in short all the small beasts that crawl on the ground—you must not eat these because they are detestable. Do not make yourself detestable with all these crawling beasts; do not defile yourself detestable with them, do not be defiled by them'. (Levit. 11:41–43)

C.1) '(1) For it is I, Yahweh, who am your God. You have been sanctified and have become holy because I am holy: do not defile yourselves with all these creatures that swarm on the ground. (2) Yes, it is I, Yahweh, who brought you out of Egypt to be your God: you must therefore be holy because I am holy'. (Levit. 11:44–45)

D.1) 'Such is the law concerning animals, birds, all living creatures that move in water and every creature that crawls on the ground. Its purpose is to distinguish the clean from the unclean; the creatures that may be eaten from those that may not be eaten'. (Levit. 11:46–47)

The last utterance (D.1) is a summary of all the utterances on dietary regulations. C.1 is an imperative statement to observe the regulations, while actual statements on the edibility and inedibility of animals are uttered in the preceding segments A.1, .2, .3 and .4 and B.1, .2 and .3. It is these segments that we should first of all analyse, however, it is important that segment C.1 states: 'Do not defile yourself with all these creatures that swarm on the ground. Yes, it is I, Yahweh, who brought you out of Egypt to be your God: you must therefore be holy because I am holy'. In this phrase, 'you' undoubtedly denotes the Israelites. There is no doubt that the dietary regulations on edible/inedible animals are addressed to the Israelites. Conversely, in the stage of Noah, God allowed the consumption of the flesh of all kinds of animals in general under the condition that blood consumption be avoided. As the Israelites are included among human beings, they had been allowed to eat all kinds of animals until the stage of Leviticus. It is this God that in the post-Exodus stage withdrew the total tolerance for eating animals from the Israelites and who ordered them to observe the restricted dietary regulations on edible/inedible animals in order to be holy. We should keep this fact in mind before beginning analysis of segments A and B, but first let me overview and clarify the forms of regulations proclaimed according to the respective animal species and the modes of expression used.

Modes of utterance in the dietary regulations in Leviticus

As can be seen at first glance, in the first large segment A, the edibility and inedibility of animal species are stated according to the following different classes of life-forms:

A.1: beasts on the earth
A.2: fishes in the water
A.3: birds in the air
A.4: winged insects on the earth

Except for the class of birds, we can find a common feature in defining the edibility/inedibility of animals. Judging by the criteria of whether or not a given animal is included in the range defined by the conjunction of certain morphological and behavioural attributes, many animals in each class are respectively described as clean and edible or unclean and inedible. Now, let's call the group defined by such a conjunction a 'category'.

At first glance, in segment A where animals are classified according to four different life-forms (beasts on the earth, fishes in the water, birds in the sky and winged insects on the earth), all animals seem to have been exhaustively taken into consideration. Nevertheless, in segment B that follows the long pronouncements in segment A, several kinds of animals are dealt with, as if the statements in segment A were not sufficient to cover all the species of animals. And every animal in segment B, classified by their respective morphological and behavioural criteria, is judged unclean and inedible.

Among the animals dealt with in segment B, we can find:

B.1.1: (Four-footed) herbivorous ungulate animals with the definition 'with hooves not cloven and non-ruminant'—Equidae (horse, ass and onager could be included).

B.1.2: (Four-footed) mammals except for the ungulate animals defined as 'walking on the flat of their foot'.

B.2: (Four-footed) reptiles and rats with the definition 'crawling on the ground'.

B.3: Any animal that moves on its belly besides those that walk with four feet or more and crawl without legs.

What kinds of animals were covered in segment B? Are they animals that cannot be classified into the four classes according to the four life-forms? If so, this could be the reason why these animals were separately treated in the supplementary section: segment B.

In this regard, it is obvious that from the definition 'anything that moves on its belly, anything that moves on four legs or more' in segment B.3 that the animals implied are insects such as centipedes, caterpillars and worms. They are not winged insects. Therefore, there is good reason not to include them in segment A.4, but to instead mention them separately in the supplementary section.

On the contrary, all the animals dealt with in B.1.1, B.1.2 and B.2 belong to the class of four-footed beasts on the earth. The 'four-footed animals with hooves not cloven and non-ruminant' in B.1.1 are Equidae. The 'four-footed animals walking on the flat of their foot' in B.1.2 are non-ungulate mammals such as dogs, cats, wolves and lions. The 'small beasts that crawl on the ground' exemplified by the lizard, gecko and chameleon in B.2 must be Reptilia of the four-footed animals, nevertheless they are dealt with separately from segment A.1. Why could they not be covered in segment A.1? With regard to such incoherent arrangement, we realise that most beasts dealt with in A.1 are ungulate animals, even though it is said that the discussion domain in segment A.1 is beasts on the earth. Then, let's suppose for the moment that the actual discussion domain in segment A.1 was limited to ungulate animals. Under such a supposition, we can find an acceptable reason why those beasts which walk on the flat of their feet (for example dogs, cats, wolves and lions) or crawl on the ground (for example lizards) were not treated in segment A.1, but covered separately in the supplementary section B: they were not regarded as members within the discussion domain of segment A.1, simply because they are non-ungulate animals. However, even after we concede to such a supposition, another question remains unanswered. Equidae, beasts with hooves not cloven and non-ruminant, undoubtedly belong to the ungulate category. Nevertheless, they are not treated in A.1, but separately in segment B.1.1. In short, we cannot help but find arbitrariness and incoherence in the arrangement of propositional statements concerning beasts on the earth. Even if segment B was a kind of supplementary section for animals not dealt with in segment A, the following question arises: according to what intention were certain kinds of beasts (Ovidae, Bovidae, Camelidae and Suidae)[2] selectively discussed in segment A.1, leaving the relative ungulate Equidae aside? In spite of the classification of animals according to the four different life-forms, if some actual propositional statements concerning a class is not expressed in the appropriate segment, but dealt with separately, we cannot help but suppose that some special intention deviated from the position of comprehensively and consistently discussing the members in the discussion domain according to objective facts.

Leaving aside those questions that emerged initially from the modes of utterance of beasts to be discussed below, let's more precisely analyse the modes of utterance on dietary regulations.

Before beginning a more precise analysis, for my convenience it is better to cite Trubetzkoy's (1958) terms to distinguish two kinds of oppositional classifications: 1) privative opposition and 2) equipollent opposition.

In privative opposition, all members in the discussion domain are classified into two groups (P/–P) according to the judgement as to whether they satisfy a unique criteria P (for example: red) or not. Members that satisfy the unique condition P are centralised as a basic reference group, while the other members, deviating from the basic criteria, are peripheralised as residual. In this form of classification, it is evident that all possible cases in the discussion domain can be exhaustively taken into consideration.

On the other hand, in equipollent opposition, members in the discussion domain are classified into plural groups (P, Q, R, S, T, etc.) according to the judgement that they satisfy plural equivalent oppositional criteria (for example: P = red, Q = orange, R = green, S = blue, T = violet). In this type of classification, though, we cannot be sure that all possible cases are exhaustively taken into account, unless we have checked if these criteria cover all the extensional members supposable in the discussion domain. In classification by equipollent opposition, the possibility for some members (for example yellow and colourless ones) to be left neglected and unclassified remains. Now, keeping such differences between the two forms of classification in mind, let me analyse each set of propositional statements in each class of segment A.

The statements in segment A.2 on fishes and A.4 on insects share the same propositional mode and give an impression of unequivocality.

In segment A.2 on the class of fishes in the water, those equipped with 'fins' and 'scales' are defined as clean and edible, while the rest not equipped with both of these attributes are defined as unclean and inedible. All members of the class are classified into two categories by privative opposition: the category which satisfies

Mode Analysis of Dietary Narratives in the Pentateuch

p = Fins   g = Scales

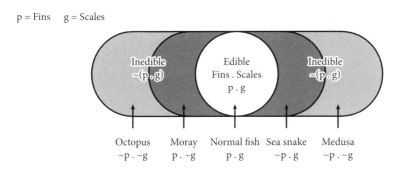

Figure 8.1 Edible/inedible fish

p = Winged   g = Four legs   r = Creeps   s = Legs to jump

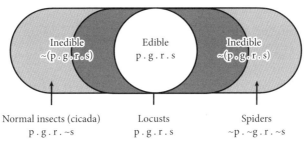

Figure 8.2 Edible/inedible insects

two necessary criteria, p: 'fins' and q: 'scales', is positively centralised as edible while the residuals that deviate from the criteria are negatively peripheralised as inedible (see Figure 8.1).

In segment A.4 on winged insects, it is said that 'All winged insects that move on four feet you must hold detestable. Of all these winged insects you may eat only the following: those that have legs above their feet so that they can leap over the ground'. Here several names of locusts are mentioned as examples of edible winged insects. In short, edible winged insects, locusts, are described as those equipped with four feet and a pair of legs to jump with, while other common winged insects that are inedible are described as those equipped with four feet, but missing a pair of legs to jump with. This descriptive method of winged insects gives us a strange and unnatural impression. Scientifically speaking, the 'six feet' feature is appropriate to describe winged insects. In spite of this, why did they adopt such an unnatural mode of description? Of course, in order to clearly distinguish the special morphological attribute of locusts, which are equipped with 'four feet' and a 'pair of legs to jump with', from common winged insects, the descriptive criteria 'four feet' could be convenient. However, we cannot ignore the fact that such a description of morphological aspects of winged insects is unnatural. For the present, however, leaving aside this unnatural aspect of morphological description to be tackled later, the mode of distinguishing between edible/inedible insects in segment A.4 appears to be the same as that of segment A.2 on fishes: those satisfying the necessary behavioural and morphological conditions are judged edible, and the rest that do not are defined as inedible—this is classification using privative opposition (see Figure 8.2).

In short, segments A.2 and A.4 commonly share the same mode of propositional statements. Members in the respective discussion domain are classified into two oppositional categories by privative opposition (P/–P). Defining a discussion domain by classifying life-forms (fishes or winged insects) and stating the necessary conditions for edibility with reference to their morphological and behavioural attributes, the members in the discussion domain are classified into two categories. The edibility and inedibility of each animal species are formally defined by differences in satisfying or not the necessary conditions P. The principle of exclusion of deviators from the centralised category seems to be applied in the distinction between edible and inedible species.

Now, let's move our attention to segment A.1 on beasts. We can find a similar way of distinction: those (Ovidae and Bovidae) equipped with the necessary two conditions, 'cloven hooves' and 'ruminant', are judged edible and those not satisfying one of these two characteristics are judged inedible. In this sense, segment A.1 also seems to share the same principle as segments A.2 and A.4. The judgement of edibility or inedibility seems to be given by formal deduction from the principle of 'exclusion of deviators from the centralised category'. Because of this, Mary Douglas once regarded these regulations as examples of the exclusion of classificatory deviators. However, as I have already noted above, if we go on reading segment B, we can find other propositional statements on the beasts on the earth, but we cannot find the same mode of classification by privative opposition as seen in segments A.2 and A.4. Among six possible cases of beasts mentioned either in segment A.1 or in segment B, only three cases are dealt with in segment A. The matter is not so simple as in segment A.2 on fishes and

Mode Analysis of Dietary Narratives in the Pentateuch

p = Ungulate g = Cloven hooves r = Ruminant

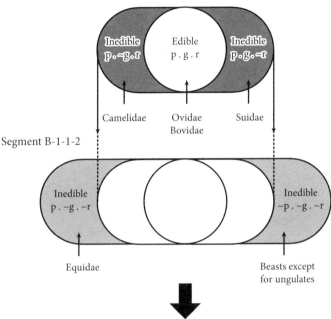

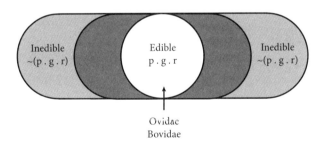

Figure 8.3 Edible/inedible beasts

A.4 on winged insects. To better understand the mode of expression regarding beasts, I list all the propositional statements concerning beasts in a simplified way according to their order of appearance.

In segment A.1, only the following three cases are mentioned:

P) The ungulate (p) beasts equipped with cloven hooves (q) and ruminant (r) (Ovidae and Bovidae) are edible (A.1.1): p.q.r = edible.

Q) The ungulate (p) animals not equipped with cloven hooves (–q) and ruminant (r) (Camelidae) are inedible (A.1.2): p.–q.r = inedible.

R) The ungulate (p) animals with cloven hooves (q) and non-ruminant (–r) (Suidae) are inedible (A.1.3): p.q.–r = inedible.

On the other hand, the edibility of other beasts not mentioned at A.1 is prescribed in segment B, as follows:

S) The ungulate (p) animals not equipped with cloven hooves (–q) and non-ruminant (–r) (Equidae) are inedible (B.1.1): p.–q.–r = inedible.

T) Other non-ungulate mammals that walk on the flat of their feet (B.1.2) or reptiles that crawl on the ground (B.2) that can be described as neither ungulate (–p), nor cloven hoofed (–q) nor ruminant (–r) are inedible: –p.–q.–r = inedible (see Figure 8.3).

Differently from the classification in segments A.2 and A.4, which is classification by privative opposition, the beasts here are classified according to equipollent opposition. Moreover, the final two prescriptive statements (S and T) are pronounced in segment B separately and distant from segment A.1. However, after reading all these prescriptive statements on beasts at A.1, B.1.1, B.1.2 and B.2, we realise that only the first category (P), ungulate animals equipped with cloven hooves and ruminant 'p.q.r', are judged clean and edible, while all the other categories (Q, R, S and T) are judged unclean and inedible. In other words, what has been globally said by these five prescriptive statements is equivalent to the following set of two statements classified by privative opposition (P/–P):

P) The ungulate (p) beasts equipped with cloven hooves (q) and ruminant (r) (Ovidae and Bovidae) are edible: p.q.r is edible.

–P) Except for Ovidae and Bovidae, the residual categories—ungulate neither equipped with cloven hooves nor ruminant and non-ungulate animals, i.e. all other beasts on the earth—are inedible: –(p.q.r) is inedible.

If the set of five prescriptive statements on beasts (P, Q, R, S and T) classified by equipollent opposition can be summarised into a simple set of two statements (P/–P), why did the Biblical writer or God not give the same message in a simple and clear mode of expression? This is the first question to emerge from my analysis. The second question is why were these categories of ungulate animals (P, Q and R) dealt with in segment A.1 while the other two categories, ungulate

Equidae (S) and other mammals except for the ungulate animals (T), were treated in segment B distinct from segment A. Being propositional statements on all potential cases pronounced separately, it is difficult to grasp what is said in short. In this regard, a third question arises: why were only the three categories of ungulates, Ovidae-Bovidae, Camelidae and Suidae dealt with in segment A.1 to the exclusion of Equidae, ungulate animals as well? Was there any reason behind such an arrangement? These questions emerge from the analysis of the mode of expression on beasts on the earth, however, for the time being, let's move on and discuss the last class, A.3, on birds.

In segment A.3 on birds in the sky, edibility and inedibility are not prescribed by reference to morphological and behavioural traits, but only by stating their individual names: 'Among birds here are those you must hold detestable; they may not be eaten, they are detestable: the tawny vulture, the griffin, the osprey, the kite, the several kinds of buzzard, all kinds of raven, the ostrich, the screech owl, the seagull, the several kinds of hawk, horned owl, night owl, the cormorant, the barn owl, the ibis, the pelican, the white vulture, the stork, the several kinds of heron, the hoopoe and the bat'. Why was the prohibition on eating them not defined by morphological and behavioural traits, instead of annunciating their species names? Such question has led to several discussions, but most are not fully plausible or acceptable. Only Bulmer proposes the following reason: it is difficult to provide unequivocal distinctive criteria of morphological and behavioural traits to distinguish between edible birds like pigeons and the inedible birds mentioned above, so the writers could not help but list the individual names of the species (1989: 316). The birds judged here to be detestable and inedible are all carnivorous. Actually, in the dietary regulations not only carnivorous birds, but also all other carnivorous animals are defined as unclean and inedible. In the narrative on dietary principles at the Noah stage where eating the flesh of all animals was approved with some reservations, the duty of an act of purification for bloodshed was prescribed. In terms of consuming flesh, bloodshed is inevitable. Carnivorous animals eat other animals without such redemptive acts, so the definition of carnivorous animals as unclean must derive from this principle.

After analysing the mode of utterance on the edibility of animals in each class, we found that animals of each class except for birds were categorised by morphological and behavioural attributes, and only one centralised category equipped with a certain set of attributes was considered edible. However, we realised that there are aberrant or incoherent modes of utterance within these rules.

Aberrant description of winged insects

Any winged insect is described by one morphological feature—'four feet'—as basic reference criteria. Edible insects, locusts, are described as those equipped with 'four feet' and 'a pair of legs to jump with', while other common insects defined as inedible are mentioned as those equipped with 'four feet' but lacking 'a pair of legs to jump with'. Even though it would be natural to describe the common winged insects as having 'six feet' and then to describe the specific morphological traits of locusts with an additional comment 'the last pair of the six feet is large to allow jumping' as a deviation from the common classification standard, 'four feet' not 'six feet' is adopted as a basic reference criteria. Why is such an unnatural criteria adopted? In other words, at the risk of an aberrant mode of description, why did they give to locusts a positive centralised position and define them as clean and edible?

Illogical array of propositions concerning beasts on the earth

Even though all the propositional statements on beasts come to prescribe only beasts with cloven hooves and ruminant as edible, and define other residual beasts as inedible, why do they not show the clean/unclean distinction of four-footed beasts by classifying members into two (P/–P) cases by privative opposition? (Question 1.1). In segment A.1, why did they treat only three cases—a) ungulates with cloven hooves and ruminant (Ovidae and Bovidae) are defined as clean and edible, b) ungulates without cloven hooves and ruminant (Camelidae) are defined as unclean and inedible and c) ungulates with cloven hooves and non-ruminant (Suidae) are defined as unclean and inedible—while ungulates without cloven hooves and non-ruminant (Equidae) and other non-ungulate mammals, both of which were defined as unclean and inedible, were not dealt with in the same segment? If the intention was to positively centralise 'ungulate animals with cloven hooves and ruminant' (Ovidae and Bovidae) as edible and to peripheralise other animals, such a scattered arrangement of related propositional statements is not appropriate. Was there any motivation to divide the propositional statements concerned in such a way? (Question 1.2). This question must be answered together with the question as to why Equidae, which are ungulate and domesticated as the animal species dealt with in segment A.1, were treated separately in segment B.

In the next section, I will try to find a reasonable answer to these questions in order to decipher the implicitly intended message.

Perlocutional meanings of Yahweh's decrees in Leviticus

First, as for the pronouncements on the class of beasts on earth in which incoherent arrangements of propositional statements was attested, I would like to focus on the following fact that has not yet been taken into consideration. In segment A.1, beasts were distinguished into clean-edible and unclean-inedible animals by classification with equipollent opposition with reference to their morphological and behavioural features, as if all the beasts on earth were taken into account. However, the species dealt with in this segment are only four categories of ungulates (Ovidae, Bovidae, Suidae and Camelidae, with the exception of hyrax and hare), which were domesticated animals in the ancient Near East. So, for the time being, let me suppose that the discussion domain in segment A.1 was limited to ungulate domesticated animals. However, in such a supposition, we cannot find the reason why the domesticated horse and ass (Equidae) defined as 'without cloven hooves and non-ruminant' were not dealt with there. Instead, these missing domesticated Equidae are discussed in the separate segment B.1 as unclean/inedible together with other unclean and inedible non-ungulate mammals that were not ordinary food animals in the ancient Near East. Now, if we take into consideration the fact that the horse and ass, even being ungulate animals and domesticated, were not ordinary food animals (even though it is archaeologically attested that they were on rare occasions eaten in small numbers according to excavated sites, and were mainly utilised for transport, riding and leather), the reason becomes clear as to why Equidae was not dealt with in segment A.1. In short, the discussion domain of segment A.1 must have been limited to domesticated food animals ordinarily consumed in the ancient Near East. Was the purpose of the utterances in segment A.1, where the distinction between clean and unclean ungulate animals is made, to bring to the fore a certain restricted range of domesticated ungulates for food in relation to the actual range of domesticated ungulates consumed in that region?

Keeping this in mind, let me recall that in segment A.1 Ovidae and Bovidae were defined as clean, while the other domesticated food animals, Camelidae and Suidae, were defined as unclean. The first two groups were important and indispensable food animals to the Israelites who were historically described as shepherds wandering in the grasslands in the neighbourhood of the dominant civilised city-states. On the other hand, the people of the civilised city-states were invariably consumers not only of sheep/goats and cattle raised by entrusted shepherds, but also of pigs raised by urban dwellers since the fourth millennium B.C., as archaeologists have demonstrated using excavated evidence (Zeder, 1991: 30–32; Pollock, 1999: 106–107). The nomadic people who wandered in the desert kept camels and consumed their meat and also consumed sheep and goats as the Israelites did. Taking into consideration such different food habits of the surrounding peoples in comparison to those of the Israelites, we can locate the implications of the statement set in segment A.1. At first glance, these statements seem to be objectively judging the cleanness/uncleanness of the respective animal species with reference to their morphological and behavioural features. However, they were intended to implicitly produce the following message: the Israelites, who were originally sheep, goat and cattle herders, are consumers of clean domesticated animals, while the dwellers of the dominant civilised city-states including Egyptians and Babylonians and other nomadic people in the desert are consumers of unclean domesticated animals.

As for the aberrant description of the winged insects, as stated above 'four feet' is adopted as a basic distinctive criteria, even though 'six feet' would be a natural way to describe common insects. At risk of unnatural description, however, common insects that lack 'a pair of legs to jump with' can be described as a deviation from those (locusts) equipped with 'four feet' and 'a pair of legs to jump with'. At the same time, locusts can be positively described as the central category.

Regarding this centralisation of locusts, it is opportune to recall that locusts are hardy wild insects used as food by pastoral nomadic people in the arid zone. Moreover, in the Old Testament, locusts were often mentioned as Yahweh's collaborators to save the Israelites on the occasion of their Exodus from the Pharaoh's captivity. Locusts were dispatched by Yahweh in order to damage the crop fields under the Pharaoh. In short, locusts were at the same time not only collaborators of the saviour of the Israelites, but also hardy wild insects consumed by the Israelites wandering in semi-arid areas. Now, as to the reason why such an unnatural mode of description was adopted, we may suppose that it was in order to define the Israelites as consumers of clean insects.

To sum up: from the unnatural mode of description of winged insects and the incoherent arrangements of prescriptive statements on beasts, we can decipher a covert motivation in God's prescriptive pronouncements on the edibility of animals: to make the Israelites recognise that they were privileged people eating only clean animals distinguishing them from the other peoples around them. In this respect, it is opportune to remember that Moses, who was the conveyer of Yahweh's orders, repeatedly admonished the Israelites not to be contaminated by the pagan customs of the neighbouring and dominant civilised peoples. If the prescriptive dietary regulations of Yahweh in Leviticus that matched the Israelites' food habits were addressed to the Israelites and implicitly suggested that those who observed such regulations could be holy, what perlocutionary message might Israelite readers have received from the dietary utterances? Being given a privileged status as consumers of clean animals and being confirmed as exclusively qualified to become holy, they might have been urged to strictly observe the dietary regulations congruent with their food habits and not submitting to the customs of the dominant pagan people.

Testament writers' intentions as reporters of Yahweh's decrees

We know that the narratives in Pentateuch are the products of writers who edited several transmitted versions with their more or less conscious intentions. What we must now identify is what these intentions were when they edited the pronouncements of their transcendent God, Yahweh, on dietary principles.

Now, let us remember that Yahweh announced three different dietary principles at historically different stages.

In the Eden stage, He gave seed-bearing plants and fruit trees as man's food after the message 'man is gifted with the qualification of governing animals because of his similitude to God'. Here man is described as a collector of plants and observer of vegetarian principles.

However, that stage ends after the expulsion from Eden when human beings were forced to toil to cultivate lands and wander through wastelands with their sheep and goats, as narrated in the story of Cain and Abel. Cain's murder of Abel triggered bloodshed on earth and the following flood narrative is told as a punishment by Yahweh cursing the wickedness of the human beings who carried out bloodshed. After the landing of Noah, Yahweh's changed mind on dietary principles is narrated. He dissolves His curse as a concession with resignation in the face of the original wickedness of human nature and approves eating the flesh of all kinds of animals with the reservation of refraining from eating blood that signifies the life of animals. However, as far as the dissolution of the curse and the tolerance of consuming flesh is conceded, surrendering in the face of the fundamental wickedness of man, His conviction as to the guilt of man remained unchanged. Even though man was allowed to freely eat the flesh of all kinds of animals, he must not have been free from his guilty conscience and therefore felt indebtedness to God. The tolerance of eating flesh had a perlocutional force for man to faithfully observe God's order not to eat flesh with blood. The pronouncements of Yahweh on dietary principles at the Eden and Noah stages were addressed to all human beings in general, including both the Israelites and the neighbouring peoples. On the contrary, Yahweh's final utterances on dietary regulations in Leviticus were addressed exclusively to the Israelites. When I tried to decipher what kind of message these last pronouncements intended to convey, I stated that the preceding narratives were arranged as if they must be referred to as anaphoric stories leading to the final utterances.

Now, by presupposing the results of the meaning of Yahweh's final pronouncements, I think that it is opportune to cite the narratives of the following episodes that the Testament writers arranged before these final statements.

Pentateuch is an ethnic history of the Israelites as descendants of Abraham, as well as historical descriptions of a process of differentiating human beings into several linguistic and ethnic groups. In the narration of their history, the writers insert the following episodes specifically regarding the Israelites.

The first episode (1) is narrated when the Israelites visited Yosef who was serving under the Pharaoh:

> After washing his face he returned and, controlling himself, gave the order; 'Serve the meal'. He was served separately; so were they, and so were the Egyptians who were in his household, for the Egyptians could not take food with the Hebrews; the Egyptians have a horror of doing so. (Genesis 43:31–32)

Then, a little further, we can find the following episode (2) in which Yosef clearly defined his group's profession as 'shepherds':

> Israel said to Yosef, 'Now I can die, now that I have seen you in person and seen you still alive'. Then Yosef said to his brother and his father's family, 'I shall go back and break the news to the Pharaoh. I shall tell him, "My brother and my father's family who were in Cannan have come to me. The men are shepherds and look after livestock, and they have brought their flocks and cattle and all their possessions." Thus, when the Pharaoh summons you and asks, "What is your occupation?", you are to say, "Ever since our boyhood your servants have looked after livestock, we and our fathers before us", so that you can stay in the Goshen region—for the Egyptians have a horror of all shepherds'. (Genesis 46:30–34)

The common theme shared by both episodes is discrimination of the dominant Egyptians towards the Israelites either regarding their occupation as shepherds or their relative food habits. However, it is narrated as the self-consciousness of the Israelites thus discriminated, and it is reported without flinching that they expressed their resolution to maintain their occupation and food habits as a basis of their self-identity. Such a resolute attitude towards discrimination was also expressed in the context of their ritual observance:

> The Pharaoh then summoned Moses and Aaron and said, 'Go and sacrifice to your God, inside the country'. 'That would never do', Moses said, 'since what we sacrifice to Yahweh our God is outrageous to the Egyptians. If the Egyptians see us offering sacrifices which outrage them, won't they stone us? We shall make a three day journey into the desert to sacrifice to Yahweh our God, as he has ordered us'. (Exodus 8:21-24)

From these narratives on the discrimination towards their occupation, food habits and sacrificial rituals, Israelite readers would be able to recognise that they were faced with a serious identity crisis and could understand the necessity of Exodus to be freed from the subordination of the Pharaoh's rule. At the same time they would be reminded that they were the descendants of the shepherds who lived only on sheep, goats and cattle.

In Leviticus, after long prescriptions on redemptive sacrificial rituals, they would read Yahweh's utterances on dietary regulations that implicitly suggested that the Israelites ate only clean animals, while the neighbouring dominant people in the civilised city centres and other nomads were consumers of unclean animals.

Given the preceding episodes which narrate the Egyptians' discrimination towards the Israelites because of their food habits and occupation, it is clear that in Yahweh's utterances on clean/unclean animal foods the readers could find a message reversing the discriminating criteria of the Egyptians towards the Israelites.

Of course, in the final part of the Noah stage it was narrated that Yahweh gave a concession to eat the flesh of all animals with His resignation in the face of the fundamental wickedness of human beings and ordered man to observe specific redemptive ritual acts. As far as the concession for eating flesh and the prescription for redemption are addressed to man in general, the Israelites, too, were without exception judged sinful and had to feel indebted to Yahweh's tolerance of the consumption of meat. After such preceding narratives, Israelite readers came to read the message that restricts the range of clean animals from all kinds of animals totally tolerated until that time and implicitly suggests that 'you are the people who eat only clean animals differently from other neighbouring peoples'. Being a distinction between clean and unclean animals narrated with reference to morphological and behavioural features, it gives an impression of presenting objective facts. The Israelite readers, being reminded that they were descendants of shepherds who kept and consumed only clean animals, thus defined, can recognise themselves as a uniquely chosen people qualified to become holy. What kind of impression might the Israelites have had on hearing such a message?

Here is an instance taken from our present situation; in a classroom, a teacher in a despising tone tells his students that they are the young generation who basically do not make an effort and deserve to repeat a year of school. Then, following this general proposition, he adds the following statement looking at a student who gets up very early in the morning: 'However, there is an exception. Those who have the habit of getting up early (7 o'clock) in the morning are diligent students, and will pass the exams'. This criteria is not sufficient to judge whether the student actually makes an effort to learn and there may be other students who make an effort, even if they do not get up early. But the student who has been selected as an example will feel chosen and appreciated by his superior and worthy of receiving rewards: he will probably be encouraged to work more diligently.

We can describe such teacher's talk as an 'utterance of temptation' according to Felman (1980). The tempted one will be lured and induced by sweet narcissism provoked by the tempter. A similar situation happens to the Israelites in front of Yahweh's words. Of course, common ordinary narcissism sooner or later bumps into reality and people realise that 'after all it was but a dream'. Instead, here, the message of temptation is given as the absolute and undoubtable words of God, so that the Israelite readers will continue to maintain their narcissism with conviction.

Incidentally, in Leviticus, preceding the narratives on dietary regulations, one finds very long prescriptions on the ritualistic rules of various sacrifices for the expiation of sins, as it is prescribed that sacrifiers be clean. Yahweh's pronouncements on dietary regulations can at first be regarded as prescriptions to obtain purity for the sacrifier. After confirming this, let me examine again the last part of the pronouncements: Levit. 11:44–45, 'For it is I, Yahweh, who is your God. You have been sanctified and have become holy because I am holy: do not defile yourselves with all these creatures that swarm on the ground. (2)Yes, it is I, Yahweh, who brought you out of Egypt to be your God: you must therefore be holy because I am holy'. It is not only said that those who observe the dietary regulations will be holy, but also that 'I' guided 'you' (Israelites) to get rid of the Pharaoh's terrestrial rule in order for 'Me' to be 'your' God. Yahweh's dietary regulations are uttered not only as prescriptions in order that sacrificers obtain a clean status, but also as those that will mark their belongingness to their God, Yahweh, and signify distance from the Pharaoh.

There is no need to say that the Testament writers as reporters of Yahweh's pronouncements are the descendants of the Israelites who received Yahweh's messages on successive dietary principles and who belonged to the professional group who executed sacrificial rituals according to the transcendent prescriptions of God. In editing the transmitted narratives, such reporters narrated not only the story of Yahweh's concession to eat all kinds of animals as His resignation to man's basic wickedness, implanting a self-consciousness of original guilt in the readers' minds, but also narrated the story of His last words on dietary regulations with a special mode of utterance in order for the Israelites to recognise themselves as the consumers of clean animals, following the episodes of the neighbouring peoples' discrimination towards their occupation and food habits. It is evident that in reporting such stories the writers intended to urge the Israelites to maintain their original food habits as a sign of self-identity without submitting to the beliefs and cultural habits of the dominant neighbouring peoples and to faithfully carry out the rituals as Yahweh and the Priestley group greatly desired in order to maintain their belief of being unblemished chosen people and their belonging to Yahweh, their saviour.

However, after my analysis of Yahweh's pronouncements on dietary regulations, I have reached the conclusion that they are expressed in special modes so that they can implicitly provoke consciousness of a privileged status in the Israelites' minds, even though these regulations are presented as a set of objective statements deduced from each animal's morphological and behavioural features. It is important that the affirmation of 'chosen people' is not given by a one-sided direct affirmation by God, but as an implicit message for the Israelites to make them recognise it by themselves as an objective truth, being driven to it by specially arranged modes of utterance. The Israelites who would read such messages, together with the memories of discrimination deriving from their occupation and food habits, might be motivated to maintain their food habits by their own initiative in order to be clean and holy. While remembering the preceding narrative on Yahweh's concession with resignation because of man's fundamental wickedness, they might be induced to observe the expiatory sacrificial rituals with a sense of indebtedness and deference to God.

Conclusion

It is true that the dietary regulations of various ethnic groups have been explained by cultural anthropologists according to the principle of exclusion of deviated or ambiguous members with reference to their cognitive classificatory system. However, the dietary prescriptions in Leviticus which distinguish between clean/edible and unclean/inedible animals is not a case where the above explanatory principle can be applied.

The general exclusion of carnivorous animals as unclean, as found in the prescriptions, may depend on the negative evaluation of blood-shedding expressed in the last part of the Noah stage as a deviation from the vegetarian principle in the ideal stage of Eden. Eating flesh without accounting for blood is judged as usurpation of life and a violation of God's order to observe expiatory rituals. The reason why carnivorous animals are defined as unclean can also be explained by the principle prescribed in the last part of the Noah stage.

Conversely, all the domesticated food animals dealt with in the dietary regulations are herbivorous ungulates. Nevertheless, only Ovidae and Bovidae are defined as clean, while Suidae and Camelidae are judged as unclean. Even though the latter negative categories apparently seem to be deviations from the former centralised positive categories by a clever arrangement of propositional statements, there is no persuasive background for the centralisation of the former categories as clean. It is but a one-sided arbitrary affirmation. From the analysis of the modes of expression we could eventually decipher that the exclusion of the latter as unclean derived from the underlying motivation to define the food habits of the neighbouring peoples in the dominant city-states and other nomadic people in the desert as consumers of unclean food. The differentiation of food habits between these peoples basically derived from their respective environmental conditions. Availing of such differences as actual facts, Yahweh's pronouncements in the dietary regulations of Leviticus succeed in giving the message to the Israelites to be consumers of clean animals, thus assuring them to be a privileged chosen people. The Testament writers, too, reported these words with the intention that the Israelite readers elicit self-confidence for their recovery from an identity crisis. The exclusion of Suidae and Camelidae as unclean in the dietary regulations of Leviticus was not the product of an exclusion principle of cognitive deviations, but rather an objective to be realised by the pronouncements as performative speech acts and the product of identity management by making use of the differences in food habits between the neighbouring peoples and themselves.

Notes

Chapter 4

1 I observed this in 1971. According to a Carpathian shepherd, if they keep a newborn far from its mother, the memory of the relationship with her will disappear within ten days after separation (from my field data of 1980).

Chapter 5

1 The so-called 'post-lactation slaughtering peak' used to demonstrate Neolithic dairying is based on the high level of culling six to twelve month old calves in the harvest profile. Vigne and Helmer suppose that traditional cattle herders who wished to exploit milk kept a large quantity of calves until weaning, who at least partly shared the milk from their mothers. But the fact that traditional herders to a large extent culled male calves of six to nine months old after weaning does not imply the existence of milk exploitation. As far as this occurred, the slaughtering peak of these ages is demonstrated in the harvest profile without evidence of milk exploitation.
2 Report presented at a symposium, 'Kachikuka to Chichi Riyou' (Domestication process and milk utilisation), held on May 16–17, 2015 at Kyoto University, organised by M. Hirata.

Chapter 6

1 'Bakharwal' literally means 'goat herder' and 'Gujar Bakharwal' is a local group that professionally engages in herding activities in northwestern India.

Chapter 8

1 All translations cited below are from the text of the New Revised Standard translation of the Israel Bible.
2 In segment A-1 where ungulate animals are mainly dealt with according to two distinct features, 'cloven hoofed' and 'ruminant', not-ungulate mammals, hyrax and hare are discussed as 'not cloven hoofed' but 'ruminant' animals. Scientifically speaking, they are not 'ruminant' and belong to the category of beasts defined in Leviticus as 'walk on the flat of their feet'. Nevertheless, why are they described as 'ruminant'? To this question, commentators on the Old Testament suppose that the reason is that the writers believed them to be ruminant, noting that they make a mumbling noise when they eat grass.

Bibliography

Amiet, P., 1980. *La Glyptique Mésopotamienne Archaïque*. Paris: CNRS.

Amoroso, E.C. and P.A. Jewell, 1963. The exploitation of the milk-ejection reflex by primitive peoples. In A.E. Mourant and F.E. Zeuner (eds), *Man and Cattle*. Occasional Paper No.18. London: Royal Anthropological Institute, 126-137.

Austin, J.L., 1979. *How to Do Things with Words*. Oxford: Clarendon Press.

Baroin, C., 1975. Techniques d'adoption en milieu animal (Daza du Niger). *L'Homme et L'Animal*, premier colloque d'ethnozoologie. Paris: Institute Internationale d'Ethnoscience, 493-495.

Bar-Yosef, O. and A. Belfer-Cohen, 1989. The origins of sedentism and farming communities in the Levant. *Journal of World Prehistory*, 3(4): 447-498.

Bar-Yosef, O. and N. Goren, 1973. Natufian remains in Hayonim Cave. *Paléorient*, 1(1): 49-68.

Bar-Yosef, O. and A. Khazanov (eds), 1992. *Pastoralism in the Levant: Archaeological Materials in Anthropological Perspective* (Introduction). Monographs in World Archaeology, No.10. Madison: Prehistory Press.

Bar-Yosef, O. and F.R. Valla (eds), 1991. *The Natufian Culture in the Levant*. Ann Arbor: International Monographs in Prehistory.

Baskin, L.M., 1974. Management of ungulate herds in relation to domestication. In V. Geist and F. Walther (eds), *The Behaviour of Ungulates and Its Relation to Management*. Morges: International Union for Conservation of Nature and Natural Resources, 24(2): 530-541.

Beck, L., 1980. Herd owners and hired shepherds: The Qashqa'i of Iran. *Ethnology*, 19(3): 327-351.

Beck, L., 1991. *Nomad: A Year in the Life of a Qashqa'i Tribesman in Iran*. Berkeley: University of California Press.

Benveniste, É., 1966. *Le Vocabulaires des Institutions Indo-Européennes*, Vol.1. Paris: Les Éditions de Minuit.

Bernot, L., 1988. Buveurs et non-buveurs de lait. *L'Homme*, 28(108): 99-107.

Bernus, E., 1981. *Touaregs Nigériens. Unité Culturelle et Diversité Régionale d'un Peuple Pasteur*. Paris: Orstom.

Blaxter, K.L., N.B. Kay, G.A.M. Sharman, J.M.M. Cunningham and W.J. Hamilton, 1974. *Farming the Red Deer*. Edinburgh: Department of Agriculture and Fisheries for Scotland.

Boessneck, J. and A. von den Driesch, 1978. The significance of measuring animal bones from archaeological sites. In R.H. Meadow and M.A. Zeder (eds), *Approaches to Faunal Analysis in the Middle East*. Cambridge, Mass: Peabody Museum Bulletin, 2: 25–39.

Bökönyi, S.H., 1969. Archaeological problems and methods of recognizing animal domestication. In P.J. Ucko and G.W. Dimbleby (eds), *The Domestication and Exploitation of Plants and Animals*. London: Duckworth, 219–229.

Bökönyi, S.H., 1976. Development of early stock rearing in the Near East. *Nature*, 264: 19–23.

Bökönyi, S.H., 1978. Environmental and cultural differences as reflected in the animal bone samples from five early Neolithic sites in Southwest Asia. In R.H. Meadow and M.A. Zeder (eds), *Approaches to Faunal Analysis in the Middle East*. Cambridge, Mass: Peabody Museum Bulletin, 2: 57–62.

Bökönyi, S.H., 1989. Definitions of animal domestication. In J. Clutton-Brock (ed.), *The Walking Larder: Patterns of Domestication, Pastoralism, and Predation*. London: Unwin Hyman, 22–27.

Bonnemaire, J. and J.M. Teissier, 1976. Quelque aspects de l'élevage en haute altitude dans l'Himalaya Central: Yaks, bovins, hybrides et métis dans la vallée du Langtang (Nepal). *Le Yak*, Paris: Société Ethnozootechnie, 15: 91–118.

Briant, P., 1979. L'élevage ovin dans l'Empire Archéménide –VIe –IVe siècles avant notre ère. *Journal of the Economic and Social History of the Orient*, 22(2): 136–161.

Briant, P., 1982. *État et pasteurs au Moyen-Orient Ancien*. Paris: Édition de la Maison des Sciences de l'Homme.

Bulmer, R., 1989. The uncleanness of the birds in Leviticus and Deuteronomy. *Man*, 24(2): 304–321.

Bynon, J., 1976. Domestic animal calling in a Berber tribe. In W.C. McCormack and S A. Wurm (eds), *Language and Man*. Chicago: International Congress of Anthropology and Ethnological Science, 39–65.

Campbell, J.K., 1984. *Honour, Family and Patronage: A Study of Institutions and Moral Values in a Greek Mountain Community*. Oxford: Oxford University Press.

Casimir, M.J., 1982. The biological phenomenon of imprinting: Its handling and manipulation by traditional pastoralists. *Production Pastorale et Société*, 11: 23–27.

Clutton-Brock, J., 1978a. Bones for the zoologist. In R.H. Meadow and M.A. Zeder (eds), *Approaches to Faunal Analysis in the Middle East.* Cambridge, Mass: Peabody Museum Bulletin, 2: 49–51.

Clutton-Brock, J., 1978b. Early domestication and the ungulate fauna of the Levant during the Pre-Pottery Neolithic Period. In W.C. Brice (ed.), *The Environmental History of the Near and Middle East since the Last Ice Age.* Cambridge, Mass: Academic Press, 29–40.

Clutton-Brock, J., 1987. *A Natural History of Domesticated Mammals.* Cambridge: Cambridge University Press.

Clutton-Brock, J., 1989. Introduction to pastoralism. In J. Clutton-Brock (ed.), *The Walking Larder: Patterns of Domestication, Pastoralism, and Predation.* London: Unwin Hyman, 116–118.

Cope, C., 1991. Gazelle hunting strategies in the Southern Levant. In O. Bar-Yosef and F.R. Valla (eds), *The Natufian Culture in the Levant.* Ann-Arbor: International Monographs in Prehistory, 341–358.

Crabtree, P.J., D.V. Campana, A. Belfer-Cohen and D.E. Bar-Yosef, 1991. First results of the excavations at Salibiya I, Lower Jordan Vally. In O. Bar-Yosef and F.R. Valla (eds), *The Natufian Culture in the Levant.* Ann-Arbor: International Monographs in Prehistory, 161–172.

Craig, J.V., 1981. *Domestic Animal Behavior: Causes and Implications for Animal Care and Management.* Englewood Cliffs: Prentice-Hall.

Davis, S.J.M. and D.O. Henry, 1974. The 1974 excavations of Hayonim Terrace (Israel): A brief report. *Paléorient,* 2(1): 195–197.

Davis, S.J.M., 1982. Climatic change and the advent of domestication: The succession of ruminant Artiodactyls in the late Pleistocene-Holocene in the Israel Region. *Paléorient,* 8(2): 5–15.

Davis, S.J.M., 1983. The age profiles of gazelles predated by ancient man in Israel: Possible evidence for a shift from seasonality to sedentism in the Natufian. *Paléorient,* 9(1): 55–62.

Davis, S.J.M., 1984. The advent of milk and wool production in western Iran: Some speculation. In J. Clutton-Brock and C. Grigson (eds), *Animals and Archaeology, vol. 3, Early Herders and their Flocks.* Oxford: British Archaeological Reports International Series, 202: 265–278.

Davis, S.J.M., 1987. *The Archaeology of Animals.* New Haven: Yale University Press.

Davis, S.J.M., 1993. The zoo-archaeology of sheep and goat in Mesopotamia. *Bulletin on Sumerian Agriculture,* 7(1): 1–7.

Delamarre, M.J.B., 1975. *Techniques de Production: l'Élevage.* Paris: Édition de Musée Nationaux.

Diakonoff, I., 1972. Socio-economic classes in Babylonia and the Babylonian concept of social stratification. In D. Edzard (ed.), *Gesellschaft im Alten Zweistromland und in den angrenzenden Gebiete*. München: Verlag der Bayerischen Akademie der Wissenschafte, 41–52.

Diakonoff, I., 1974. Slaves, helots, and serfs in early Antiquity. *Acta Antiqua*, 22: 45–78.

Digard, J.P., 1973. A propos des aspectes économique de la symbiose nomades sédentaires dans la Mésopotamie Ancienne: le point de vue d'un anthropologue sur Moyen-Orient Ancien. *XXe Congrès Intern. D' Sciences Humaines en Asie Afrique du Nord*, Mexico.

Digard, J.P., 1981. *Techniques de Nomades Baxtyâri d'Iran*. Cambridge: Cambridge University Press.

Digard, J.P., 1990. *L'Homme et les Animaux Domestiques*. Paris: Fayard.

Dor, R., 1982. Une recherche en cours: Les huchements du berger turc. *Production Pastorale et Société*, 11: 13–21.

Dor, R., 1985. Les huchements du berger turc. I: Interpellatifs adressés aux animaux de la cour et de la demeure. *Journal Asiatique*, 273(3–4): 371–424.

Douglas, M., 1957. Animals in Lele religious symbolism. *Africa*, 27(1): 46–58.

Douglas, M., 1966. The abomination of Leviticus. In M. Douglas, *Purity and Danger: An Analysis of Concepts of Pollution and Taboo*. London: Routledge and Kegan Paul, 1–57.

Douglas, M., 1975. Deciphering a meal. In M. Douglas, *Implicit Meanings*. London: Routledge and Kegan Paul, 249–275.

Douglas, M., 1999. *Leviticus as Literature*. Oxford: Oxford University Press.

Driver, G.R., 1955. Birds in the Old Testament. *Palestine Exploration Quarterly*, 87: 5–20.

Ducos, P., 1978. 'Domestication' defined and methodological approaches to its recognition in faunal assemblages. In R.H. Meadow and M.A. Zeder (eds), *Approaches to Faunal Analysis in the Middle East*. Cambridge, Mass: Peabody Museum Bulletin, 2: 53–56.

Durand, J.M. and D. Charpin, 1980. Remarques sur l'élevage intensif en Iraq ancien. In M.T. Barrelet (ed.), *L'archéologie de l'Iraq*. Paris: CNRS, 131–153.

Echallier, J.C. and F. Braemer, 1995. Nature et fonctions des 'desert kites': Données et hypothèses nouvelles. *Paléorient*, 21(1): 35–63.

Engels, F., 1884. *L'Origine de la Famille, de la Propriété Privée et de L'État*. Paris: Édition Sociale.

Evershed, R.P. et al., 2008. Earliest date for milk use in the Near East and Southeastern Europe linked to cattle herding. *Nature*, 455: 528–531.
Felman, S., 1980. *Le Scandale du Corps Parlant*. Paris: Seuil.
Fijn, N., 2011. *Living with Herds: Human-Animal Coexistence in Mongolia*. Cambridge: Cambridge University Press.
Finkelstein, J.J., 1968. An old Babylonian herding contract and Genesis 31:38f. *Journal of the American Oriental Society*, 88(1): 30–36.
Follansbee, E., 1939. The story of the flood in the light of comparative Semitic mythology. *Religions*, 29: 11–21.
Foucault, M., 1980. Du gouvernement des vivants. *Annuaire du Collège de France, 80 année, Histoire des systèmes de pensée, année 1979-1980*, 449–452.
Foucault, M., 1981. Omnes et singulatim: Towards a criticism of political reason. In S. McMurrin (ed.), *The Tanner Lectures on Human Values, t. II*, Salt Lake City: University of Utah Press, 223–254.
Foucault, M., 1982. The subject and power. In H. Dreyfus and P. Rabinow (eds), *Michel Foucault: Beyond Structuralism and Hermeneutics*. Chicago: The University of Chicago Press, 208–226.
Frymer-Kensky, T., 1977. The Atrahasis epic and its significance for our understanding of Genesis 1–9. *Biblical Archaeologist*, 40: 147–155.
Fujii, S., 2001. *Mughi to Hitsuji no Kokogaku* (Archaeology of wheat and sheep). Tokyo: Doseisha.
Fujii, S., 2013. Chronology of the Jafr prehistory and protohistory: A key to the process of pastoral nomadization in the southern Levant. *Syria*, 90: 49–125.
Fujii, S., 2015. Sedentary, transhumant and nomadic pastoralism: From the archaeological survey in Jordan. Reported at a symposium *Kachikuka to Chichi Riyou* (Domestication process and milk utilization), held on 16–17 May, 2015 at Kyoto, organised by M. Hirata.
Geist, V., 1971. *Mountain Sheep: A Study in Behaviour and Evolution*. Chicago: University of Chicago Press.
Geist, V., and F. Walther (eds) 1974. *The Behaviour of Ungulates and its Relation to Management*. Morges: International Union for Conservation of Nature and Natural Resources.
Gelb, I., 1973. Prisoners of war in early Mesopotamia. *Journal of Near Eastern Studies*, 32: 70–98.
Gilead, I., 1992. Farmers and herders in southern Israel during the Chalcolithic period. In O. Bar Yosef and A.M. Khazanov (eds), *Pastoralism in the*

Levant: Archaeological Materials in Anthropological Perspectives. Madison: Prehistory Press, 29–42.

Glatzer, B., 1977. *Nomaden von Gharjistān*. Wiesbaden: Steiner Verlag.

Grayson, A.K., 1995. Eunuchs in power: Their role in the Assyrian bureaucracy. In M. Dietrich and O. Loretz (eds), *Vom Alten Orient zum Alten Testament*. Kevelaer/Vulyn: Butzon und Bercker/Neukirchener, 85–98.

Greenfield, H.J., 1988. The origins of milk and wool production in the old world: A zooarchaeological perspective from the central Balkans. *Current Anthropology*, 29(4): 573–593.

Grice, H.P., 1975. Logic and conversation. In P. Cole and J. Morgan (eds), *Syntax and Semantics*. New York: Academic Press, 41–58.

Harding, G.L., 1953. The Cairn of Hani. *Annual of the Department of Antiquities of Jordan*, 2: 8–56.

Habel, N.C., 1988. The two flood stories in Genesis. In A. Dundes (ed.), *The Flood Myth*. Berkeley: University of California Press, 13–28.

Hahn, E., 1896[2016]. *Die Haustiere und ihre Beziehungen zur Wirtschaft des Menschen, eine Geographische Studie*. Leipzig: Drucker and Humbolt.

Hämmerly-Dupuy, D., 1968. Some observations on the Assyro-Babylonian and Sumerian flood stories. *Andrews University Seminary Studies*, 6(1): 1–18.

Hasdeu, B.P., 1976. *Etymologicum Magnum Romaniae*. București: Editura Minerva.

Hatt, G., 1919. Notes on reindeer nomadism. *Memoirs of the American Anthropological Association*, 6(2): 75–133.

Haudricourt, A.G., 1969. Domestication of animals, cultivation of plants and human relations. *Social Science Information*, 8(3): 163–72.

Haudricourt, A.G., 1977. Notes d'ethnozoologie: Le rôle des excrétats dans la domestication. *L'Homme*, 17(2–3): 125–126.

Haudricourt, A.G., 1978. Ecologie et agriculture Asiatiques. *La Pensée*, 198: 131–132.

Helmer, D., 1989. Le développement de la domestication au Proche-Orient de 9500 à 7500 BP. *Paléorient*, 15(1): 111–121.

Helmer, D., 1991. Étude de la faune de la phase Ia (Natoufien final) de Tell Mureybet (Syrie), fouilles Cauvin. In O. Bar-Yosef and F.R. Valla (eds), *The Natufian Culture in the Levant*. Ann-Arbor: International Monographs in Prehistory, 359–370.

Helms, S. and A. Betts, 1987. The desert 'kites' of the Badiyat Esh-Sham and North Arabia. *Paléorient*, 13(1): 41–67.

Henckel, A. and A. Schöne, 1967. *Emblemata: Handbuch zur Sinnbildkunst des XVI. und XVII. Jahrhunderts*. Stüttgart: J.B. Metzler.

Hesse, B., 1995. Animal husbandry and human diet in the Ancient Near East. In J.M. Sasson (ed.), *Civilizations of the Ancient Near East*, Vol. I. New York: Scribner, 203–222.

Hole, F., et al., 1969. *Prehistory and Human Ecology of the Deh Luran Plain: An Early Village Sequence from Khuzistan, Iran*. Memoirs of the Museum of Anthropology, University of Michigan, 1. Ann Arbor: University of Michigan Press, 262–331.

Hole, F., 1989. A two-part, two stage model of domestication. In J. Clutton-Brock (ed.), *The Walking Larder: Patterns of Domestication, Pastoralism, and Predation*. London: Unwin Hyman, 97–104.

Hongo, H., J. Pearson, B. Öksüz and G. Ilgezdi, 2009. The process of ungulate domestication at Çayönü, Southeastern Turkey: A multidisciplinary approach focusing on *Bos* sp. and *Cervus elaphus*. *Anthropozoologica*, 44(1): 63–78.

Hunn, E., 1979. The abominations of Leviticus revisited. In R.F. Ellen and D. Reason (eds), *Classifications in their Social Context*. London: Academic Press: 103–116.

Imanishi, K., 1995[1948]. *Bokuchiku Ron Sonohoka* (On nomads and others). Revised edition, Akitashoten. Tokyo: Heibonsha Library.

Inamura, T., 1995. *Ryama to Arupaka—Andesu no Senjyumin Shakai to Bokuchiku Bunka* (Llama and Alpaca: Society of the Andean Aborigines and their pastoral culture). Tokyo: Kadensha.

Ingold, T., 1986. *The Appropriation of Nature: Essays on Human Ecology and Social Relations*. Manchester: Manchester University Press.

Ingold, T., 1994. From trust to domination: An alternative history of human-animal relations. In A. Manning and J. Serpell (eds), *Animals and Human Society: Changing Perspectives*. London: Routledge, 1–22.

Ingold, T., 2000. *The Perception of the Environment: Essays on Livelihood, Dwelling and Skill*. London: Routledge.

Ishighe, N., 1970. Koushi no Kuchikase to Rakuda no Burajaa (Mouthcuff to calf and bra for camel). *Kikan Jinruigaku* (Anthropological quarterly), 1-2: 102–108.

Ishighe, N., 1973. Dentouteki shokujibunka no sekaiteki bunpu (World distribution of traditional food cultures). In N. Ishighe (ed.), *Sekai no Shokuji Bunka* (Food cultures in the world). Tokyo: Domesu Shuppan.

Jarrige, J.F. and R.H. Meadow, 1980. The antecedents of civilization in the Indus valley. *Scientific American*, 243(2): 122–133.

Jewell, P.A., C. Milner and J.M. Boyd (eds), 1974. *Island Survivors: The Ecology of the Soay Sheep of St. Kilda*. London: Athlone Press.

Khazanov, A.M., 1984. *Nomads and the Outside World*, (translated by J. Crookenden). Cambridge: Cambridge University Press.

Killen, J.T., 1964. The wool industry of Crete in the late Bronze Age. *Annual of the British School at Athens*, 59: 1–15.

Kirkbride, D., 1966. Five seasons at the Pre-Pottery Neolithic village of Beidha in Jordan. *Palestine Exploration Quarterly*, 98(1): 8–72.

Kirkbride, D., 1975. Umm Dabaghiyah 1974: A fourth preliminary report. *Iraq*, 37: 3–10.

Kohler-Rollefson, I., 1989. Changes in goat exploitation at 'Ain Ghazal between the Early and Late Neolithic: A metrical analysis. *Paléorient*, 15: 141–146.

Konagaya, Y., 1983. Mongoru niokeru kachiku henoyobikake (Vocal calling of Mongolian shepherds towards domesticated animals). In Department of Geography of Kyoto University (ed.), *Kukan, Keikan, Imeiji* (Space, landscape and image). Kyoto: ChijinShobou, 197–205.

Konagaya, Y., 1989. Sogen ni ikiru Onnatachi (Women living in Steppe). *Kikan Minzokugaku* (Ethnological quarterly 50), Senri: National Ethnological Museum: 6–25.

Konagaya, Y., 1991. *Mongoru no Haru* (Spring in Mongolia). Tokyo: Kawadeshobo Shinsha.

Konagaya, Y., 1996. *Mongoru Sogen no Seikatsu Sekai* (Livelihood in the Mongolian Steppe). Tokyo: Asahi Shinbunsha.

Kuzuno, H., 1990. *Tonakai no Shakaishi* (Society of reindeer herders). Tokyo: Kawai Shuppan.

Lakoff, G. and M. Johnson, 1980. *Metaphors We Live By*. Chicago: University of Chicago Press.

Leach, E., 1969. *Genesis as Myth and other Essays*. London: Jonathan Cape.

Lechevallier, M., 1978. *Abou Gosh et Beisamoun: Deux gisements de VIIe millénaire avant l'ère chrétienne en Israël*. Paris: Association Paléorient.

Ledda, G., 1975. *Padre Padrone: L'Educazione di un Pastore*. Milano: Feltrinelli.

Legge, A.J. and P.A. Rowley-Conwy, 1987. Gazelle killing in Stone Age Syria. *Scientific American*, 255: 88–95.

Lent, P.C., 1974. Mother-infant relationships in ungulates. In V. Geist and F. Walther (eds), *The Behaviour of Ungulates and its Relation to Management*. Morges: International Union for Conservation of Nature and Natural Resources, 24(1): 14–55.

Leroi-Gourhan, A., 1964–1965. *Le Gestes et la Parole*, Vols. 1–2. Paris: Albin Michel.
Lot-Falk, E., 1953. *Les Rites de Chasse chez les Peuples Sibériens*. Paris: Gallimard.
MacEwan, G.J.P., 1983. Distribution of meat in Eanna. *Iraq*, 45(2): 187–198.
Maekawa, K., 1979. Animal and human castration in Sumer, I. Research Institute for Humanistic Studies, Kyoto University, *Zinbun*, 15: 95–140.
Maekawa, K., 1980. Animal and human castration in Sumer, II. Research Institute for Humanistic Studies, Kyoto University, *Zinbun*, 17: 1–56.
Maekawa, K., 1982. Animal and human castration in Sumer, III. Research Institute for Humanistic Studies, Kyoto University, *Zinbun* 18: 95–122.
Maekawa, K., 1983. The management of fatted sheep (*udu-niga*) in Ur III Girsu/Lagash. *Acta Sumerologica*, 5: 81–111.
Maekawa, K., 1994. The management of fatted sheep (udu-niga) in Ur III Girsu/Lagash. Supplement 2 (BM 87494). *Acta Sumerologica*, 16: 165–176.
Marmon, S., 1995. *Eunuchs and Sacred Boundaries in Islamic Society*. Oxford: Oxford University Press.
Matsubara, M., 1983. *Yuboku no Sekai-Torukokei Yubokumin Yurukku no Minzokushi kara*, vol. 1–2 (World of nomadism: View from the ethnography of Turkish Nomad Yöluk). Tokyo: Chuokoronsha.
Matsubara, M., 1988. *Seizou Kiko-Yousuko Genryu wo yuku* (Travel in the Tibetan Area: Around the headwaters of the Yangtze River). Tokyo: Chuokoronsha.
Matsui, T., 1980. *Pashutun Yubokumin no Bokuchiku Seikatsu—Hokutou Afuganisutan niokeru Duranikei Pashutun Zoku Chosa Hokoku* (Pastoral life of the Pashtun Nomads: Survey report on the Durrani Pashtun Tribe in Northeastern Afghanistan). Kyoto Daigaku Jinbun Kagaku Kenkyusho Chosa Hokoku 33 (Survey Report 33), Research Institute for Humanistic Studies, Kyoto University.
Matsui, T., 1989. *Semi Domesutikeshon* (Semi-domestication). Tokyo: Kaimeisha.
Meadow, R.H., 1981. Early animal domestication in South Asia: A first report of the faunal remains from Mehrgarh, Pakistan. In H. Härtel (ed.), *South Asian Archaeology 1979*. Berlin: Dietrich Reimer, 143–179.
Meadow, R.H., 1984. Animal domestication in the Middle East: A view from the eastern margin. In J. Clutton-Brock and C. Grigson (eds), *Animals and Archaeology 3. Early Herders and Their Flocks*. Oxford: British Archaeological Reports, 309–337.
Meadow, R.H., 1989. Osteological evidence for the process of animal domestication.

In J. Clutton-Brock (ed.), *The Walking Larder: Patterns of Domestication, Pastoralism, and Predation*, London: Unwin Hyman, 80–96.

Mitamura, T., 1963. *Kangan* (Eunuchs). Tokyo: Chuokoronsha.

Morgan, L., 1877. *La Société Archaïque*. Paris: Anthropos.

Nakao, S., 1966. *Saibai Shokubutsu to Nokoo no Kighen* (Cultivated plants and the origin of agriculture). Tokyo: Iwanami Shoten.

Nakao, S., 1967. Noko kighen ron (On the origin of agriculture). In S. Morishita and T. Kira (eds), *Shizen—Seitaigakuteki Kenkyu* (Nature: Its ecological studies). Tokyo: Chuoukoronsha, 329–494.

Nakao, S., 1992. *Chichi Bunka no Keifu* (Genealogy of milking cultures). Tokyo: Chuouhouki Shuppan.

Noth, M., 1962. *Exodus: A Commentary*. Kent: SCM Press.

Nozawa, K., 1987. Kachikuka no seibutsugakuteki imi (Biological implications of the domestication of animals). In K. Fukui and Y. Tani (eds), *Bokuchiku Bunka no Genzou-Seitai, Shakai, Rekishi* (Towards an understanding of pastoralist cultures: Ecology, society and history). Tokyo: Nihon Hoso Shuppan Kyokai, 63–107.

Ohta, I., 1982a. Man-animal interaction complex in goat herding of the pastoral Turkana. *African Study Monographs*, Supplementary Issue, Kyoto University, 1: 13–41.

Ohta, I., 1982b. Bokuchikumin niyoru kachiku houboku no seiritsu kikou (How herding is realised: Its emerging mechanism). *Kikan Jinruigaku* (Anthropological quarterly), 13(4): 18–56.

Oppenheim, A.L. and L.F. Hartman, 1945. The domestic animals of ancient Mesopotamia—according to the XIIIth tablet of the series HAR .ra = hubullû. *Journal of Near Eastern Studies*, 4(3): 152–177.

Paine, R., 1994. *Herds of the Tundra: A Portrait of Saami Reindeer Pastoralism*. Washington, DC: Smithsonian Institution Press.

Payne, S., 1975. Faunal change at Franchthi cave from 20,000 B.C. to 3,000 B.C. In A.T. Clason (ed.), *Archaeozoological Studies*. Amsterdam: North Holland Pub.: 120–131.

Peters, J., A. von den Driesch and D. Helmer, 2005. The upper Euphrates-Tigris basin: Cradle of agro-pastoralism. In J.-D. Vigne, J. Peters and D. Helmer (eds), *First Steps of Animal Domestication: New Archaeozoological Approaches*. Oxford: Oxbow Books, 96–123.

Pollock, S., 1999. *Ancient Mesopotamia*. Cambridge: Cambridge University Press.

Riney, T. and G. Caughley, 1959. A study of home range in a feral goat herd. *New Zealand Journal of Science*, 2: 157-170.

Ryder, M.L., 1993. Sheep and goat husbandry with particular reference to textile fibre and milk production. *Bulletin on Sumerian Agriculture*, 7(1): 9-32.

Scrimshaw, N.S. and E.B. Murray, 1988. The acceptability of milk and milk products in populations with high prevalence of lactose intolerance. *The American Journal of Clinical Nutrition*, 48(4): 1142-1159.

Shikano, K., 1984. On the stability of the goat herd in the pastoral Samburu. *African Study Monographs*, Supplementary Issue, Kyoto: Kyoto University Press, 3: 59-69.

Shikano, K., 1991. Ningen to kachiku no kankei karamita bokuchikuron no kokoromi (Tentative treatise on pastoralism viewed from the relationship between man and domesticated animals). In J. Tanaka and M. Kakeya (eds), *Hito no Shizenshi* (Natural history of man). Tokyo: Heibonsha, 233-251.

Simoons, F., 1970. The traditional limits of milking and milk use in Southern Asia. *Anthropos*, 65: 547-593.

Snell, D.C., 1986. The rams of Lagash. *Acta Sumerologica*, 8: 133-217.

Soler, J., 1973. Sémiotique de la nourriture dans la Bible. *Annales. Économies, Sociétés, Civilisations*, 28(4): 943-955.

St. Croix, F.W. de., 1972. *The Fulani of Northern Nigeria*. Farnborough: Gregg International Publishers.

Tani, Y., 1976a. Bokuchiku bunka kou (Treatise on the pastoralist culture). *Zinbun Gakuhou* (Journal of humanities), 42: 1-58.

Tani, Y., 1977. Itaria chuubu sanson iboku hitsuji no kanri nitsuite—Omoni Abruttsuo Cherukueto mura chosayori (On the management techniques of transhumant shepherds in the mountain villages of Central Italy: Mainly from fieldwork in Cerqueto village in the province of Abruzzo). In Y. Aida and T. Umesao (eds) *Yoroppa no Shakai to Bunka* (Society and culture in Europe), Kyoto: Research Institute for Humanistic Studies, Kyoto University, 117-167.

Tani, Y., 1979. Shusei to bunka no aida—Nansei Yuurasia no hitsujikaiwo tazunete (Between ethology and culture: After visiting shepherds in southwestern Eurasia), *Kikan Minzokugaku* (Ethnological quarterly), 8: 6-23.

Tani, Y., 1980. Man-sheep relationship in the flock management techniques among North Carpathian shepherds. In Y. Tani (ed.), *Preliminary Report of Comparative Studies on the Agrico-Pastoral Peoples in Southwestern Eurasia*. Kyoto: Kyoto University Research Institute for Humanistic Studies, 67-86.

Tani, Y., 1982. Implications of the shepherd's social and communicational interventions in the flock: From field observations among the shepherds in Romania. In Y. Tani (ed.), *Preliminary Report of Comparative Studies on the Agrico-Pastoral Peoples in Southwestern Eurasia*. Kyoto: Kyoto University Research Institute for Humanistic Studies, 1–18.

Tani, Y., 1983. Hito ga hajimete Chichi wo shibotta toki (When man succeeded in milking for the first time). *Kikan Jinruigaku* (Anthropological quarterly), 14(2): 152–157.

Tani, Y., 1985. Jiremma heno shuhou (Tactics inducing dilemmas). *Shisou*, Feb.: 22–41.

Tani, Y., 1987a. Preliminary notes on the flock management techniques of the Bakharwal and the Ladakhi shepherds in northwestern India. In S. Sakamoto (ed.), *A Preliminary Report of the Studies on Millet Cultivation and its Agro-Pastoral Culture Complex in the Indian Subcontinent (1985)*. Kyoto: Research Team for the Studies on Millet Cultivation and its Agro-Pastoral Culture Complex in the Indian Subcontinent, Kyoto University, 78–88.

Tani, Y., 1987b. Two types of human interventions into the sheep flock: Intervention into the mother-offspring relationship and raising the flock leader. In Y. Tani (ed.), *Domesticated Plants and Animals of the Southwestern Eurasian Agro-Pastoral Culture (2): Pastoralism*. Kyoto: Kyoto University Research Institute for Humanistic Studies, 1–42.

Tani, Y., 1989a. The geographical distribution and function of sheep flock leaders: A cultural aspect of the man-domesticated animal relationship in Southwestern Eurasia. In J. Clutton-Brock (ed.), *The Walking Larder: Patterns of Domestication, Pastoralism, and Predation*. London: Unwin Hyman, 185–199.

Tani, Y., 1989b. Group organization and herding techniques of the Bakharwal in Kashmir. In S. Sakamoto (ed.), *A Preliminary Report on the Studies on Millet Cultivation and its Agro-Pastoral Culture Complex in the Indian Subcontinent II (1987)*. Kyoto: Research Team for the Studies on Millet Cultivation and its Agro-Pastoral Culture Complex in the Indian Subcontinent, Kyoto University, 81–94.

Tani, Y., 1989c. Mode analysis of the dietary darratives in the Pentateuch. Research Institute for Humanistic Studies, Kyoto University, *Zinbun*, 24: 314–353.

Tani, Y., 1991. Kachiku kanri karamita Indo Atairiku—Yudouhitsuji ketsujo to yuchiku nougyo (Indian Subcontinent viewed from the management techniques of domesticated animals: Deficiency of the castrated herd guide-wether and agriculture with livestock raising). In S. Sakamoto (ed.), *Indo*

Atairiku niokeru Zakkoku Saibai to sorewomeguru Nouboku Bunka Fukugou (Millet cultivation in the Indian Subcontinent and the agro-pastoral culture complex). Tokyo: Gakkai Jimu Center, 223–277.

Tani, Y., 1992. Kachiku to kaboku—Kyosei osu yudou hitsuji no chiriteki bunpu to sono imi (Domesticated animals and serfs: Geographical distribution of the castrated herd guide-wether and its meaning). *Zinbun Gakuhou* (Research journal of humanities), 71: 53–96.

Tani, Y., 1995a. Koukogakuteki imideno kachikuka towa nandeattaka—Hito—hitsuji/yaghi kanno intarakushon no Katei toshite (What was the domestication archaeology identified? Viewed as an interactional process between man and sheep/goats). *Zinbun Gakuhou* (Research journal of humanities), 76: 229–274.

Tani, Y., 1995b. Chichi riyou notameno sakunyu wa ikanishite kaishi saretaka (How was milking for human consumption initiated?). *Seinan Ajia Kenkyuu* (Journal of Southwest Asian studies), 43: 21–38.

Tani, Y., 1996a[1976]. *Bokufu Furanchesuko no Ichinichi—Itaria Chubu Sanson Seikatsushi* (One day in the life of Shepherd Francesco: Life histories of people in the mountain villages of Central Italy), revised edition. Tokyo: Heibonsha.

Tani, Y., 1996b. Domestic animal as serf: Ideologies of nature in the Mediterranean and Middle East. In R. Ellen and K. Fukui (eds), *Redefining Nature: Ecology, Culture and Domestication*. Oxford: Berg, 387–415.

Tani, Y., 1997. *Kami, Hito, Kachiku—Bokuchiku Bunka to Seisho Sekai* (God, man and domesticated animals: Pastoral culture and the Old Testament). Tokyo: Heibonsha.

Tani, Y., 1999. Chukintouniokeru yaghi/hitsujino kachikuka no katei saikou—Boshikankeiheno futatsuno kaijoghihou no kaishiki to sono imi (Rethinking the initial stage of domestication of sheep/goats in the Near East). *Minzokugaku Kenkyuu* (The Japanese Journal of Ethnology), 64(1): 96–113.

Tani, Y., 2005. Early techniques as a forerunner of milking practices. In J. Mulville and A.K. Outram (eds), *The Zooarchaeology of Fats, Oils, Milk and Dairying*. Oxford: Oxbow Books, 114–120.

Tani, Y., 2010. *Bokufu no Tanjo—Hitsuji/ Yaghi no Kachikuka no Kaishi to sonoTenkai* (The birth of the shepherd: The beginning of sheep/goat domestication and its development). Tokyo: Iwanami Shoten.

Tani, Y., and N. Ishighe, 1969. Fezanniokeru oasisu nougyo to bokuchiku seikatsu

(Agricultural and pastoralistic life in an oasis village in Fezzan). In K. Yamashita (ed.), *Dai Sahara* (The Great Sahara). Tokyo: Kodansha, 132–147.

Tani, Y., T. Matsui and S. Omar, 1980. The pastoral life of the Durrani Pashtun nomads in Northeastern Afghanistan. In Y. Tani (ed.), *Preliminary Report of Comparative Studies on the Agro-Pastoral Peoples in Southwestern Eurasia*. Kyoto: Kyoto University Research Institute for Humanistic Studies, 1–31.

Tei J., 1992. *Yuboku—Tonakai Yubokumin Saame no Seikatsu* (Nomadism: The life of Saami reindeer herders). Tokyo: Chikuma Shobou.

Telcianu, R., 1939. *Terminologie Oireasca in Comuna Maieru, Judeţul Bistriţa-Nasaud* (Classificatory terminology of sheep's colour patterns in the village Maieru, province of Bistriţa-Nasaud). PhD dissertation, University of Cluj-Napoca, Romania.

Trinchieri, R., 1953. *Vita di Pastori nella Campagna Romana* (Life of shepherds in the Campagna Romana). Roma: Fratelli Palombi.

Trubetzkoy, N.S., 1958. *Grundzüge der Phonologie*. Göttingen: Vandenhoeck and Ruprecht.

Uerpmann, H.P., 1978. Metrical analysis of faunal remains from the Middle East. In R.H. Meadow and M.A. Zeder (eds), *Approaches to Faunal Analysis in the Middle East*. Cambridge, Mass: Peabody Museum Bulletin, 41–45.

Uerpmann, H.P., 1989. Animal exploitation and the phasing of the transition from the Paleolithic to the Neolithic. In J. Clutton-Brock (ed.), *The Walking Larder: Patterns of Domestication, Pastoralism, and Predation*, London: Unwin Hyman, 91–96.

Umesao, T., 1965. Shuryo to bokuchiku no sekai I -II (World of hunting and husbandry I-II). *Shisou*, Feb.: 10–29 and Apr.: 66–88.

Umesao, T., 1966. Datoga shakai niokeru kachiku hoboku to kachikugun (Herding and herds of Datoga). In J. Kawakita, T. Umesao and S. Ueyama (eds), *Ninghen—Jinruigakuteki Kenkyu* (Man: Anthropological studies). Tokyo: Chuokoronsha, 423–463.

Van de Mieroop, M., 1993. Sheep and goat herding according to the Old Babylonian Text from Ur. *Bulletin on Sumerian Agriculture*, 7: 161–182.

Van Driel, G., 1993. Neo-Babylonian sheep and goats. *Bulletin on Sumerian Agriculture*, 7: 219–258.

Van Driel, G. and K.R. Nemet-Nejat, 1994. Bookkeeping practices for an institutional herd at Eanna. *Journal of Cuneiform Studies*, 46: 47–58.

Vigne, J.-D. and D. Helmer, 2007. Was milk a 'secondary product' in the Old

World Neolithisation process? Its role in the domestication of cattle, sheep and goats. *Anthropozoologica*, 42(2): 9–40

Vladuțiu, I., 1961. Almenwirtschaftliche viehhaltung und transhumance im Brangebiet (Südkarpaten, Rumänien) (Alpine economic cattle breeding and transhumance in Bran area (Southcarpthia, Romania)). In L. Földes (ed.), *Viehzucht und Hirtenleben in Ostmitteleuropa. Ethnographische Studien* (Husbandry and shepherds' life in east-central Europe, ethnographical studies), Budapest: Akadémiai Kaidó, 197–241.

Vreeland, H.H., 1957. *Mongol Community and Kinship Structure*. New Haven: Human Relations Area Files.

Vuia, R., 1964. *Tipuri de Păstorit la Romîni* (Types of Romanian shepherds). București: Editura Academiei.

Watanabe, K., 1992. Nabû-u salla, Statthalter Sargons II. in Tam(a)nūna (Government official of Sargon II, Nabû-usalla in Tam(a)nūna). *Baghdader Mitteilungen*, 23: 357–369.

Watanabe, K., 1995. Shin Assiria jidai no kangan—Insho wotegakari ni (Eunuchs in the age of New Assyria: Referring the seals as clues). In Ancient Orient Museum (ed.), *Bunmeigaku Genron* (The principles of civilisation). Tokyo: Yamakawa Shuppan, 211–233.

Wheatley, P., 1965. A note on the extension of milking practices into Southeast Asia during the first millennium A.D. *Anthropos*, 60: 577–590.

Zarins, J., 1989. Pastoralism in Southwest Asia: The second millennium B.C. In J. Clutton-Brock (ed.), *The Walking Larder: Patterns of Domestication, Pastoralism, and Predation*. London: Unwin Hyman, 127–155.

Zeder, M.A., 1991. *Feeding Cities: Specialized Animal Economy in the Ancient Near East*. Washington: Smithsonian Institution Press.

Zeder, M.A., 1994 After the revolution: Post-Neolithic subsistence in northern Mesopotamia. *American Anthropologist*, 96: 97–126.

Zeder, M.A., 2005. A view from the Zagros: New perspectives on livestock domestication in the Fertile Crescent. In J.-D. Vigne, J. Peters and D. Helmer (eds), *The First Steps of Animal Domestication: New Archaeozoological Approaches*. Oxford: Oxbow Books, 125–146.

Zeder, M.A., 2006. A critical assessment of markers of initial domestication in goats (Capra hircus). In M.A. Zeder, D.G. Bradley, E. Emshwiller and B.D. Smith (eds), *Documenting Domestication: New Genetic and Archaeological Paradigms*. Berkeley: University of California Press, 181–208.

Index

Abruzzo shepherds, Italy, 58, 61, 95, 136
Abu Gosh, 42, 43, 59
accidental death in the entrusted herd
 allowance of, 132–133, 135, 152
 skins as evidence of, 132, 134, 135, 152–153
accounting texts of the herd entrusted to shepherds
 of the Old Babylonian period, 125–134
  supplying rams from outside, 130, 133
 of Prince Arsham, Neo-Babylonian period, 137–139, 144, 148
  owner's share of female newborns, 137–138
  owner's share of male newborns, 137–138
 of private owner, Neo-Babylonian period, 139–154
  loss, 140–141, 148–150
  owner's share of female newborns, 194–195
  owner's share of male newborns, 194–195
  premium, 140–141, 148
  shepherd's share of female newborns, 146–147
  shepherd's share of male newborns, 146–147
  why the loss of male lambs is always zero, 141, 149–150, 153–154
  why the premium of male lambs is always zero, 141, 148–149
accumulative interactional process between humans and animals, xv, 10
adoption strategies, 60–63, 72, 81–84, 113
 shifting method in, 62, 82
agricultural expansion towards hillsides, 23–25, 30–31
alpaca *see* llama and alpaca
Amdo Doma (shepherds), Tibet, 107
Arabi shepherds, Afghanistan, 99, 106
archaeozoological markers of domestication, 18–21
Ardan (shepherds), Bistriţa-Nasaud, Romania, 101–103, 107
Aromani shepherds, Greece, 103, 106
attitudes towards animals (ancient Japanese), ix–xii
attitude towards animals (Mongolian shepherds), xii–xiii, 58, 61–62, 68, 88, 107, 113–114, 162

Bakharwal shepherds, Kashmir, India, 64, 70, 93–94, 106–107, 136
Baxtyâri shepherds, Iran, 55–61, 99, 106
beasts on the earth edible/inedible

with cloven hooves and non-ruminant as inedible, 174, 180, 182, 184–186
with cloven hooves and ruminant as edible, 174, 180–182, 184–186
that crawl on the ground as inedible, 175–177, 182–183
with non-cloven hooves and ruminant as inedible, 174, 180, 182, 184–186
ungulate animals with hooves non-cloven and non-ruminant as inedible, 174, 176–177, 182, 184–185
that walk on the flat of their foot as inedible, 174, 176–177, 182
beginning of agriculture, 12, 17, 23
beginning of sheep/goat domestication,
 how, 13, 17, 25, 31–40
 when, 10–13, 17, 22–23
 where, 13, 22–23
Beida, 46, 59
Beisamoun, 12
bio-control
 classificatory, 44, 54, 69, 74
 collective, 50, 74
 personal, 60, 63, 72, 74, 113
body size reduction, 19–20
Bovidae, 78, 177, 181–183, 185, 192

Camelidae, 78, 174, 177, 181, 183, 185, 192
Carpathian shepherds, Romania, 64, 66
castration, 73, 95–97, 99–100, 104–105, 108, 111–112

categorical identification of domesticated animals and slaves and serfs (as movable property) *see* Large household chief in the ancient Near East
changes in horns, 21
'collect and kill' hunting, 32, 34
collective sharing of home range in the same artificial enclosure, 33–34, 38–39, 52, 71
contractual relationship between herd owner and entrusted shepherds
 annual share as entrusted shepherd, 146–147
 annual share as herd owner, 135, 144–145, 147
 loss allowance by eventual accident, 132–133, 135, 140, 148, 150
 premium for shepherd, 140–141, 148
Crete, Micaenean period, 131
Cretan shepherds, Greece, 100–101, 103, 106
culling of male yearlings, 4, 41–44, 71, 117–118, 130

daily herding
 beginning of, 44–50, 71
 favourable conditions for, 45–49
 and imprinting failure, 52
 separate herding of weaned lambs from the main flock in, 13, 69–70
daily seclusion (or separation) of newborns from mother ewe group, 5, 13, 53–56
Datoga, East Africa, 80
delivery

during herding in the field, 52, 71
at harbouring site, 52, 71
dense aggregation of adult ewes, 53, 55, 57–58
desert kite *see* kite site
developmental stages of human subsistence economies
  hypothesis of, 11
dietary principles in the Pentateuch
  approval of eating (all animals') flesh with reservations, 171–172, 187–189
  three different stages of, 165
  in the Eden stage, 167–168, 171–172, 187, 192
  in the Leviticus, 165, 187
  in the Noah stage, 161, 167, 169, 171–172, 157, 192
  vegetarian principle, 169, 172, 187, 192
dietary regulations in Leviticus,
  aberrant description of winged insects in, 180, 184, 186
  covert motivation of, 186
  and differences of food habits between Israelites and surrounding people, 172
  illogical array of propositions in, 184
  as last discourse on dietary principles, 167
  mode of utterance of, 167, 173, 176–185
  as performative speech acts, 166
  as a report of 'God's utterances addressed to Israelites', 172, 187, 188

segment A of, 174, 176–177, 185
segment B of, 174–177
distribution system of meat, 119, 139
domesticated animals and serfs *see* categorical identification of domesticated animals and slaves and serfs (as movable property)
domesticated animals (sheep/goats)
  attachment to artificial site, 46
  attachment to man, 47–48
  compared to feral sheep/goats, 39
  compared to reindeer, 48–49
  formation of flock boundary in, 48–49
domestication process
  definition of, xv
  as mutual involvement between man and animals, 14
domestication (sheep/goats)
  as collective sharing of home-range in the same artificial enclosure, 33–34, 38–39, 52–53, 71
  definition of, xiii
  environmental and technical conditions favourable to the beginning of, 23–31
  how it began, 13, 17, 25, 31–40
  hypothesis 1, 'drive in hunting', 31–34
  hypothesis 2, 'intimacy establishment with flock as a whole', 34–37
  motivation of, 37–38
  negative effects of, 41, 50–59, 71–73
  positive effects of, 41, 50, 71
  when (sheep/goats), 13, 17, 22–23
  where (sheep/goats), 13, 17, 22–23

Drehem system, 121
drive-in hunting, 25–34

edible/inedible (animal) species in Leviticus, 173–186
 beasts on the earth, 174, 176, 178, 182
 birds in the air, 174, 176
 by classification by morphological and behavioural criteria, 176, 186
 fishes in the water, 174, 176, 179–180
 winged insects on earth, 174, 176, 179–180
entrusted shepherds,
 eat owner's male sheep (and bring its skin), 152–153, 159
 labour resource of, 155–157
 management strategies of, 122, 150–154
 reserved room for entrusted shepherds to manipulate reality, 132, 134, 150, 157, 159
 substitution strategy of, 152
entrustor-entrustee relationship
 deception-suspicion in the, 154–155, 159
Equidae, 176–177, 181, 183, 185
equipollent opposition, 178
 in the classification of beasts on the earth, 182, 185
eunuch, 93, 96–98, 105, 110, 112–113
 definition and function of, 97
 and guide-wether, 95, 97, 105
European attitude towards animals, xviii, 89
ewes
 as productive capital, 86

to keep alive, 5, 118, 124, 137
exclusion of cognitive anomaly (deviation), 166
expansion of agriculture towards hillsides, 23, 30

familiarity (of sheep) with man *see* domesticated animals' attachment to man
fattening, 121–125, 131, 138, 160
feeding cities
 according to the selective preference for meat from the city side, 118, 124
 Banesh stage (B.C. 3300–2800), 117–119
 example in Tal-e Malyan, 115–121
 Kaftari stage (B.C. 2400–1800), 117–120
 relationship between pastoralists and city dwellers seen from, 115–121
feral sheep/goats
 behavioural characteristics of, 15, 51
 compared to domesticated sheep/goats, 51
flock
 self-anchoring to human camp (residential) site, 3, 33, 35–36, 48–49, 66
 formation of flock boundary, 48–49, 71
followership of sheep/goats, 47, 93–95, 97, 100, 103

gene isolation, 20

Index

Genesis
  dietary principle at Eden stage in, 167–168, 171–172, 187
  dietary principle at the post Noah stage in, 161, 167, 169, 171–172, 187, 189
  God's entrustment of animals to man in, xiii–xiv, xviii, 114, 161, 187
  God's changing mind on the dietary principle in, 171
  identity crisis of the Israelites in, 189, 192
  total allowance to eat all kinds of animals in, 162, 171–172, 187–189
  story of Jacob and Laban in, 150–154
God
  absolute belongingness of the animals' life to, 162
  as entrustor of the control of animals to man, xiii–xiv, xviii, 114, 160–161
  resigning in the face of the wickedness of human nature, 171, 187
guide-wether, 93–99, 105–110, 160
  and eunuch, 97, 110
  geographical distribution of, 98, 105–110
  how to train, 95, 103
  as a model of eunuchs, 105, 110

herd guide technique
  elaboration of, 98, 104–105
  using castrated goat, 99, 105
  using goats' natural characteristic to promptly react, 98–99, 105
  using instructed castrated goat, 99, 105
  using instructed castrated ram (herd guide-wether), 93–95, 102–103, 105, 112–113
  using mother-offspring bond of sheep, 100, 105
  using plural instructed ewes (*fruntașa*), 101–105
  using provisioned ram or ewe, 101, 105
herd guide-wether and eunuchs
  homology of the role between, 96–97, 110, 112
  which is the technical model for inventing the other?, 98, 105, 110, 112–113
home range
  of domesticated sheep/goats, 34, 38–39, 41, 52–53
  of feral sheep/goats, 39
  of wild progenitor of sheep/goats, 39, 41, 52

identification of strayed sheep, 63–67
imprinting, 51–52, 54, 60
  failure, 60
  incomplete imprinting after delivery in the herding field, 52
intimacy establishment with flock as a whole *see* domestication, hypothesis 2, 'intimacy establishment with flock as a whole'

Israelites
  as chosen people qualified to
    become holy, 190, 192
  as consumers of only clean animals,
    190, 192
  identity crisis of, 189, 192

Kailash shepherds, Tibet, 107
Kashmiri nomads, India, 61, 136
Kirghiz (nomads), Kirghizstan, 107
'kill and collect' hunting, 32, 34
killing profile
  after the beginning of
    domestication, 18
  after the beginning of milking, 69
  before the beginning of
    domestication (hunting stage), 18
  of the consumed animals in the city,
    117–120
  at the primordial village in
    Mesopotamia, 118
  at the stage of Natufian Culture,
    26–27, 32
killing strategy
  after the beginning of
    domestication, 13, 41–44
  of hunters, 13
kite site, 28–29
Kurdish shepherds, Turkey, 100, 103,
  106

Ladakh shepherds, India, 107
large household chiefs in the ancient
  Near East, 98, 110–114, 160–162
  categorical identification of
    domesticated animals and slaves
    and serfs (as movable property)
    of, 110–112, 114, 160
large urban herd owners (large
  household chiefs)
  annual share as owner, 138, 144–145
  distant from the herding place of
    the entrusted shepherds, 132–133,
    150–151
  relationship between large urban
    herd owners and entrusted
    shepherds, 126, 133, 139–155,
    161
  reflection of large urban herd
    owners in the passages in the Old
    Testament, 161–163
Leviticus
  belongingness of animals' lives to
    God in, 162
  dietary regulations in, 165–192
  guiding principle behind, 165
  mode analysis of dietary regulations
    in, 176–184
  sacrificial ritual in, 189, 191
llamas and alpacas, 78, 83
  reason of deficiency of milking
    from, 83
locusts, 174, 179, 184, 186
  as hardy wild insects for pastoral
    people, 186
  as Yahweh's collaborators, 186

males as circulating goods, 131, 138,
  159
memory of shepherds of individual
  animals, 64–65
  age order of siblings, 64

colour pattern, 64
the mother-offspring relational tie,
  64–65
middleman between urban herd
  owner and entrusted
  shepherd, 127, 135, 138, 157–158
milk ejection reflex inducing devices,
  79–81
  for cows, 79–84
  parallels with adoption strategies,
    81–82
milking
  beginning of, 10, 37–38, 77
  of cows, 77–82, 84
  milking facilitation (allowance)
    inducing devices, 6, 67–68
  the Near Eastern pastoralists as
    unique initiators of, 7, 77–84
  of sheep/goats, 37, 67–68
  socio-cultural meaning of, 84–87
  and ideological avoidance of meat
    eating (vegetarianism), 85
multilayered structure of herd
  entrusting *see* middleman
mutual recognition between mother
  ewe and her offspring, 51, 60
  how to establish, 52, 60

nursing assistance
  against newborn's death in the ewes'
    harbouring site,
    53–54, 72
  and adoption strategies, 72
  for delivery during daily herding,
    52, 58
  for delivery at night, 53, 58, 71
  and the eventual injury and death of
    newborns, 53–54, 72
  as newborn seclusion from the
    mother ewes' group, 52–54, 58, 72
  as responses to the negative effects
    of domestication, 50–60
  at sucking-suckling time, 5, 54–59,
    72

orphans
  adoption of, 60–63, 72, 113
  de facto, 60
  real, 60
Ovidae, 177, 181–183, 185, 192

Pashtun nomads, Afghanistan, 61–62,
  70, 99, 106
pastoral power, xvi
pasu (*paśu*), 110
perlocutionary meaning (force)
  of the narratives of dietary
    regulations in Leviticus, 171–172,
    185–191
  of the narrative of Yahweh's
    approval of eating flesh, 171
  of reporting Yahweh's decree by
    Testament writers of Leviticus,
    187–191
  of Yahweh's decree in Leviticus, 185
physiological impediment (hurdle) to
  milking
  of Camelidae, 78
  of cows, 78–79
  how to clear (overcome) *see* milk
    ejection reflex inducing devices
pigs, 174, 186

for urban dwellers (in ancient
    Mesopotamia), 186
privative opposition, 178
  in classification of edible/inedible
    beasts, 182, 184
  in classification of edible/inedible
    fishes, 179–180
  in classification of edible/inedible
    insects, 179–180
professional shepherds
  birth of, 70, 73
  deficiency of professional shepherds
    in Japan, xi

Qashqa'i nomads, Iran, 3, 57, 61–62,
    99, 136

rams
  as circulating goods, 119, 131, 134,
    138, 158–159
  concentrated in the city, 125
  culling yearlings (at maturity), 5,
    18–19, 44, 71
  discharge of rams from the mother
    ewes' group, 124, 134, 138, 158
  and milk as profit, 58
  as objects of complementary
    economic interests between
    shepherds and temple cities, 131
  seasonal separation of breeding,
    68–69
  supplement of rams from outside,
    130, 133, 138, 158–159
  as tribute, 125–126, 131, 160
  for wool textile industries, 122,
    130–131, 158

reindeer, 14–15, 48
  behavioural characteristics
    compared to domesticated sheep/
    goats, 48
  frequent transfer into other groups,
    48
  relationship between urban herd
    owner and entrusted shepherd,
    122, 125, 133, 136, 139–140, 154,
    158, 161–162
Reptile, 176

Saami (reindeer herders), 15, 34–36,
    48–49, 66
Sarakatsani shepherds, Greece, 58,
    101, 103, 106
Scarcity of material tools of pastoral
    nomads, 11–12
self-anchoring to the human
    campsite, 3, 33–34, 38, 46
self-consciousness of original guilt,
    191
separate herding of weaned lambs
    from the main flock, 13, 51,
    69–70
sheep herds in the temple cities of the
    ancient Near East
  entrusted, belonging to a private
    owner in the Neo-Babylonian
    period, 139–154
  entrusted, belonging to Prince
    Arsham in the Neo-Babylonian
    period, 134, 137–139
  entrusted, belonging to the temple
    in the Old Babylonian period,
    125–134

externally entrusted, 135, 158
internally retained, 124, 134, 138, 158
for wool, 122, 130–131, 158
shepherd's memory of the mother-offspring relationship, 64–65, 72
Siberian hunters, 85, 88, 114, 162
strayed sheep
  identification of, 63–67
Suidae, 177, 181, 183, 185

taming by food provisioning, 47–48
Tilişca shepherds, Sibiu, Romania, 102–103, 107
Topalu shepherds, Dobrogea, Romania, 107
transfer into other flock
  in the case of domesticated sheep/goats, 49
  in the case of reindeer, 48–49
Tuareg, Niger, 61

Umm Dabaghiyah, 45, 59
Ur, Old Babylonian period, 125–134
Ur, third dynasty, 122
Uruk, Neo-Babylonian period, 134–138
Uzbecki shepherds, Afghanistan, 99, 106

Vlach shepherds, Greece, 106

Yöluk nomads, Turkey, 61, 64, 106